All Good Things

All Good Things

From Paris to Tahiti:

Life and Longing

Sarah Turnbull

GOTHAM
BOOKS

GOTHAM BOOKS
Published by the Penguin Group
Penguin Group (USA), 375 Hudson Street,
New York, New York 10014, USA

USA | Canada | UK | Ireland | Australia | New Zealand | India | South Africa | China

Penguin Books Ltd, Registered Offices: 80 Strand, London WC2R 0RL, England
For more information about the Penguin Group visit penguin.com.

First published in 2013 by HarperCollins Publishers Australia Pty Limited by the same title.

LIBRARY OF CONGRESS CATALOGING-IN-PUBLICATION DATA
has been applied for.

ISBN 978-1-592-40868-9

Printed in the United States of America
10 9 8 7 6 5 4 3 2 1

Set in ITC Baskerville Std

While the author has made every effort to provide accurate telephone numbers, Internet
addresses, and other contact information at the time of publication, neither the publisher
nor the author assumes any responsibility for errors or for changes that occur after
publication. Further, the publisher does not have any control over and does not assume any
responsibility for author or third-party websites or their content.

Penguin is committed to publishing works of quality and integrity.
In that spirit, we are proud to offer this book to our readers;
however, the story, the experiences, and the words
are the author's alone.

ALWAYS LEARNING   PEARSON

For Frédéric and Oliver

PROLOGUE

When I'm in waist deep, I stop for a moment to take it all in.

It's another flawless daybreak; there isn't a whisper of breeze. In the distance, hovering above the coral reef, the fine mist and spray of broken waves glow like a halo; around me the lagoon spreads a silvery skirt. The surface is so still I feel almost guilty disrupting it. While the temperature may have cooled overnight it is hardly cold, and on this liminal fringe it's difficult to discern between air and water. I don't even really feel wet, rather wrapped in the softest silk. Through the crystalline surface, patterns appear magnified and fascinating: the delicate whorls on my own finger pads; the hermit crabs scurrying out of my way, so well camou- flaged they look like sand, shifting and blossoming around my feet.

But this ritual has become essential. Briskly, I adjust my swimming goggles. Overhead a couple of seagulls circle, in- terested only in the tiny fish that spray into air when I dive in.

These first few seconds underwater are like a rebirth. Or maybe they're more like one of those near-death experiences that survivors liken to being drawn into a tunnel of beauty and brilliance, only here there are no walls, no limit to the luminosity which spreads in every direction. Either way, the unburdening is instantaneous. In the opaline rush of streaming water, a weight I can't name loses its grip and gets left behind in the fizz of my wake.

One two three breathe. I count my way through the first hundred meters. It takes a few minutes for my limbs to remember the rhythm but pretty soon I'm longer, looser. It's schoolgirl freestyle: nothing fast or fancy, just enough to earn me third or fourth place in the 50-meter sprint at annual carnivals. But for a shallow breather like me, swimming is fantastic— more than yoga or running or any gym class, it gets me drawing in deep lungfuls of air, and on a good day it feels like someone's thrown open the windows on that locked and empty space below my stomach. It was my preferred exercise in Paris, too, which is why I was so thrilled we found a house right on the lagoon.

After heading straight out for a couple of hundred meters, at a large head of mustard-colored coral I tack parallel to the shore, keeping an eye out for the stroppy clownfish who doesn't take kindly to encroachments on its territory. On the sand below, stingrays prowling for shellfish have left winding trails, like spaceships that came and went in the night. The bottom looks close, though you can't trust distances underwater. Try as I have to pencil-drop to the lagoon floor, my feet never quite touch, though the local spear fishermen descend twenty meters or more without air tanks and flippers.

Early on, an obligation to be adventurous had made me try new directions. Once I struck out for the coral reef 800 meters offshore, toward the glistening frill of freshly cracked waves that delineates lagoon and deep sea. Another time, instead of turning left I headed in the opposite direction for the islet Motu Ahi. The distances weren't greater than usual and as life changes go these experiments were inconsequential. Yet somehow those swims had felt all wrong and the days got off to a shaky start. I'd learned my lesson. Now, faced with the freedom of swimming in any direction, I stick to my route like a sure-footed mountain goat, all too aware of the hazards of leaving the trail.

People talk about switching off when they exercise but it is during my morning swims I feel most switched on. Not to reality—at least not realities onshore. Out here the novel that's going nowhere seems blissfully far away. In this womb of water there is no sense of solitude or emptiness. Even time—whose sluggish pace on land I have come to dread— acquires a playful fluidity, streaming through my fingers in ribbons so satiny and seamless I am barely aware of them.

Instead I switch on to myriad small miracles: the fine comb of a tiny fish fin; the dark grace of a spotted eagle ray, more skybound than waterborne. Or the startled schools that flutter nose-down, like striped snowflakes, when I reach the shelf. The mere sight of the deeper blue waters, looming like a shadowland, sets my heart racing. The drop is only about twenty meters but after the glass shoals it feels like an abyss. My eyes swivel anxiously, scanning for sharks. They're only harmless reef varieties, no more than one and a half meters in length, though underwater everything looks bigger. As tests of courage go, it is unremarkable. But these days I'm grateful for any sense of accomplishment, and for me this shelf is a valued challenge, an essential part of my morning ritual.

As abruptly as it fell, the bottom rises again to a shallow garden. The coral is nothing to rave about; the colors are dull and tweedy. Yet between the branches, in the crannies and caves, it's all go. There's so much life nibbling, hiding, watching, slithering, darting through tentacles of sea anemones whose tips cling but don't sting when you brush them.

At the navigation marker for boats, I turn back. My heart starts racing again—not from fear but unbounded pleasure. The return journey is my favorite leg of the swim. With each breath I glimpse the sandy shoreline, fringed with coconut palms, and if I turn my head far enough I can see Mount Mouaputa, watching me unblinkingly with the eyehole that perforates her summit. I stay out deep: *right in the boat lane*, as Frédéric pointed out, unimpressed. Though by then I'd been swimming for too many months to start worrying about it. At this hour there's never so much as a pirogue on the lagoon anyway.

Here, over the gently ribbed sandy plain, color and light and volume amp up to create a whole new register of stunning effulgence. Were I an artist, I might be tempted to paint it—look at the wondrous, weightless infinity Monet created out of a garden pond! The water is not simply turquoise; it segues constantly from yellow to honeydew-melon green, from aqua to peacock blue to ultramarine. It's impossible to say where one shade begins and another ends. Into these radiant splashes and spills the sun has cast a shimmering net.

Each diamond-shaped loop undulates, as if to its own song, and because there are millions of them, because the net is infinite, the impression is of something pure and vital, as if this dazzling, dancing filigree of light were the ocean's pulse or breath.

Science tells us it's just bending light: sun rays refracting upon hitting the water, as they do on penetrating glass or in the thin, hot air above a road. Science tells us a lot of things. To my mind, the sight—which is felt as much as seen—is enough to inspire belief in God and miracles. And I do believe, fervently—right up until I get out.

I swim the final few hundred meters as fast as I can. Not from a desire for this to end but because my energy is boundless. I feel strong to the core; mighty. I'm flying, gliding, falling. No longer swimming but intent on grasping one of the wands of light, with all my heart wishing I might melt into this wondrous mirror, become part of it, dissolve, before my feet touch land.

Because the temptation to stay in is strong I get out briskly. No lingering in the lagoon—it's one of my rules. I rinse off quickly under our outdoor shower, positioned between two tall palms. Frédéric jokes that, like having bird poo land on you, getting struck by a coconut might bring good luck—but this is one superstition I'd rather not put to the test.

Though when you want something badly, when you really long for something, you might try almost anything.

ONE

Inside the church, which stood on a cobbled square in Paris, there were prayer candles for one euro each and slightly bigger ones for two. But perhaps when it comes to getting God's ear, you get what you pay for. The ten-euro candles towered over the tea lights and, when lit, their ruby-colored glass jars glowed rich rose-gold in the dark interior. A sign promised they burned for nine days straight. They weren't cheap yet I didn't think twice before slipping my pink banknote into the collection box. It wasn't as if my countless one-euro prayers had done us any good.

A few people knelt in the pews; others lit their own votive offerings. Like me they were probably here to beg a favor. *Le lieu des causes perdues*, the place of lost causes: that's how a Parisian friend had once flippantly referred to Notre-Dame des Victoires. Before I got to know the place, her words had seemed apt, but now I'd never use such an unsympathetic description.

It had none of the breathtaking reach or delicate sculpting that had made the Paris cathedral of similar name a world-famous tourist attraction. In comparison, Notre-Dame des Victoires was small, exteriorly plain and rather squat. Yet from the first time I'd pushed through those high, swinging entrance doors that shut out the sound of chattering passersby and tooting traffic, it was obvious this wasn't an ordinary place of worship. Inside there was all the poetic drama of a seventeenth-century painting: even as my eyes adjusted to the darkness, they could scarcely take in the radiance. Classified as a basilica, for centuries Notre-Dame des Victoires has been a place of pilgrimage. There were prayer candles everywhere, rising in tiered banks around Mary and other saints, throwing out so much flickering light that the solid stone walls rippled like water.

In the beginning I'd puzzled over the protocol of prayer. Should I close my eyes? It was one thing to opt for the tall ten-euro candles but whom exactly was I seeking to impress? Saying the words "Dear God," even silently, felt awkward, too forward. An introduction might be in order, given we weren't exactly well acquainted. Perhaps it was more seemly to begin with an unselfish prayer: a cure for cancer or malaria, an end to homelessness? Though God, if He did exist, must be busy and might well appreciate me getting straight to the point.

These days I was no longer self-conscious. It wasn't as if there was a sign prohibiting agnostics from entering; you weren't required to think of Him at all. The wick of my candle flared in the flame of another. On its own my offering might have looked lonely. In this holder, though, it was part of a chorus of candlelight that filled my eyelids with orange brilliance as I said my prayer.

⌒⌒

I'd been secretly lighting candles in churches for a few years but it wasn't until renovations forced us to move out of our apartment for a few months that the habit became expensive. Friends who lived most of the time in San Francisco kindly offered Frédéric and me the use of their Paris home, which happened to be directly on my favorite square, Place des Petits-Pères, and right next door to Notre-Dame des Victoires. It was then I started dropping into the church three or four times a week.

From our temporary abode it was a ten-minute walk back to our own apartment to check on progress. After we moved out, the floorboards were ripped up and the workmen started knocking down walls, though sometimes it was difficult to see what was happening for the dust in the air. We were not only renovating but also enlarging our home. Recently, we'd managed to buy the only other residence on the top floor, though "residence" is perhaps too grand a word. Formerly a *chambre de bonne*, or maid's quarters, it was not much bigger or brighter than a prison cell. Curiously configured, the meager surface area of 13 square meters was spilled into two tiny "wings" either side of a toilet. A friend who lived in the country happened to be staying with us the first time we were able to tour the room as new owners. While our hearts privately sank, Jean-Michel surveyed the small windows and water-stained walls with undisguised hilarity. *"Magnifique, c'est Ver-*

3

sailles!" To illustrate the ludicrously small scale, he backed his bulky frame into the toilet, proclaiming boisterously from the throne it was *parfait* for a garden gnome.

The nickname Versailles stuck, but even so, in Paris every square centimeter of additional space counts. An architect drew up plans. Once the common wall came down, part of the room next door would form a new kitchen. That left the other area, all 5 square meters, though it did at least have a small window. "A walk-in linen room," suggested the architect. "Or one of those pantries that Anglo-Saxons like," he added, looking at me. But being first-time renovators, we had not considered details such as where to store the flour or honey. Anyway, we had other ideas. "You could get a cot in there," Frédéric had said, peering at the wee rectangle on the floor plan. "Do you think?" I'd responded hopefully.

As the work on our apartment advanced, scaffolding went up outside our peeling building. The whole neighborhood was being spruced up, in keeping with a general *embourgeoise-ment* that had already swept other parts of inner Paris. Most exciting of all, after years of traipsing up six floors and twelve flights of stairs, was the decision to install a lift. The *projet* had long been opposed by a silver-haired tyrant of the local rag trade who happened to own the lower three floors. "What do I care about a lift?" he'd snorted at one body corporate meeting. "You don't think I'm ever going to *live* in this place, do you?" In the end, rising property prices convinced him to sell. One by one, the sweatshops were converted back into private homes, and the Chinese and Turkish seamstresses were replaced by couples and families who quickly tired of dragging kids and groceries up the stairs. Not long after, engineers and builders could be seen inside, jotting down measurements and making pencil marks on the stairwell walls.

⌒⌒

Apart from our apartment and Maddie, our beloved West Highland terrier, our responsibilities were minimal. I was in my early thirties, Frédéric in his early forties, but neither of us owned a car. Instead we flew around on his handsome navy-and-chrome Kawasaki 1100. Without nannies and baby-sitters to worry about, friends knew we could be relied on to embrace any last-minute plan. At dinners we made quite an entrance, arriving windswept and leather clad, causing laughter with our offerings of tulips, say, whose heads had been blown off en route. *"Oh, qu'elles sont jolies!"* our hosts would exclaim jovially at the stalks. Maddie, who adored the motorbike, had her own party trick. At traffic lights, her pointy ears and black nose would pop out of the carry case as she drew herself up, cute but commanding, to the surprise and delight of passersby.

A new elan had swept the whole city it seemed to me. You could feel it on Friday nights, standing curbside in the rush of wind as ever growing numbers of skaters took to the streets. People came from all over the continent and from across the Channel for the thrill of being part of the 15,000-strong crowd that whooshed around the city like a current. A few years earlier the story had been very different: Paris had lost its mojo, its fantasy, according to the international press. It was little more than a beautiful, stuffy museum, sniffed influential fashion magazines. And I must admit, on trips away I saw their point: London did seem excitingly eclectic in comparison, New York so savvy and fast-paced. It had taken the new millennium for Paris to remind the world what it stood for—those celebrations were the turning point to my mind. As the seconds were counted down, streams of light shot from the Eiffel Tower, beginning at the base and rising up the lattice stem. Instead of an eruption of gaudy pyrotechnics, on the count of midnight there was a spellbinding blooming. That's the only way I can describe the marvelous gold petals and shoots; it was as if the whole display were a rare and natural phenomenon. We were in Sydney at the time but even watching it on television made my skin tingle. The detractors were won over, too, and there was lots of gushing in the media about French savoir-faire and the City of Light.

And yet in our enviably carefree existence a new poignancy had begun to color old rituals. There were my tall prayer candles at Notre-Dame des Victoires. There were the medical appointments, tests and injections, along with whatever else I was giving a whirl: acupuncture, Chinese herbs, the naturopath in London I saw a few times, with her gentle, upper-crust accent, crystals and hanging plants strung up in macramé. Strolling about our neighborhood, I tried to avoid Bonpoint, the baby and children's wear boutique. The clothes were very beautiful, very bourgeois, very Parisian—not the sort of kit I'd dress a child in. Yet the mere sight of its windows triggered visions of a little girl buttoned up in the red woolen coat or twirling in a spotted skirt. At the entrance to the Palais-Royal gardens, where I'd always loved to walk, I had to speed up passing the old-fashioned toy shop. It sold wooden puzzles, puppets and dolls and magical paper lamps that projected jewel-like colors from cut-out clowns and animals. So enchanting were they that we very nearly bought one. Then Frédéric hesitated.

"How about we wait," he said, sounding wistful. "Let's buy one to celebrate the birth of our first child."

⌒

When Frédéric arrived home from work one evening, he flopped into an armchair, even though we were running late to meet friends for dinner. It was almost nine but sunlight poured like honey through our west-facing window. Late spring had always been my favorite time of year in Paris. The tulips at the Palais-Royal gardens were past their prime and any moment there'd be an eruption of lilacs and peonies. With the summer solstice still a month away, the days promised to get even longer. Frédéric gazed distractedly into the sparkle of dust motes.

"They've asked me to set up a new office," he announced. "Overseas."

As far as I knew, his law firm was not in the habit of sending people abroad, so this came as a surprise. Perhaps the plan to extend farther into Eastern Europe had been reignited. Ukraine had been mentioned in the past. Frédéric had already gone to Kiev a few times to help redraft laws, and one year just before Christmas I'd joined him there for a week. My memory was of bone-chilling winds funneling down stark Soviet boule-vards. Despite the cold, we'd both agreed then that Eastern Europe would be interesting, for a while. My thoughts skipped along. I'd have to get myself one of those astrakhan coats, some good thermal underwear, maybe some Australian sheep sk—

"Tahiti," he said, raising his eyebrows.

"Ta-HEEdee?"

Frédéric nodded.

Perhaps the suggestion wasn't so random. French Polynesia was a French territory so presumably the laws were also French. And Frédéric worked for a French firm. Still, I found it hard to reconcile thoughts of work in a place that evoked luxury resorts and poolside piña coladas—or was it mai tais there? The other Tahiti association that sprang to mind didn't fit with the images of limpid lagoons at all. I still recalled the furor during my first year in France when Jacques Chirac—wanting to begin his presidency with a show of might, no doubt—decided to resume nuclear testing in the Pacific.

"Why there? I mean *what's* there?" I asked uncertainly.

Frédéric shrugged. "Lots of little islands." He wasn't exactly bubbling with curiosity but we went and knelt around our globe lamp. There was still so much daylight in the room it barely brightened when we switched it on. Frédéric flicked the orb and Earth spun: Ocean would have been a better name, I thought, so much of its surface is blue. My finger went instinctively for Australia. I've always loved the way my country stands out on the world map; simply watching television news graphics of a spinning globe gives me a thrill. Former empires and even superpowers pass in a blur of borders and undistinguished form yet Australia stands boldly alone, independent and important—at least that's the impression it gives.

Not in our backyard. The headline from 1995 came back to me: that was the furious message broadcast by Australian newspapers after the decision to resume nuclear testing was announced. Do your dirty experiments somewhere else, in other words, not in our neighborhood. French Polynesia mustn't be far from Australia then? My finger made circles around New Caledonia.

Frédéric stabbed a point way east. "No, over here."

My first thought was that it wasn't in anyone's backyard—least of all France's, of course. The territory floated in a vast oceanic no-man's land between South America and the east coast of Australia. Beside a minuscule dot, in faint, spidery font, was written "Tahiti," though some cartographical imperative meant the town "Pape'ete" was printed in type twice as big. A nearby pinpoint bore the name Rai'atea. Far to the northeast, drifting toward Mexico, were the Marquesas. The rest of the islands, however many there were, had not been marked.

"It'd be the end of my career," muttered Frédéric. "*Pas sérieux du tout.* It's a total backwater."

He was right, I thought. On the world map French Polynesia looked like punctuation—entirely optional. Some people are obsessed with islands, especially remote ones: "islomaniacs" Lawrence Durrell called them. But the faraway lands that had captured my childhood imagination were up magic trees and through secret closets. I hadn't been much into island adventure stories, unless you count *Lord of the Flies*.

"And I wouldn't be able to continue my research," I added.

It had taken a while and a number of false starts but finally I was fired up about an idea for my next book. The inspiration for my historical novel was a remote village in rural Brittany that in the late nineteenth century became the unlikely home to a flourishing artists' colony. Already I had folders of facts about Breton peasants, including notes made at libraries and exhibitions. The last thing I wanted was for my new momentum to be interrupted.

It wasn't that we hadn't considered leaving Paris. On occasion we'd talked about *one day* living in Australia *for a while*, though these discussions always stumbled over the issue of what Frédéric—trained in French law—would do there. On holidays and work trips, inspired by history and landscape, new people and different food, we often indulged in flights of fancy. We would help rebuild war-torn Sarajevo; we would buy a crumbling *riad* in Marrakech and spend holidays restoring the traditional home. On the Greek island of Sifnos, after too much retsina, we came up with the idea of opening a guesthouse. Invariably the sparks went out upon our return home. Really we weren't that motivated to leave Paris, we were just greedy for multiple lives.

But the suggestion of a move now rekindled these old dreams.

"I wouldn't hesitate if it was India," started Frédéric.

"Istanbul would be fantastic." I'd always wanted to go back to Turkey, only this time not as a backpacker.

"Beirut."

"Bucharest," I offered after a pause. We'd met in Romania and both of us had a soft spot for the place.

Frédéric looked thoughtfully around our freshly renovated, repainted apartment. "It'd be a shame to leave now that it has been redone."

"Now that we've got a lift, you mean." We laughed, though this wasn't a joke. Having recently moved back home after four months of building work, we still blinked in astonishment when those automatic doors slid open and abracadabra, there we were, transported to the top floor. No more having to lug suitcases and groceries up 120 steps; no arguing over whose turn it was to take Maddie out for a last pee. The lift had changed our lives. Instead of cursing or accusing because someone had forgotten to buy butter, we vied for the chance of another ride. I'll go. You went last time. No really, it's my turn, let me.

Apparently we had until after the summer holidays to make up our minds, though they felt pretty made up. Like a little wave, the Tahiti proposition had lightly licked our shore and then retreated. Or so it seemed. In reality perhaps it was more like a ripple, as when a pebble plops into a pond.

TWO

I have been to hot places, lived in equatorial Singapore as a child, traipsed through desert country in the Northern Territory in summer. But Paris in a heatwave is something else. The congestion of buildings, crowds, cafés and streets—ordinarily so charming—grows claustrophobic and stifling. That summer I half expected the gilt domes to drip like scoops of ice cream. There was no breeze, not even a light one, and pollution draped a dirty quilt over the city. It was 2003 and the main news item was the Allied invasion of Iraq—that was until *la canicule*, the record heatwave, swept Europe. With no fixed holiday plans, we installed Maddie in her carry case, hopped on Frédéric's motorbike and rode south, in search of fresh air and open skies.

We kept to country roads and out-of-the-way areas with fewer tourists. Even so it seemed an act of charity that any *chambre d'hôte*, or small hotel, took us in: two sweaty motorcyclists spattered in bugs and grime, and one scruffy, panting fur ball. (*C'est un chien?* was the impertinent but possibly genuine response at one B & B when we asked if they took dogs.) Along the way, temperatures crept into the 100s and beyond. Of all Europe, France had the highest death toll and later, when the figure was announced, it seemed scarcely possible: 15,000 people, most of them elderly, died during the heatwave. Oblivious to any drama, we splashed about in town fountains, along with laughing children and parents and grandparents. At service stations we stood, fully clothed, under giant mist machines that had been erected hastily. We stopped by streams, sheltering beneath thick canopies of oak and chestnut trees to eat picnic lunches: baguette; one or two cheeses; *saucisson*; a glass each of rosé, followed by biscuits dipped in dark chocolate that ran all over our fingers. Once, finding no decent shade, we ate in a blessedly dark and cool Romanesque church in the middle of sun-fried fields.

I've always found the French countryside to be gently reassuring, and in this most unforgiving of summers it was no different. Even in sparsely populated areas, there's always a trusty farmhouse nestled in a glen or a steeple poking up from behind a hill. Driving through some rural pockets feels like entering one of Monet's haystack paintings; it's as if time has stood still. Occasionally, passing fields dotted with bales, Frédéric pulled over and we removed our helmets then continued on. I used to consider this habit of his reckless and would primly protest but now, with the wind on my face and my hair streaming like a comet, I felt more alive than I had in ages. "IT SMELLS GREAT," I hollered, high on the cereal scents. Frédéric's elated reply flew past my ears: *"MERVEIL-LEUX!"*

Did the French countryside have a transformative effect on us? How was it that the prospect of leaving became more tantalizing at the very time we were seduced by France's loveliness? I recall thinking on that two-week trip that this was what life should be: not a permanent holiday but an adventure. Perhaps the telling moment was when we turned around and started back toward Paris and felt our playful spirits sinking. Back to what? I wondered. Viewed from a distance it seemed that our life wasn't really going forward. When we stopped for lunch or to buy a cold drink or visit a village our talk turned again to Tahiti. Only now the conversations started to play out differently.

"I'd be my own boss there at least," reflected Frédéric, who in truth had never felt at ease within big city law firms.

I nodded slowly. "I suppose I could get all my book research done before we leave. Then in Tahiti I can just write."

"It's not like Paris is *going* anywhere. Time flies."

"Two years is nothing."

Later, somewhere in Auvergne at a Café des Sports on a square rimmed by plane trees, the subject of our dream destinations came up again. "The thing is," I said slowly, thinking it through, "we haven't been offered India or Istanbul." I took another sip of a bitter espresso. "It's pointless thinking like that."

Frédéric nodded. "Anyway, what are we going to do? Stay put for the sake of a lift and an IKEA kitchen?"

He meant to be funny but the mention of our renovated apartment made me think of our tiny spare room and I felt a pang of sorrow. With no other use for it, the space had become a dumping ground for items that in the past would have been stored in our cellar—wine, spare mattresses, suitcases. Mostly, the door was kept shut.

⌒

It was dark when we got back to Paris and when we switched on our globe lamp, this time Earth lit up like a crystal ball. Dry, desert countries like Australia glowed the mustard gold of Van Gogh's haystacks. The Pacific Ocean looked not empty but positively magnetic. The scattered dots of French Polynesia now seemed like promising seeds. An image straight from a glossy travel magazine came to mind: palm-fringed islands, smooth and golden as blinis on a platter.

"How many did you say there were?"

"One hundred and eighteen. Spread across an area the size of Europe," recited Frédéric, who'd done some homework.

Remaining in Paris was starting to seem like the dull, safe option. Whereas moving to Tahiti was more in tune with riding *sans* helmet down a country road with the wind in our hair. You only live once, we kept saying.

⌒

Quel rêve! What a dream. It wasn't the only reaction from friends but it was the most common one when, several weeks after our holiday, we announced our move. The mere sound of those three light-as-air syllables, Ta-hi-ti, was like pushing play on a favorite old movie, one whose familiar scenes continued to delight. People joked and smiled as though we'd announced a sabbatical or an extended holiday. All that swimming, all that fresh fish and tropical fruit. "You'll be able to get coconut milk straight from your garden," enthused one friend, a keen cook. (It's an indication of how little I knew of tropical islands back then that I thought all the splashing liquid inside the nut was coconut milk.) *"Belles femmes, très, très belles,"* sighed a Senegalese taxi driver, winking at Frédéric in the rearview mirror. "Always in bikinis. Only bottoms. No tops in Tahiti."

The small island seemed to tap into a huge human longing, though whether the longing was very deep or very shallow was hard to say. Like Paris, it made people dream. If the lure of Paris lies in glorious civilization, history, art and architecture, Tahiti is its antithesis, evocative of beauty and romance of a wholesome, natural kind.

People's reactions fanned our enthusiasm. Stepping outside each morning, I became more aware of the manic tooting and shouted arguments on the busy thoroughfare that swept past our building. Wouldn't it be nice to get away from the noise and pollution for a while? Wouldn't it be lovely to swim laps in a tropical lagoon rather than in an indoor public pool wriggling with other people's hair and snot? Wasn't Tahiti famously *fertile?* Picturing the lushness and the turquoise water I was reminded of something I'd read about colors and their symbolism. Blue: the color of calm and healing. Green: the color of new beginnings.

By October it was like someone had switched on a propeller. Having allowed us time to procrastinate, the law firm wanted Frédéric in Tahiti as soon as possible.

I wrote lists of things to be done, lost them and wrote new ones. The most complex travel arrangements revolved around Maddie, who required endless veterinary appointments prior to a stay in quarantine before being granted entry to Tahiti. Frédéric made a show of grumbling about the expense—the million-dollar dog, he called her—yet when a friend kindly offered to mind her for as long as we were away, he looked appalled. "She's part of the family," he spluttered, "we can't go without Mads!"

To celebrate our departure, a few weeks before the removalists were due we invited sixteen friends over for dinner. It was an informal evening, a fitting hybrid of French and Australian influences, with Thai curries on the menu and plenty of cheeses for afterward—no one ever seemed to mind that the flavors didn't strictly go together. I covered the hired tables in cheap, shimmery Indian fabric and Frédéric decorated them with careful arrangements of flowers and candles. From the outset Paris dinner parties had been an enlightening source of cultural experience to me and this one, our very own and last, was no exception.

An American couple were the first to arrive, surprising us by being five minutes early. Over the next forty-five minutes the other English-speaking guests turned up. At half past nine, an hour and a half after we'd invited people, I glanced around the half-empty room.

"Who's missing?" asked our dear friend Alicia, picking up on my anxiety.

"The French," I answered bluntly. Except for Jean, none of our French friends had arrived.

She waved a hand to indicate there was nothing to worry about.

"They'll get here soon."

And they did. Remarkably, although our tardy friends had traveled from different corners of the city, all nine turned up within five minutes of each other, as if invited to a function that began sharply at a quarter to ten. There was a clamor of good-humored complaints as they poured through the door.

"About time!" Anne loudly exclaimed, voicing my thoughts precisely until she made her point clear: "About time you guys got a lift."

"How often have you made us walk up those bloody stairs?"

"And now they've finally got one they're going, *les salauds*."

Everyone had a story about the traffic, the metro, the buses. There were no apologies for being late: it was Paris' fault; it was our fault for living in the inner city, where parking was impossible. Suddenly the room was noisier, fuller. Ashtrays were requested and a new round of mojitos had to be poured. By the time we sat down to dinner it was 10.30 pm and clouds of cigarette smoke had built up overhead.

"Can you believe how rude they were?" At two in the morning, after everyone had gone, Frédéric sank into an armchair. For a moment I was surprised. It was unlike him to be cross with latecomers. *L'homme du dernier moment*, Man of the Last Minute—among his friends Frédéric's lack of punctuality was a source of teasing, though to me it was only ever exasperating. "As if you don't have enough to do when you're trying to feed that many people." He shook his head disdainfully. "Imagine doing that."

Who knows how many misunderstandings go undetected in a marriage; who could say how many times we had wrongly presumed to know the other's meaning? Were it not for his next words this would have been another of those occasions. I'd forgotten all about our American friends. But not Frédéric.

"Imagine arriving five minutes *early*," he muttered crossly.

⌐⌐

It was our first major move together since we'd met eight years before and though this made it exciting, it was also stressful. While everything had to be packed up to rent out our apartment, not everything would fit in our shipping container. Many boxes and pieces of furniture would remain behind, locked in the cellar. But decisions about what to take and what to leave highlighted fundamental personality differences. Frédéric, a natural hoarder, could not bear the idea of parting with anything—even for a few years. An entire day was devoted to constructing a special box in which to pack his model ship, an impossibly fragile meter-long three-mast replica of the one sailed by the French explorer La Pérouse. A lovely Louis XVI console table—80 kilos of marble miraculously supported by long, fluted legs—was earmarked for the journey, too. As were childhood collections of shells, Tintin comics and our playful paintings on glass, cherished mementoes we bought together in Romania.

By contrast, having moved around many times as a child,

I was an old hand at sorting and culling. True, I did go a bit mad buying books to take to Tahiti. And I suppose fragrant candles weren't strictly a necessity. But my trove was modest next to the piles of belongings tagged for Tahiti by Frédéric. There were tense mutterings on both sides. "You've got to be joking," I'd say, sifting through one of his boxes. "Did you move my Jules Verne collection back into the Paris pile?" he accused me at one point.

The disagreements might have been petty but there was a cultural underdrift to them. To listen to Frédéric I was like New World tumbleweed: no family history, no roots. Whereas to hear me speak he was a member of an old European snail species weighed down by memories, keepsakes and heirlooms. If neither perception was fair or true, briefly we both came perilously close to living up to our respective caricatures.

When all was packed and done, I walked. I'd always got around in Paris mostly on foot, and during those last weeks my trails looped all over the inner arrondissements. Time flies and two years is nothing—yet one cold evening in the courtyards of the Louvre, I detected a note of finality in the way my winter boots beat on the cobblestones. Earlier in the day I'd cursed the city after a squabble at our local dry cleaners. The owner had been indignant when I pointed out that the black inky marks they'd put on our white quilt covers hadn't washed out. "That's our system, Madame," she'd retorted haughtily. "We have to stamp each item so we know who it belongs to." The illogic was infuriating; the idea of dry cleaners leaving stains instead of removing them made me want to shout.

But now, enclosed by the softly lit courtyard, all I felt was love. Dear Paris, thank you for opening my eyes. For showing me the grace and beauty in small things: a spray of flowers and vines, sculpted in stone above an entrance; a massive wooden door, worn smooth and shiny from human touch. No other city inspired in me the same surging emotion. I knew of none as dazzling, nor any other that could look quite as flat and monotone. But then constancy in appearance, in feeling, in anything, can be dull, which to the French is unforgivable. My years in Paris had not been dull. I looked up at the Louvre's sculpted facade with a lump in my throat. Good-bye cherubs; good-bye angels; farewell pontiffs, kings and queens. I felt a little stab of regret that I'd never bothered to find out who these important figures were.

In those last weeks I popped into Notre-Dame des Victoires so often that in my memory one visit has merged with another. After lighting a prayer candle—admittedly not always a tall ten-euro one—I remained in the rose glow, straining my eyes and tilting my head until my neck ached. In the beginning the ex-voto plaques hadn't much interested me but once I got started, reading them became part of the ritual. In this place of pilgrimage the walls and arches, even the risers between steps, were tiled with messages. There were more than ten thousand plaques in all, in thanks for sight restored or health recovered, for lives spared in war. Though my favorite was number 3585, down a dimly lit aisle to the left of the nave.

LOVE AND RECOGNITION
TO MARY AND JOSEPH
THROUGH THEIR INTERCESSION
I HAVE THE JOY OF BEING
MOTHER TO SEVERAL CHILDREN

Below were three dates, spread throughout the 1860s, and beside each one was an initial: L, E and M. Louise, Emile and Maurice? Louis, Edgard, Marie? Whoever they were, their mother had clearly struggled to have them, otherwise she wouldn't have gone to the effort and expense of posting a plaque. *Three* children: Frédéric's magic number. My heart always swelled at the sight of those initials and once or twice I'd had to brush away a tear that escaped. You didn't have to be a believer to want to hear the message, soberly engraved on stone and marble thousands of times over.

Miracles do happen.

There was one last thing to be done before we got on the plane. Since it opened in October, everyone had been raving about the Gauguin exhibition—the largest collection of the artist's oeuvre from his many years in French Polynesia. Given the serendipitous timing, we had to see it. Apparently many Parisians felt the same way because at the Grand Palais the queues that extended from the glass entrance doors were longer than any I'd seen at a major exhibition.

Despite the crowds, once we finally got inside the atmosphere was almost churchly. In the expressly dimmed rooms,

Gauguin's Tahitians—mostly women, many of them naked or semi-naked—shone like icons. The colors were not just rich, they were incandescent: lustrous shades of ruby and amber, rose-pink, yellow and nut-brown threw light and heat onto our faces, stretching across the darkness like a trail of bonfires on a beach.

The story of Paul Gauguin's escape from the confinement of overcivilized Europe to idyllic Tahiti, along with his lust for young native girls, is as famous as any of his paintings. No other person, it is said, has done more to fan fantasies about the island. The nudity on the walls of these rooms was largely a product of his imagination, though. By the time the artist arrived in Pape'ete in 1891, Tahitians were buttoned up in missionary clothes. Not finding the perfect, primitive culture he had sought, Gauguin chose to paint not what he saw but what he'd hoped to see.

Throughout my adolescence, two of Gauguin's Tahitian women sat on my wall, filling my bedroom with their solid, comforting presence. The picture must have been precious to me because I paid to have it framed. Now, face-to-face with the original, I studied *Women on a Beach*. Unlike many of his other subjects, the pair in this painting was fully clothed. Here were the same heavyset islanders in the floral sarong and pink Mother Hubbard dress that looked too hot for the beach. But for all its familiarity, to my adult eyes the painting was puzzling.

A knot formed in the traffic flow as visitors were forced to step around me. One woman clicked her tongue disapprovingly. I clicked back. With our departure imminent, I was looking for answers. What had the artist wanted to say? Was

Women on a Beach in part a comment on the elusive nature of paradise? The truth is, for much of his time in Tahiti Gauguin felt frustrated and disillusioned. It struck me that the women didn't look very friendly. Were they bored? Disgruntled? What was it that drew me to the painting all those years ago? The outlined, flat forms now struck me as inert: I preferred animated daubs and trowelled-on paint. How strange that Gauguin had become known around the globe as an ambassador for Tahiti when his pictures hardly offered a typical postcard view, I thought. Despite the rich pigments it was a moody picture. Even the lagoon was not turquoise or aqua but moss-green.

A lid of cloud had closed over the city by the time we stepped back outside. This was one of the shortest days of the year and it was already getting dark. If the exhibition had raised unsettling questions, the wintry chill and skeletal trees made my excitement for our move bounce up again. Bring on radiant color and sunshine! Bring on yawning blue sky and sea breezes strong enough to wipe clean any slate. Oh yes, I was ready—even if I wasn't sure quite what awaited me.

THREE

"Loom" doesn't capture it. Nor is it enough to say the island "rose up" from the ocean. It burst through the surface, not like land at all but a surge of pure energy, caught mid-motion as if by a spell.

"*C'est vraiment* Jurassic Park, *non?*" Frédéric yelled into the wind. We were standing on the top deck of the *Aremiti IV*, one of the fast ferries that go back and forth between Tahiti and Mo'orea. A strong swell barreled portside into the boat and we had to grip the rail as she rolled and leaned. It was not yet ten in the morning but already sunlight rebounded off everything, making it hard to look at the water and the white deck. Since the ferry had set a straight course out of Pape'ete's port we now had a clear view of our destination.

"It looks kind of scary," I finally shouted back. Somehow the photos we'd looked at in Paris hadn't prepared me. The island made me think of a heartbeat stopping and starting. There was not one mountain peak but many, and they jabbed morphing cumuli then plunged to Earth, only to soar straight up and needle the clouds again. So much for the blini-islands my mind had conjured up back in front of our globe lamp.

Frédéric had already had a week on his own to get used to the scenery, whereas only a few hours ago I'd stepped from the plane into the pillowy damp of Pape'ete's night. People complain about languor in the tropics but to me the combination of heat and humidity creates a sense of suspense. The very first thing I did was take a big, deep breath. The hot air smelled of peat and overripe mangoes and salty ocean. A tropical thunderstorm was coming, for sure.

The journey from Paris had taken twenty-two hours and had been beset by the usual airport delays—some or other strike at Charles de Gaulle then the interminable security and travel document checks at Los Angeles. But at Pape'ete there was no waiting for transit buses or disembarkation bridges; we simply walked across the tarmac straight to the entrance of the terminal, where three men in straw hats and bright floral shirts sang and strummed. Ukuleles have never been my favorite instrument but the music was infectiously jovial, if a bit frenetic for three in the morning. A woman with long black hair handed flower buds to passengers as lines formed for passport control. *Yo-rah-nah*, she repeated, or so it sounded, though I knew from my language book it was spelled *'ia ora na*. That was the extent of my Tahitian: hello.

The impression of having stepped into a postcard continued in the arrivals hall, where the first thing Frédéric did was hang two milk-white floral manes around my neck. I felt a bit silly, decorated like a tourist, though in fact many locals were being greeted with garlands, too. They were surprisingly heavy and cool: he'd bought them at the market earlier in the day, Frédéric explained, and the vendor had told him to keep them in the fridge for freshness. Not frangipanis but the same small flower I'd been given by the lady with the long hair, only now the fragrance was many times more potent. Added to my lack of sleep, the jet lag and the hot, charged air, the sweet scent made me light-headed, like I'd had a couple of stiff drinks.

But now on the ferry, with the wind whipping my hair, I felt utterly alert. Mo'orea's reputed beauty and proximity to Tahiti, along with the fact that it was much less developed than the main island, were among the reasons we'd decided to live there. From this distance it appeared uninhabited: an upward swathe of uninterrupted green. Even allowing for erosion and land slips, this must be pretty much how Mo'orea has looked for millennia, and I couldn't help thinking of earlier sea voyages. The first Polynesians had sailed to these islands not in dugout canoes as I'd imagined but large double-hulled ships— wind-powered predecessors of the waterjet-propelled catamaran we were on now. Determined not to arrive completely ignorant, in Paris I'd bought a few books and read of the existence of Tahiti's kings and queens and those extraordinary voyages of the first Polynesians. After decades of speculation, it is now accepted that their ancestry goes back to southern Asia, and not South America.

Tellingly, until then my only knowledge had been of the later explorations by Europeans. It was after one of his three long stays on Tahiti that Captain Cook sailed on to Australia. Though of all the foreign lands seen by the white men during

these extraordinary circumnavigations, it was Tahiti that inspired the most rhapsodic reviews.

"Cook's Bay is over there, round a few points," announced
Frédéric, as if reading my thoughts. The bay was renowned
for its spectacular scenery and we'd considered renting a
house there until someone revealed it was also the wettest
spot on the island, owing to the clouds that frequently clung
to its peaks. "Cook actually anchored at the next bay, Opunohu," continued Frédéric, who'd evidently been reading up
too.

The mountains grew taller as the ferry drew closer. Any
lingering thoughts of history were banished by signs of modern life: cars skirting around what must be the narrow ring
road; windows blinking sun signals; houses, or rather shacks
by the look of some of them, built right on the sand. Suddenly Frédéric pointed: "That's our beach, over there."

I looked left to where a stretch of blond sand fairly glittered in the sun. Sitting a little back from the shore, hidden
among leafy trees and coconut palms, was a white house with
a pale green roof.

Our house. On a beach. By a lagoon. On an island.

Frédéric glanced at me anxiously. Arriving one week ahead
of me had put him in the role of tour guide. On top of this,
he probably felt responsible: it was his job that had led us
here and he wanted me to be happy and to like it. My silence
must have worried him. But the wind on the upper deck
made anything but snippets of conversation difficult. Plus

honestly, I felt too much to express. I was excited, definitely. But also awed and intimidated.

Arriving somewhere by air makes you feel mighty. Looking down at a perfect quilt of fields or the many squiggles and inlets of a harbor, or even the plunging creases and folds of an alpine range, you feel all seeing, all knowing. Whereas arriving by boat, I discovered, makes you feel small. It wasn't just the impressive heights ahead: there were the mysterious inky depths and the vastness of the ocean. For ten years we'd lived in a charmingly congested *quartier* in a city where parks came pocket-sized and where Montmartre—elevated by the creamy domes of Sacré-Coeur basilica—was the closest thing to a mountain. By contrast, Mo'orea appeared not so much one of nature's creations as Mother Nature herself, rising up to greet us or maybe scare us away.

It was precisely the radical change we'd sought, as Frédéric now indirectly reminded me. Pointing to some hills to the right of the bay into which we were heading, he said: "They look like a pregnant woman lying on her back, don't you think?" He was always seeing shapes and faces in clouds and landscapes. "They're her boobs; that's her stomach there."

But there was no time for me to make out anything. The ferry had charged through the island's gateway, the main pass that cut the encircling reef, and over the smooth lagoon it seemed to take off. From that point on, our arrival was a sequence of vivid tableaux: the teal water below, whipped up like egg whites by the ferry's engines; blokes with massive tattooed arms and practiced aim lassoing pylons; a colorful ribbon of disembarking passengers dressed in everything from loose-fitting frocks to surf shorts, thongs and bare feet, base-ball caps and pandanus hats. Tahitian floral shirts abounded but there wasn't a tie or business suit to be seen.

There was plenty of noise and action, though. As we edged down the pedestrian ramp a series of blasts sounded from the belly of the ferry: cars, trucks, motorbikes and scooters fired up their motors in readiness to drive off. Clack clack went their wheels down the ramp; toot toot sounded a few horns. The disembarking vehicles seemed to get tangled up with those waiting to board; there were shouts and hand signals and right in the middle of this, one fellow stopped his car, blocking traffic both ways, and strode over to a ute. I waited for the sort of altercation that was a common sight on the boulevard that swept past our building in Paris. But all that was exchanged was a swinging bundle of pineapples for a friendly bag of something else. The other drivers smiled and waited and called out greetings.

"Well," I mused, after taking in the scene, "we're definitely a long way from Paris."

For some reason we both found this funny. Of everything I'd seen in the last few hours it was this simple show of Polynesian patience, this jovial fruit swap, that seemed most exotic.

It's just like in the photos, Frédéric had said of our house when we'd spoken over the phone. And at first glance it was. There it stood on short stilts, bright white as if freshly washed, and covered in splashes of pink and crimson and orange bougainvillea. It was newish, possibly one of those kit homes that apparently were popular in the territory, colonial in style with a wide, encircling veranda and iron lacework decorating the eaves. There was nothing grand about it, but it was very pretty and cheerful.

Stepping through the front door, I got a shock. Not because of the interior; to be honest I didn't even notice it. Rather, from what I could see straight ahead, outside, through windows and sliding glass doors: an aqueous shimmer so bright you might need sunglasses in the house. "It's right there!" I exclaimed, amazed. In the photos the lagoon hadn't looked nearly so close. It seemed unfathomable that a real estate agent would *under*sell a water view—in Sydney a distant suggestion of blue was enough to prompt superlatives about a not-to-be-missed harborside property. Not wanting to spoil the surprise, Frédéric had continued to downplay the proximity but in reality the beach was at the bottom of our garden. I stood on the back porch, taking it all in. Less than a kilometer away, across the gently ruffled surface of the lagoon, a pretty frill of spray and breaking waves marked the reef. My eyes skipped back to the shoreline, sparkly in the sunlight. Why, it couldn't be more than . . .

I kicked off my sandals then and ran down the three porch steps and over a stretch of buffalo grass no more than five meters wide, through a small opening in the back fence that we could easily close to stop Maddie wandering, onto soft sand and straight into water that made me shriek in delight.

"It's so WARM!"

"Eighty-two degrees," Frédéric said, catching up. "All year round. In a really hot spell it can get even warmer."

Having never been a cold-water person this was all the enticement I needed. We hurried inside, found our bathing suits and then plunged in—or rather waded in, as we had to go quite a distance before the water rose up to our chests. It was the same ocean I'd swum in much of my life yet the lagoon couldn't have been more different from the Pacific that pounded the east coast of Australia. It wasn't just the warm temperature or the absence of barreling waves but its taste and texture. There was no salty bite, no zing on your skin. Instead the sea water was light and soft, as if *monoi* coconut oil had been added to it, I would think later.

The next morning we were having a leisurely breakfast on the beach, sitting at the plastic table Frédéric had bought expressly for this purpose, when a large Polynesian man appeared around the side of our house. Frédéric had already met our landlord, Alain, and his wife, Aima, who lived just across the road. They seem really nice, he had assured me over the telephone. Dressed in shorts and a singlet and thongs, Alain mopped his brow with a threadbare towel draped around his neck and shoulders, and shuffled his weight from one foot to the other, a bit awkwardly. "They're called solo," he explained, holding out a bag heavy with papaya. "They're small but sweet."

We all sat down and made small talk about the house and the stunning view, about the wet season, which so far had been unusually dry. Alain explained the mysterious sprinkling that we'd felt despite there not being a rain cloud in the sky. "*Mouches pisseuses,* they're a real pest," he said, pointing directly above at the thick branches and foliage that provided welcome shade. "They love the *mape* tree." A recent colonizer from California, the grasshoppers had rapidly spread across the island, where they spent their days chomping leaves and peeing. After a few minutes, Alain lightly slapped the arms of the chair and made to get up. "How about coming for dinner one night soon? Are you free Thursday?"

My eyes met Frédéric's and neither of us could help smiling. It wasn't as if we had to check our social diaries. We'd arrived in the territory not knowing a soul. This early invitation was a welcome surprise. "That would be lovely," I replied enthusiastically.

A kindly man, there was no doubt, but somewhat solemn and reserved: that was my first impression of Alain. Perhaps he feared his new tenants would live up to the Parisian reputation for being difficult and demanding. Possibly our neighbor had mixed feelings about the French full stop: underlying resentments exist in any colonized territory. This was the kind of second-guessing I used to do during my first years in France. It's hard in a new culture to know what people are really thinking.

⌐⌐

When Thursday arrived, the northeasterly was blowing hard enough to send newspapers flying like confetti around our back porch. But at Alain and Aima's place *côté montagne,* as the mountain side of the road is called, there was no sea breeze at all. On their front patio the air was still and thick and the iced rum punch made by Alain's mother, Guite, slipped down easily. "Heaven's above, my poor flowers need rain," she grumbled good-naturedly. "*Oh là là*, when it starts it's really going to pour."

Our closest neighbors were all directly related to Alain, and at dinner there was his sister Moetu, too. That was how Polynesians lived apparently, in family groups. The women looked feminine and elegant, wearing hibiscuses behind their ears and loose frocks in patterned fabrics which threw green next to magenta, fuchsia next to orange, bright blue next to yellow and red. Trimmed with lace, they appeared a jazzed-up version of the old missionary-style dresses. Aima had a gentle face and a tinkling laugh like running water, while Guite had the sort of stately dignity that some women acquire in old age.

As the evening wore on the atmosphere grew more relaxed and it occurred to me the initial reserve I'd sensed in Alain the day we'd met might have been shyness. When I teased Frédéric about his inability to cook anything more complex than an omelette—a fact that, to tell the truth, did not greatly amuse me—Alain came to his defense. Guite, who lived alone, chortled and shook her head as if she herself knew something of the hopelessness of men. When our landlord was chided by his mother for his failure to attend church, Frédéric patted Alain's shoulder sympathetically. "While you're off praying," he teased the women, "he's cooking your dinner."

As we were leaving, Aima handed me a paper bag. "My stepfather has a small vanilla plantation," she explained. "Maybe one day you'd like to go there." The instant I opened the bag, the scent bolted out like a genie from a bottle: a gloriously heady melange of fine old leather and the pink musk stick lollies I'd loved as a child. The vanilla beans felt surprisingly soft between my fingers. In the moonlight, they shone like dark, polished wood.

There must have been fifteen or so plump sticks in the paper bag and I knew enough about vanilla prices to understand the generosity of the gift. First papaya, now this, offered to virtual strangers without fuss or fanfare, as though sharing was the most natural thing in the world. With no friends and no family in the territory, this unexpected welcome from our neighbors was precious. Walking home I couldn't help wondering what we might give back in return.

The car windows were down, the Cranberries were turned up and there was so much white, supernatural moonlight that the ferns and plants along the roadside had a shiny, plastic appearance. It was our first full Saturday together on Mo'orea and to celebrate we'd decided to head to the other side of the island, to find somewhere to eat among a cluster of small hotels and restaurants. After checking distances we'd left the map at home. Apart from a few interior dirt roads there was only the one tarred ring road around the coastline. With no traffic lights or intersections on the island, navigation wouldn't be a source of disagreement in the car. Left or right out of our drive—that was the only decision to make. On this night it didn't matter. From our place, our destination, Hauru Point, looked to be exactly midway around Mo'orea; half an hour away we estimated. "Left," I'd said.

The wind that rushed through the car was warm, the palm trees that flashed by looked like something dreamed up by Dr. Seuss: strange, long-necked creatures in wild wigs. On the left side, between houses, the lagoon sparkled with moon-light. On the right side of the road, neon bulbs lit outdoor areas where large family groups sat around tables eating and drinking. Behind rose the mountains, blacker than anything. By day, when the contrast was more obvious between *côté mer* and *côté montagne*, between the ocean's horizontality and the heights of the interior, the island seemed to have a split per-sonality.

"Watch out!" I hadn't meant to scream but the shadow shot out from nowhere and we missed it by barely a meter. Dressed in a dark hoodie, on a bike about three sizes too small for him, the youth rode straight for us on the wrong side of the road. I thought maybe it was a deliberate provoca-tion but then we overtook more kids on bikes who seemed equally oblivious.

"Where's the closest emergency ward?" I asked, already imagining the terrible possibility of hitting one of these night riders.

"Pape'ete. There's a helicopter for emergencies." This piece of information must have been offered by someone; it was not the sort of detail Frédéric would fret about. "It takes five minutes."

After about half an hour street lamps suddenly appeared along the roadside, along with a few small hotels and a string of shops. But for a Saturday night the tourist strip at Hauru

Point seemed awfully quiet. It was the middle of the wet season and *fermé* signs hung in many restaurant windows. The few places we stopped at were empty and at one glance we decided to continue on.

A scooter with no headlights overtook us, though its tinny hum sounded more like an outboard motor on the lagoon. "I see it, I see it," Frédéric said impatiently, swerving to avoid a hobbling dog, though he couldn't avoid the crabs—a great army of large mud crabs, hundreds of them, scrambling sideways across the road. It was the strangest sight. "You could try herding them to the other side," Frédéric suggested, slowing right down. In the end we rolled right over them, wincing at the sound of their shells crunching beneath the wheels. Upset to have killed something, Frédéric glanced forlornly in the rearview mirror, but with no street lamps along the roadside, whatever carnage lay behind remained in obscurity.

After we'd been driving for almost an hour we'd nearly given up hope: in a few minutes we'd be back at the house. Finally we came to a restaurant gaily strung with fairy lights, outside which was a lineup of parked cars. For a moment it seemed we might be too late; the mostly Polynesian diners seemed to be settling their bills. But a tall, handsome woman ushered us to a table. Within no time we were served grilled tender mahi mahi that came with a ginger sauce and steamed vegetables—more Chinese style than French.

We were home just after nine. In Paris we'd have been stepping out to a bar or bistro about now. Yet apart from our house, there wasn't a single light on in the neighborhood; there was barely a sound except from barking dogs. We sat on our front steps, staring at the shadow mountain behind Alain and Aima's house, reflecting on the evening. It seemed a bit magical. All we'd done was keep driving straight ahead and now here we were back where we started. "Lap number one," announced Frédéric, like a race track announcer, vowing to keep count of our tours of the island.

"What do you suppose those teenagers were doing hanging about that little bridge?" I asked.

"What teenagers do everywhere probably—smoking, drinking, maybe fighting." *Paka*, the local weed, was a big problem among youth across the territory. "*Paka* and beer, the mix makes them crazy," Alain had told us, shaking his head.

Frédéric was still pondering the crabs, though he appeared to have got over his guilt. "I wonder if you can eat them."

"Aren't they the same as the one in our garden?" I asked doubtfully. A large irritable crab lived beneath the grand old *mape*, the Tahitian chestnut tree that stood in our backyard. Our arrival had obviously caused offense because when one of us strayed too close it shot an indignant spray of sand from its burrow.

⌒

The six Polynesian removalists who jumped out of the truck to deliver our belongings from France were more than burly, they were fearsome. Most of them had no necks and nearly all were covered in tattoos, except on their faces; several looked as if they could kill simply by sitting on you. From their stern expressions they clearly meant business. With a sinking heart, I pictured our boxes of crockery tossed like handballs from one to the other, our furniture carelessly knocked and scratched. Frédéric's beloved model ship, which he'd treasured for twenty years, would be smashed to pieces in no time—if it wasn't already. I would try not to say I told you so.

We'd already heard jokes about slow island time and Tahitian work ethics but these guys didn't stop. Our packing boxes were hefted onto shoulders as wide as shelves; pieces of furniture that had required two removalists in Paris were lifted single-handedly. Yet despite the fast pace, every time they entered the house the men slipped out of their thongs, leaving them lined up at the door, where they put them on again to fetch more loads from the truck. It seemed a lot of bother, especially with a queen-sized bed balanced on your back, but it was confirmation of a custom we'd taken note of when we went for dinner at Alain and Aima's house. No shoes inside.

And then amid this manly scene of strength and muscles, I witnessed from the kitchen window an incongruous sight. The heaviest, fiercest-looking bloke—a professional weight-lifter, he later told us—carefully picked a bud from one of our gardenia bushes and slipped it behind his ear. Possibly you have to have seen his shoulders, the massive legs, to appreciate the wonder of the gesture. Soon several of the removalists appeared at the door wearing the same delicate white blossoms that at the airport I'd thought were an affectation for tourists—*tiare* they were called.

It was a joy to discover that Frédéric had taken no notice of me in Paris. Box after packing box was opened to reveal items I'd listed as contraband. I hadn't realized how important it would be to have our own belongings in a strange environment but I could have clapped with delight to see our kooky, colorful Romanian glass paintings and the old ceramic bowls that must have held couscous for whole villages in Morocco, along with the handsome volumes of Jules Verne. Not a single thing was broken, not a plate or cup. Pleased as anything, Frédéric put the model ship in pride of place on the console table.

It turned out I'd packed enough reading material for a desert island—a fact that did not go unnoticed. One particularly bulky box labeled "SARAH'S RESEARCH" caught Frédéric's eye. Peeling off the masking tape, he found it was brimming with history books that I'd bought to help fill in the background for my novel. "*The Bretons at Home,*" he read, "*Il y a un Siècle la Bretagne*; *Breton Folk*; *La Vie Quotidienne des Paysans en Bretagne*; *Vêtements et Costumes en Basse–Bretagne.*" As he flipped through the pages of one, his eyebrows flew up in surprise. "How much information do you need on nineteenth-century Breton *bonnets*?"

I wasn't going to admit I'd gone overboard. "It's good to have all the facts at your fingertips," I replied airily.

We spent evenings fiddling and arranging. Down came the gaudy floral curtains, all except the ones in the bedroom. Up went our paintings and photos. Together, Frédéric and I managed to heft the leggy console table and its marble top to a new position, only to decide it belonged back where it was. At night we lit a musk-scented Diptyque candle we'd been given as a going-away gift. In Paris these full-bodied fragrances used to permeate the whole apartment. But here the candle was overpowered by the briny sea breeze, along with the gentle *hupe* that blew in the late afternoon from the valleys, bringing with it notes of wild ginger and sultry ylang-ylang.

⌒

But it was another delivery two weeks after our packing boxes and furniture arrived that made the house feel more like home. A dog may not talk but there is a whole soundtrack to its company—the rooms had felt empty and quiet without the patter of paws, the jingling identity tag, the sighing, farting and snoring, the snuffling and wuffing during twitchy dreams. It had been almost six weeks since we'd bid a teary farewell to Maddie, who had stared back at us in confusion from a cage in the back of a government transport van. All pets entering French Polynesia are required to do quarantine in a country approved by the territory. I'd picked the home of Queen and corgis, figuring that a British center would surely have a dog-mad Barbara Woodhouse figure to attend to Maddie's needs.

The stocky terrier that was led out to us on a leash at Faa'a airport looked very similar to the one we'd left, only better groomed and distinctly more roly-poly. The quarantine center had given us almost daily updates on Maddie's cunning hunger strike, for which she had been rewarded with an exclusive diet of her favorite treat, the one thing that drove her wild with greed: cooked chicken. Otherwise she was the same perky, bright-eyed Mads. For once Ms. Independence didn't put on a pained expression or do her rigor mortis routine on being picked up and cuddled. She yelped in joy and licked our ears and wriggled so much we all fell to the ground in a laughing heap.

Back at the house the buffalo grass seemed to throw her. She froze, one paw midair, as if trying to summon some ancestral memory of it—so much scratchier than tarred street and age-worn cobblestones and polished parquet. Then Maddie went off like a rogue cracker, ricocheting around the garden, squirting her scent over as much new territory as possible. Unabashedly colonialist, she made it clear there would be no sharing it: the wild chickens and roosters were promptly dispatched over the fence in an indignant squawking flap. I can't say I was sorry to see them go. They'd been waking us at odd hours of the night, and Maddie was praised and petted for her troubles.

Later that day Frédéric and I sat on the beach with a glass of wine, entertained by the sight of our four-legged friend stalking the hermit crabs that would obsess her. Closer and closer she crept, with the stealth and patience of a tiger. "Go Mads, go," I cheered, when finally she lunged. The wily crabs waved and scuttled easily into the water. "That was close!" Ignoring our teasing, Maddie crouched back down on the sand and the pantomime with the crabs began all over again.

Our other entertainment was gazing at Tahiti. The view of the main island had come as a surprise, along with the proximity of the lagoon, that first time I raced from our porch onto the beach. In the photos sent by the real estate agency, Tahiti had looked indistinct and distant. In reality, it was only fourteen kilometers away—though even that sounded farther than it actually appeared to the eye. Across the narrow stretch of ocean, the island rose like a great pyramid; a massive, masculine counterweight to Mo'orea's slender peaks and femininity.

Back in Paris, when we were deciding between houses, I would have said any water view would be fantastic. The importance of seeing land had only dawned on me a few days before as we drove around Mo'orea. After wiggling around bays and inlets for about twenty minutes, the coastline turned a corner, at which point the diminishing wedge of Tahiti disappeared altogether. The swathe of uninterrupted ocean had looked like a landscape painting bereft of subject. The emptiness made me shiver. "I could go mad looking at that all day," I'd confessed to Frédéric, even though the lagoon was indisputably lovely and there was the reef in the distance.

Tahiti was company. Solid and reliable, the island was also a study in evanescence, registering endless variations in weather, light and mood. There was always something to watch—a plane coming into land, a sunset. If I felt a pang of aloneness when Frédéric headed off to Pape'ete to work each morning, in the late afternoon it was fun to watch the returning ferries growing from tiny dots into bigger ones. From their size and shape I tried to guess which was in front: the game, boxy *Moorea Express* or the larger *Aremiti IV*, which Frédéric caught. It was one of many local mysteries that both boats left at exactly the same time.

"It looks like a Cézanne painting," I said, staring at the island. With the sun slipping behind us, blue and violet ran into Tahiti's folds, rivers and ravines; salmon and gold dusted the slopes where houses and buildings had the warm glow of pale stone. In this lovely tricksy light they could have been

French hilltop villages. Smoke rose here and there along the coastline, drawing blond curls on the background slopes. When I'd asked Alain what people burned in their backyards he'd replied coconut husks, household rubbish, anything.

All day cumulous castles had been bulging and building up over Tahiti's peaks. Now, at their most vertical and magnificent, they began dissolving into thin bands and streamers as if the effort of appearing so puffed up and self-assured had proven exhausting. As we watched, the sun threw all its remaining strength at Tahiti to produce feverish luminosity: saffron and flamingo pink with deep ripples of indigo and cobalt. Like an old face, the island wrinkled, growing wiser and more ancient before our eyes.

Sumptuous sunsets. Palm-fringed private beach. Lagoon on our doorstep. Sweet papaya by the bagful. Vanilla beans bundled up like lush and fragrant firesticks.

I know, I know.

Paradise.

FOUR

During the day, while Frédéric was working at Pape'ete, I kept company with my artists and stalwart Bretons. Reached out to them you might say: truth be told, it felt like they had gone into hiding since our arrival on the island. My "novel" wasn't much of a story yet, only a scattering of scenes. But before leaving Paris a cast of nineteenth-century characters had formed in my mind, including a headstrong Breton lass and a lanky Australian painter, who had fled the uncouth colony for the center of the art world only to find himself in a rural backwater of pigs and peasants, situated on a rugged coast thrashed by chill winds and waves.

Through the window the lagoon throbbed with color, still and satiny. Initially I'd tried working on the veranda but the glare outside made it impossible to see the computer screen. My office was a corner of the living room: it's the sort of domestic detail that doesn't raise an eyebrow until one day it's cited in court as a reason for divorce. Officially the arrangement was on trial. For the moment I was making an effort to keep my papers tidy and to avoid calling Frédéric *maniaque*; Frédéric was trying to refrain from passing critical comment or staring pointedly at my "monsters," as he called my piles of books and notes. We both agreed the living room was the best option. Our mezzanine level was too hot to work in and the spare room was rather dark.

My head felt itchy and I sweated just thinking about those elaborate lace bonnets, clumping clogs and coarse dark skirts. Perhaps my pasty Bretons needed a moment to acclimatise to the tropical heat. Amid the palm trees and dark-skinned Polynesians my novel's setting did feel a little incongruous. Yet the true history of this artists' colony in Brittany had inspired me the moment I'd read about it: how amazed the Celtic-speaking farmers and fisherfolk must have been to see urbane painters from all over the world arriving in droves with their easels. I loved the idea of writing about artists, who with their insecurities and egos, failings and strengths, provide a vivid reminder of what it means to be human. I had a fascination for color, too, probably because it was the subject of so many conversations with Frédéric. He is color-blind—a vexation for one whose hobby is painting. Distinguishing red from green is a problem, of course, but many other complementary colors are also indistinguishable to him, depending on the light. Once in Paris he returned from a day of painting *en plein air* and proudly unveiled his work, raving about the glorious sunset that he had tried hard to capture. I hesitated, before coming out with it. "Freddie," I said as gently as I could, pointing to his sky, "you've painted it gray, not pink."

It became our habit to take a glass of wine onto the beach when Frédéric got home from work for an end-of-day debriefing.

"Regarde ça!" he exclaimed one evening, as a dazzling full moon rose above the horizon, like a massive sunflower blooming in outer space. Across the lagoon it rolled a gold runner of light right up to our feet. Straight ahead the dark bulk of Tahiti was just visible. Tiny pricks of light were strung like Christmas decorations along the island's coastline and up the low slopes.

"What's the latest from Pape'ete?" I asked after a pause. "Any news?"

He shook his head.

"Still waiting on a date for the court case."

His voice was tinged with frustration. A last-minute campaign to prevent him from practicing in the territory had been instigated by a pair of influential local lawyers—not Polynesians, interestingly, but *popa'a-*, the Tahitian word for white foreigners, which refers to the "grilled" appearance of sunburned European skin. It was nothing personal, they'd told him imperiously, but your arrival is *"ni souhaitée, ni souhaitable"*: neither desired nor desirable. Newcomers across many professions met with the same hostility from established French residents, apparently. The objections would be overruled soon enough, everyone knew, but the court case meant an unwelcome delay in the process of setting up office.

Changing the subject, he asked: "What about you, how did you get on with your writing?"

I nibbled a fingernail, staring at the moonlight, which no longer looked gold but like silver tinsel stretched straight across the water. "Okay, I guess." I attempted a joke. "Wrote a really good paragraph without a single 'e.'" This was one of the playful exercises recommended in a fiction manual to help writers free up their minds: that morning my task had been to describe the view from my window. "Lagoon," "sand" and "coconut palm" were fine but "blue" was out, as was "green," "turquoise," "sea," "ocean," "shimmer," "gardenia," "beach" and virtually every other word that popped into my head. After fifteen minutes of this supposed fun, I was stabbing the keyboard in frustration.

From the way his spine straightened I sensed Frédéric was about to get swept up in one of his characteristic waves of enthusiasm. It couldn't have been easy finding the right words of encouragement, knowing how badly I wanted this idea to work.

"Think of yourself as a tube of green mustard," he announced. It took me a moment to work out he meant Japanese wasabi paste—with all the fresh tuna we ate on the island it had become a mealtime staple. "Squeeze, squeeze, squeeze . . ." Pressing his thumb and fingers together he went on miming and squirting until a silent chant had taken up in my head: *limites, limites*, righto that's enough, his mother used to say firmly when as a boy Frédéric took a story or joke too far. In the darkness he didn't notice my incredulous expression. Was this meant to inspire me, this imaginary green poo of words?

"Something will come out, eventually," he assured me solemnly.

Squeeze I did at my desk, though my thoughts frequently drifted. I suppose it wasn't such a big leap, from one life goal to another. Book and baby: I'd never dared speak them so boldly but my aims for the next two years were clear in my mind before we moved. That both goals were big challenges I did not doubt: I'd never written a novel and so far my body hadn't shown much inclination toward pregnancy, even with the assistance of doctors. Yet it didn't occur to me that it might be too much to ask—of myself and also of the island. Where there's a will, there's a way; so the proverb went anyway. On occasion at my desk I spoke sternly to myself. Sarah, you have to learn to be a better sleeper. You must breathe more deeply. Stop worrying. Then it will happen naturally.

Trying to get pregnant naturally wasn't something we'd given much of a go in Paris. Once my test result came back with its single but significant anomaly, we were advised not to dally. We saw a couple of infertility specialists before finding the right one. The first came with high recommendations and a long waiting list. On the day of my appointment, we sat for forty-five minutes in a waiting room with high ceilings patterned like doilies. The walls were hung with oil paintings of voluptuous women with dimpled, creamy flesh, peach cheeks and rosebud mouths. Frédéric's lips curled. "They remind me of Renoirs," he sniffed. "Chocolate-box pictures." We might have saved ourselves further wait. The cloying prettiness was, in Frédéric's humble opinion, a sign of extremely bad taste and though he didn't say so, it was apparent that to his mind this was an undesirable trait in one meant to help us make a baby. When finally we were granted our allocated minutes, the doctor delivered an eloquent speech then quickly ushered us out. "Next time, next time," he said dismissively when I tried to ask a question. "No next time," we huffed on the street outside.

Eventually we found Dr. B, a small, warm man who not only spoke but also listened and patiently answered our questions. Infertility specialists are fond of statistics and charts, and the ones he showed us were probably no more hopeful than the success rates given by the previous doctor. I can't say. Early on I developed a habit of tuning out when it came to the probability of me getting pregnant. Like me, Frédéric had looked around Dr. B's airy office and taken heart. The African fertility statues that stared at us, squat and goggle-eyed, from handsome shelves were a vast improvement on the faux Renoirs. And so it was with optimism that we had commenced IVF treatment—the panacea for fertility problems, I'd thought then. There were countless tests and intrusions and the daily injections of hormones left a rash of pin-sized bruises across my stomach. But really the only part I dreaded was going to Clinique de la Muette for the main procedures. It was a maternity hospital and the elevator to the wards was often full of children and fathers bearing flowers, on their way to meet the latest addition to the family. The contrast between their brimming excitement and our fragile hopes was almost unbearable and I all but turned my back on them.

Still, after each failure there was the prospect of another attempt, which kept the dream alive. Though I'd heard it described as a roller coaster, doing IVF felt more like being on an ever-turning Ferris wheel. The nurses told me I coped well with it. And so it had appeared for a time.

⌐

Accustomed as I was to working from home, it was clear to me early on that extra discipline and rigor would be required on Mo'orea. Compared to our Paris apartment in our inner-city neighborhood with its cafés and buzzing street life, this house on an island where we knew nearly no one felt intensely isolated. Time had a curious elasticity—hours could drip by but then suddenly I'd wonder where the day had gone. In an effort to be more productive, I wrote a timetable that included allocations for coffee breaks, e-mailing and my writing exercises. Although it was regularly modified, the first line never changed: 7 am SWIM.

When Frédéric roared off on his motorbike, cutting it fine again for the 6:50 am ferry, beeping twice for good-bye, I was up and about. If the rush of traffic for the first boat to Tahiti hadn't woken me, the sun usually did: it poured through the red floral curtains, which lit up like cellophane. Dressed in my bathing suit, blinking at the brightness, I'd stop at the steps to put on my plastic sandals—*nouilles* as they were known locally, and they did feel a bit like cooked noodles. It had been a while since anyone had spotted a stonefish in the waters directly in front of our house, Alain had said, but I wasn't taking any chances. The cunningly camouflaged fish was very hard to see and stings were excruciating, potentially even fatal.

For the moment I had a city girl's suspicion of the creatures I came across in the lagoon. The sea urchins looked prickly to say the least and the sausage-like sea cucumbers slumbering on the sandy floor were vaguely repulsive, I thought. A slight nip on my ankle one morning made me spin around fast, only to be confronted by a clownfish smaller than my hand, quivering its fins in outrage. Who are you, how dare you? it seemed to say, then ridiculously it charged again, relenting only once it had chased me from the vicinity of its coral patch. The first time I encountered a spotted eagle ray gliding straight for me I'd flapped and flailed, recalling warnings about stings and tails. It swerved sharply, and with two or three powerful wing flaps, accelerated toward the reef. I was sorry then to have frightened it away. Diamond shaped, with a bill-like nose, big eyes and a dark coat patterned with small white spots, it was in fact a most curious, graceful creature. I hoped we'd meet again.

Wednesdays were the only days my routine differed slightly. On these mornings, round about seven a bicycle rattled and jangled into our driveway. Back then our doors were always open and if I wasn't in the lagoon I'd hear a loud sigh, heavy but not unhappy. Oh-aay, it sounded like. Another day, here I am, life goes on: that sigh conveyed all these things to me though it may have meant none of them. Then my name would drift through the house, called from outside: Sah–rah.

It was much more leisurely than the clipped way the French said it, with the middle "r" scraped from the back of the throat. Polynesians made a trill of the letter, a bit like the Spanish, by tapping the tongue on the roof of the mouth.

Like many other good things that had occurred since we arrived, Nelly came to us by way of Alain and Aima. When we were first introduced, she'd kept her eyes on the ground and had barely said a word, leading us to wrongly assume she didn't speak much French. Her looks were quintessentially Tahitian: long, thick black hair and a face that was unlined despite six children. Though only a year or two older than me, she would soon be a grandmother. In repose her face could look quite sad yet when she smiled it expressed such kindness and natural loveliness that somehow a year would pass before I even noticed her two missing front teeth.

The initial plan was that she'd come every Wednesday morning to iron Frédéric's work shirts. But this arrangement did not take into account Nelly's dogged thoroughness. *Laisse, laisse* leave it—she'd say, gently but firmly, when I told her not to worry about sweeping or changing sheets. With each week Nelly's responsibilities expanded until she was spending the whole morning cleaning and organizing our home. She had a thing about airing—no doubt a sensible precaution during the wet season. Sometimes I got out of the lagoon to find that Nelly had single-handedly dragged our queen-sized mattress onto the back lawn, along with cushions and Frédéric's heavy, dust-ridden rugs which hadn't seen sunlight since Iran or Afghanistan.

Like all Polynesians she preferred dark, woody interiors that were decorated with high color. The sagging, faded blue sofa Frédéric had bought second-hand straight out of university caused her no end of distress. "*Popa'a-* are different," she said wonderingly one day, shaking her head. I waited, curious to know what she saw as our strange manners and ways. "You like sad colors." Thinking to help, from a box I dug up the creamy canvas material I'd bought in Paris precisely for the purpose of covering the couch and armchairs. But Nelly brushed me off with another of her *laisse, laisse,* leave-it-to-me replies. The plain, pale fabric was neatly refolded and put back in the packing box. Instead she covered every centimeter of the couch and matching armchairs with whatever bright material she could find: sari silk I hadn't even meant to bring with us, batik tablecloths, scarves. When that didn't do the job, she dragged a large potted bougainvillea from outside and plonked it directly in front of the sofa in place of our coffee table. By the time I got home, papery flowers were already beginning to drop but Nelly's face was flushed with pride. "Not so sad now, is it?" she asked, nodding in satisfaction at the incongruous tree in the middle of the room.

"I thought we were paying for someone to do the ironing, not decorate the house," Frédéric remarked drily after we'd swept up the floral confetti and lugged the heavy pot back into the garden. Yet it was already apparent to both of us our home *would* be sadder without Nelly's weekly visits, her unselfconscious humming, the shallow dishes of *tiare* gardenia buds she left in the bathroom, not to mention the hibiscus flowers on our pillows. Here where we had no family or old friends, Nelly was an important part of our lives. It was the fact she cared as much as anything. Often she constructed elaborate floral arrangements, with bougainvillea and frangipanis and whatever else was in bloom. Poking stems through leaves, she built floor upon floor, creating whimsical towers of ephemeral beauty.

⌐⌐

The days grew hotter and clammier but the storm that had seemed imminent the night of my arrival still didn't come. I'd imagined the wet season would be similar to the monsoon in Singapore. There, a daily thunderstorm used to roll in around four and roll away again around five, so punctually you could set your watch by it. Another look at our globe lamp confirmed my poor grasp of geography: Singapore sat virtually on the equator whereas we were almost 2000 kilometers below it.

From our shore I watched each day as clouds built dark towers and brooding fortresses over Tahiti. But by the next morning they'd either have vanished altogether or melted into milder, amorphous forms that would bulk up again in the afternoon. The wet season was drawing to an end, the island was supposed to be at its most fecund, yet the ground was resolutely dry. Even our hardy bougainvilleas had to be brought back to life with regular hosing. Across the road Guite was despairing about her flowers. Morning and night she would water her garden, fretting that she wouldn't have much for her floral arrangement for church that week.

Then one evening in March, as we were sitting on our back patio, the gentle sea breeze turned into a gusty north-easterly that instantly dried and cooled our damp foreheads. The change must have been building for hours but it felt like someone had flicked a switch. My ears popped from all the electricity. Waves pounded the reef, sending whitecaps scudding across the lagoon and vibrations traveling through the air. Ferns shimmied and shook, coconut palms tossed their heads like impatient ponies, the rubbery papaya tree arched acrobatically.

When the rain fell the power of it was thrilling. Water rolled down our iron roof, falling over the eaves in fat glass ropes that glittered under the bright garden lights. The percussive din was so loud we had to shout to be heard. The next morning Tahiti had disappeared: rain and cloud had rubbed it out. It was Saturday and Frédéric and I raced into the lagoon like we had my first day, only this time it was not the warmth that made me squeal. "Feel how *cold* it is!" Though in fact only the surface layers had cooled; underneath the water temperature was the same as ever.

Just as it had seemed rain would never come, now it seemed it would never stop. I enjoyed the belated beginning of the wet season tremendously. The air felt fresh and energized and at my desk I felt recharged, too. Glorious waterfalls soon dropped down Mo'orea's sheer mountains like twisted bedsheets from a window. Was it the lack of other distractions on the island that made the rain, sunsets and full moons more dramatic? Did everything appear bigger viewed from a small dot in the ocean? Already I sensed that in our new life the natural world was a powerful presence.

FIVE

Pape'ete was my big day out. For a change of scenery and to ease the sense of isolation, once or sometimes twice a week I caught the early ferry to Tahiti with Frédéric. I worked in a spare room at his office. "It can be your city bureau," he offered. It says something about my new life that I took more care to dress up for what, in reality, was a provincial town than I ever had on a daily basis in Paris. Grooming was required: lipstick, mascara, perfume. A nice dress or a skirt and top made a change from the usual sarong and singlet, as did sandals instead of thongs. On the ferry over, Frédéric seemed to know half the passengers already and exchanged *'ia ora nas* with the crew. He was on particularly friendly terms with one fellow with a gold earring like a pirate's, for whom he collected Maddie's grubby fur clippings. The guy was delighted. Apparently he used it to fish for bait that was attracted to white hair—off-white in Maddie's case.

Frédéric had always said that given a second life he would

happily settle down as mayor of a village, and watching him wave, chat and shake hands I saw he'd be a natural. The atmosphere on the *Aremiti IV* was jolly: Polynesians dug into buns and cakes smothered in coconut icing, and the espresso from the small shop wasn't bad either. A taped broadcast welcomed passengers in Tahitian, French and English. To the tune of "Ebony and Ivory"—a rather sappy instrumental version—the ferry headed over the sunken slopes of Mo'orea's ancient volcano, through its gateway, Vai'are Pass, and across the deep valley of ocean toward Tahiti.

"An ugly, plundered-looking town"—that's how the famously acerbic American writer Paul Theroux described Pape'ete (pronounced Pa-peh-eh-teh, though a lot of French *popa'a-* say Pa-pet). The main problem to my eyes was that it wasn't really anything. There was little sign of either Polynesian charm or colonial ambition in the peeling facades and low-story offices, built on the cheap in the sixties and seventies. There were boulevards named after Tahitian royalty, and being a French territory there was the requisite avenue Charles de Gaulle. But these traffic-choked arteries had no sweep or grandeur, nor were they scruffy in an exotic way. Though it was right by the water, downtown Pape'ete did not have the feel of a port or harbor town. The island's ring road—six lanes wide at this point—sliced along the coast, for the most part squandering the marvelous location.

Yet it was the *only* town for 4000 kilometers. Auckland, the closest city by plane, was a six-hour flight. This geographical reality may have colored my vision, for to me the sight of Pape'ete was always uplifting. It helped that my first glimpse of it was always from the water. With the morning sun skipping down the high slopes above the town, the island looked as fresh as a bowl of limes and lemons. If the odd unsightly development stood out, too large and too prominent, the natural setting still managed to triumph.

In times past Pape'ete was apparently renowned for its nightlife and legendary bars where Polynesians danced and drank with white sailors, adventurers and entrepreneurs. Now it was dead after dark but in the morning, full of people, the town exuded an infectious energy. From the moment the *Aremiti IV* ferry docked at the wharf it was all go. A fellow with an officious whistle and a furious glare ensured chaos as vehicles poured off the ferry into the line of traffic waiting to board. The ring road was solid with vehicles converging on town: utes and scooters, four-wheel drives and "trucks" as the quaint local buses were called. Yet even in the big smoke at rush hour, many islanders refused to be rushed.

"Stop being such a Parisian," I said, elbowing Frédéric one morning as he impatiently tried to overtake three women ambling along the walkway. To say they were solid or stout would be to do them a polite injustice: with their thighs rubbing and weight swaying from side to side it seemed possible that they might shift the earth's center of gravity. Given the focus on Tahiti's legendary svelte *vahine*, meaning woman or women, there was something stirring about the way the trio defied the stereotype. Unable to get around them, we had to slow our own pace to the leisurely slap of their thongs.

My town days soon fell into a pattern. First stop on arrival was one of the few *papeteries* that stocked English-language newspapers for tourists. If I was lucky the plane from Los Angeles would have flown in the latest issues of the *Interna-*

tional Herald Tribune. At US$7 a copy the paper was an indulgence; the French publications were much cheaper. But for years I'd read the *IHT* every morning. While there was no yearning for fancy shops or fully stocked supermarket shelves or cinemas, continuing this little ritual from my old life somehow was important. It made little difference that the news was often eight days out of date.

Still, at that price, the newspaper had to be eked out like rations, not devoured in one sitting. I was careful to read only a few pages under the whirring ceiling fans at the corner café. It wasn't clear to me whether I chose this particular place because of the waiter or in spite of him. Mincing around the covered terrace with a string of fresh flowers crowning his head, he did little but scowl and his hauteur could rival that of any old-school Parisian *serveur.* Table service was beneath him. He didn't paint his nails or dress in the flamboyantly camp way of many *rae rae* but his effeminate manner suggested he belonged to this curious Polynesian transgender tradition. In the past it was customary in each village for one boy to be raised as a girl to care for siblings and perform women's work. While this selection no longer takes place, *rae rae* were a common sight working in bars, restaurants and resorts. The impression was of widespread acceptance but later a Marquesan transvestite painted a more poignant picture. Many *rae rae* who come to the capital from outer islands end up in prostitution, he said.

Back at the bureau I'd struggle along 'til lunch, trying to get my cast of Bretons and painters to interact. Meanwhile in the room next door, Frédéric was often on the phone. If I

listened hard I could hear his pen on the paper, not taking
notes but sketching a caricature, usually of the client or col-
league on the other end of the line. It was a habit he'd long
practiced, although one I hadn't seen in action until now.
Magistrates with bulbous noses, local French notaries made
to look like petty criminals with angled eyebrows, a Tahitian
matriarch with an authoritative glare—his legal pads were
covered in cartoon faces that had to be hidden before anyone
came by. On a long-distance phone call to the head office
one morning he sketched his boss, a cigar-puffing, jowly
Frenchman fond of red wine and rich food and prone to
roaring rages. It was one of Frédéric's better likenesses I
thought—not unkind but not exactly flattering either—and
on impulse he faxed the drawing to the unwitting subject,
assuring me that his boss would "appreciate the joke." I'd
only met him once but privately thought this was unlikely. It
seems I was right because in their next conversation the caricature was passed over coolly.

Sometimes a work contact or another lawyer Frédéric had
met would join us for lunch at one of the busy cafés where,
despite the heat, the *plat du jour* might be a rich *blanquette de
veau* or even a hearty *boeuf bourguignon*. Polynesians seemed
to embrace these copious cold-climate dishes, though there
was always raw tuna salad on the menu and usually tuna car-
paccio, served with olive oil, fresh limes, grated carrot, to-
mato and ginger. In the afternoon, I often popped out to buy
food items we couldn't get on Mo'orea. By this time the sun-
drenched streets were listless. Cafés either closed or morphed
into bars that at sundown would start to look seedy. After
standing up in the heat all day, the whole town seemed to

want to slump. It was a good time to be inside, browsing and buying at the town's covered market.

Much is made of it in tourism guidebooks for it's one of the few buildings with any charm. Its cast-iron frame looped around the entrances in a leisurely way; inside, its glass paneling and worn timber cladding made me think of a grand nineteenth-century pavilion crossed with a garden shed. Unlike markets in Asia or elsewhere, there was no shouting or pushing, no hard sell, no bartering. There was plenty to lure tourists—shell necklaces; woven hats from the southern Austral archipelago; *monoi* oil infused with *tiare*, frangipani, vanilla or sandalwood. But the attraction for residents was the fresh produce: the tuna, bonito, mahi mahi and swordfish; the fruit stalls piled with papayas, custard apples, several types of bananas including the red *fei* for baking, pyramids of Tahitian limes and all sorts of root vegetables. *Tiare*, wrapped in palm leaves or woven into garlands and crowns, were sold at tables outside. One elderly *mamie* with wiry white hair sold a stunning variety of heliconia—Sexy Pink was the ill-suited English name, as though these sculptural beauties were a cheap lip gloss. "I knew you'd come today, *tu vois*, I saved these last ones for you," she'd say, pointing to three tumbling, twisting bracts in dusty pink and pale green.

From the market I'd walk to the wharf with the long stems thrown over my shoulder like a fishing rod, my exotic catch bobbing behind me. By the time Frédéric boarded, the homebound ferry would be rumbling and revving its engines, preparing to pull away. *"Attends, l'avocat!"* the fur-fisherman would yell, pointing to the familiar figure bolting down the quay. On he'd leap, out of breath but still looking crisp in his white shirt, to friendly salutations from the crew and an exasperated look from his wife. *L'homme du dernier moment* indeed.

⌒

Life bubbled along. We began to understand more about the sensitivities and divisions that ran through the territory. Elections were imminent, revealing how local politics was dominated by parties with opposing positions on the relationship with France: pro-independence and pro-autonomy. The incumbent president, Gaston Flosse, led the latter camp. With interest we watched him interviewed on the nightly news. Journalists proceeded timidly, respectfully. White-haired with glasses, the Polynesian president had a round face that might have passed as avuncular were it not for something about the eyes: a shrewdness or craftiness that made me think of an old tomcat, timing his pounce.

Before leaving Paris we'd been told a lot about Gaston Flosse—been warned you might say, though on the positive side his energy and diligence were frequently admired. In power for more than twenty years, he apparently ran the territory like a fiefdom. There were colorful stories about lavish parties at his palatial official residence, where fine champagne flowed like water and a bevy of beauties, all former Miss Tahitis, entertained guests. More ominously, questions had been raised about the still unsolved disappearance of a local journalist, Jean-Pascal Couraud, who had led a very public campaign against the president. Later, allegations would be made that he was tortured by members of the territory's special task force, fiercely loyal to Gaston Flosse. While there was no evidence whatsoever that the Polynesian president had given any such orders, the fact that rumors of foul play persisted says something about his perceived power.

"It's not like we're moving to some dodgy dictatorship in central Africa," I'd exclaimed disbelievingly before we moved.

Chuckling, Frédéric had reminded me that many of the dodgy African dictatorships were once French territories, too.

Professionally speaking, Frédéric might have been better off living on Tahiti, rubbing shoulders day and night with the territory's business leaders. His job was to bring in clients, after all. But politics and big business were meshed in a tight community of longtime French residents and wealthy *demis*, as islanders of mixed Polynesian and European heritage were called. Even before leaving Paris, Frédéric saw advantages in not living in the thick of this elite. The old "missionaries, mercenaries and misfits" label was too sweeping and outdated a description for the French population. But Tahiti was far enough away from *la métropole*, as mainland France is known, to offer a clean slate to anyone seeking reinvention. The island had its share of not quite squeaky clean entrepreneurs, so it was said. After dark, only the occasional small plane flight linked Tahiti and Mo'orea, which gave us a good excuse not to attend the official soirées and cocktail parties. They'd drive you mad, Frédéric assured me.

Still, we weren't hermits. Some evenings I was busting to get out of the house, and at first we gratefully accepted any invitation. The social pool on Mo'orea was limited but already we had spent a few very enjoyable evenings with people who hopefully would become friends. Several times we found ourselves at cocktail parties that combined elements of a day-time television soap with traces of Graham Greene's expatri-ate scenes: outdoor parties lit with lanterns and fairy lights, where women with fake eyelashes and possibly fake boobs flirted and vied for male attention. It was impossible to say whether it was all innocent fun or so-and-so really was sleep-ing with his wife's best friend. Perhaps I lack the imagination to appreciate how such games might keep marriages alive, but it seemed to me the undercurrents of sexual restlessness were matched by a general air of ennui. After a while I grew more discerning. "I might be desperate to get out of the house but I'm not *that* desperate," I told Frédéric.

One night we found ourselves on our way to a dinner where apart from the hostess, whom Frédéric had met just once, we knew no one. As our Renault Clio jounced up an unlit dirt track with a gradient that cried out for a four-wheel drive, and Frédéric swerved like a rally driver to avoid can-yons and boulders, the journey seemed to herald adventure. I tried to imagine the kind of person who would live perched on a remote mountainside. Someone a bit alternative. A leftie-greenie type, perhaps. I pictured a fifty-something woman, carefree and elegant in a kaftan, hoop earrings and bangles.

Sandrine met us at the door in pearls, heels and a nicely tailored skirt. Ushering us inside, she chattered so fast it was pointless trying to get a word in. "You must want to see the house first, *on va faire le tour.* Oh I see you like books," she trilled, as Frédéric eyed her shelves. "Well, I am *une femme de lettres,* you know." There was no one except us inside but she lowered her voice to a whisper. "You can live in the tropics, friends—I hope you don't mind me calling you friends—but you must not go to seed."

Outside on a candlelit balcony, our fellow guests sat in cane lounges; at the far end a table was set for eight, with fragile wineglasses, neatly folded napkins and silver. It was all very French and formal, with a sprinkling of *tiare* flowers for a tropical touch, yet something about it made my heart sink. Is there such a thing as a too perfect table? At home Frédéric fiddled endlessly with flowers and candles and settings, after all, and I found his attentions endearing.

After cheek kisses and handshakes, conversation resumed idly about recent holidays back in France.

"Did you get to the Gauguin *expo* in Paris?"

"Yes, wasn't it *sublime?*"

"Marvelous. His colors blew me away."

"It's ironic that they named a high school after him here, don't you think?" I piped up. "I mean, a street and shops you can understand, but *Lycée Paul Gauguin?*" Flattered to have everyone's attention, I went on in a light voice. "I suppose Gauguin would have loved it, having his name on an institution filled with teenage girls!"

Lips pursed in reproach.

"Mais non, enfin!"

"When are people going to stop going on about him being a pedophile?"

"He was a master."

Unwittingly, I'd been provocative—or perhaps not so unwittingly. Gauguin was a sore point among certain Polynesian writers and academics resentful of this dubious foreigner who around the world had become emblematic of their islands. In downtown Pape'ete there was a street named after him, shops and restaurants and a cruise ship, but it was the territory's top high school that most raised ire. Though whether or not I was aware then of the controversy I'm not sure. Skilfully steering the conversation back to France, our hostess turned to a woman still tsk-tsking disapprovingly.

"Did you get caught out by the strikes?"

"*Oh là là, oui!*" She puffed out air through her lips. "It was a nightmare. We had to wait six hours for our connecting flight from Charles de Gaulle."

"Isn't the mood in France morose?"

"All our friends keep saying how lucky we are to have left!"

A fellow with a neat, gray beard sank back into his cane armchair. "France is going downhill," he said with satisfaction. "We're better off here."

In the space of a few minutes the talk had swung from indignant defense of Gauguin, venerable pillar of French culture, to this gloomy picture of the mother country that bore little resemblance to the functioning place we had left not long before. Yet I understood these contradictions and impulses. In moments of doubt in France, had I not found comfort in remembering my pet dislikes about Australia—the omnipresent sport, the soulless shopping malls, the sensational news and current affairs programs and so on? And yet the sight of its distinct giant form on a spinning globe could provoke pangs of pride and homesickness. The decision to abandon your mother country and live abroad is one that brings with it episodic soul searching. For *popa'a-* in French Polynesia, perhaps, the need for vindication is even greater. On the French scale of social and political importance, Paris sparkles at the pinnacle. Below it lie the provinces. Spread far and wide at the very bottom are France's overseas territories, out of mind and out of sight.

I might not have won much support for my remarks about Gauguin but I'm happy to say it was a comment made by Frédéric that caused consternation over dinner. The conversation turned to politics—an unwise topic, perhaps, but difficult to avoid with the territorial elections only weeks away. Not that there was any doubt as to who would win: Gaston Flosse had recently managed to push new electoral laws through the French parliament, all but guaranteeing him victory. When Frédéric stated that we had attended a rally on Mo'orea held by the President's arch rival, the pro-independence leader Oscar Temaru, the admission was about as welcome as a gob of glistening spit on the table.

"You went to a rally of the *Tavini party*?" The guest who had got most worked up over Gauguin now curled her lips in horror. Pond-sized Tahitian pearls glared darkly from her ears.

"Yes," he started, "out of curiosity we—"

"You know the first thing Temaru will do if he gets into power," she cut in. "He'll kick us out!"

"He can't. This is a French territory, don't forget." A man in a red floral shirt chopped the air with his hand. "It's *our* money that pays for the schools and hospitals, for everything. *On est en France, quand même.*"

"We've just got here; Sarah and I can't vote," Frédéric reminded them. "It's just interesting to hear what all the main players—"

"If *he* gets in we're leaving for good."

"Don't worry, he won't," muttered her husband.

The bearded fellow, a bigwig notary apparently, turned to Frédéric. The table had split in two and we had been cast in the enemy camp, among those who advocated separating from France. "So, so, so," he said with a tight, unfriendly smile. "The new lawyer in town is an *indépendantiste*."

Maybe Oscar Temaru did want the French out. But it was hard to reconcile the other guests' fears with the discussions we'd had with some of Temaru's supporters, who seemed more interested in a change of leadership than his politics. Nelly had swatted the air when I asked if she wanted the territory to be independent: "No, no, no! Our kids don't want to go back to eating *uru* and taro. We need the French," she continued. "They've given us good things, like teachers and doctors."

"One day, maybe," Alain had shrugged, as we bobbed in the lagoon on a Sunday morning. "But right now independence is a pipe dream."

My father is a very reasonable, diplomatic man, who always sees the best in everybody; my mother, on the other hand, is a woman of heartfelt likes and equally exuberant dislikes. That night I was my mother's daughter.

"Christ," I grunted in the car as it lurched down the mountain. "I'm not going there again."

Frédéric chuckled. "Don't worry, we won't be invited back."

At home, though, he reflected on the evening in a way that took me by surprise. When I walked into the bathroom, there he was peering closely at the mirror. "Do I look as old as them?" Frédéric asked worriedly.

"As old as who?"

"The other guys at the dinner. They're my age, you know." Frowning, he appraised his hair. "God, I've gone gray."

While Frédéric had always paid attention to his appearance, this sensitivity to aging was new. Several times lately I'd caught him examining his reflection as if surprised by this familiar but altered version of his true self. There was no refuting the fact that more salt sprinkled his hair, particularly at the sides. It was a source of lighthearted banter—he'd claim it made him look old; I'd say it made him look more like George Clooney. He'd threaten to dye it; I'd say do that and I'll leave you. When he fussed over the white strands, I'd remind him he was lucky to still have hair at all. It's all in the eyes, I had told him more than once: youth, beauty, honesty, intelligence, goodness. The skin around could wrinkle and mottle but what mattered were those two oval windows.

"They seemed much older," I assured him, truthfully. "*Much*." I gave his bum a friendly slap. "Now stop being vain!"

Though there was more to it than vanity, I knew. In truth, I had my own issues with age and the passage of time. I had done ever since hearing the words "There's no time to lose."

SIX

Hurrying past the handsome buildings, I had felt upbeat. On that November afternoon in Paris some four years before our move to Tahiti, there was no portent in the air, which had smelled of armpits in the metro but in the gentrified 7th arrondissement had a rarefied freshness. I'd breathed in gratefully. It was the sort of day my mother would have said didn't know whether it was Arthur or Martha. The sky was a pale gray canvas that dimmed at whim and occasionally brightened to take on a pearly luster. En route to an appointment, thoughts of our plan to start a family had wafted pleasantly across my mind.

Dr. G, my gynecologist, had taken a minute or two to glance through my test results. Standard tests, blood and ultrasound, just to make sure everything was okay. Idly, I had admired the floor, waiting. The parquet was more like marquetry for the intricacy of its pattern and variety of timbers. Everything here murmured Old Establishment: the district, the quiet street, the spacious office, the tall, dignified windows with shutters, the fancy ceiling moldings. Dr. G fitted with the territory, too. Her plain doctor's coat couldn't quite disguise the designer labels and good grooming underneath. Unfailingly professional and pleasant, she was also direct and slightly intimidating.

"*Mmmm. Ce n'est pas très bon*, it's not good at all," she had muttered half to herself, then looked up from the stapled sheaf of results and fixed me with a grave, unflinching look.

"Your ultrasound's fine; there's no sign of any obstructions." Her mouth had pulled into a tight seam. "But there's a problem with your blood result. Your FSH level is extremely high."

She pronounced the letters the French way, *ef es arsh*, though she may as well have said ABC for all they meant to me. Follicle-stimulating hormone. My level was 19.8, which didn't sound a cause for concern to me but apparently was way too high for a 33-year-old. The ensuing explanation sounded increasingly like a discussion of an unproductive henhouse: talk of too few eggs and eggs of poor quality and low fertility. I was shocked. "*Ménopause*," I'd blurted in disbelief at one point. "At my age?" I thought there must have been a mix-up but, briskly, Dr. G had assured me that early menopause was a possibility.

Wrapping up, she'd told me that infertility treatment was our best chance at having children. In my memory's eye, the scene closed on her next words, though she must have said good-bye. *Il n'y a pas de temps à perdre.* There's no time to lose.

After, I'd stood on the long island of neat grass running up the Esplanade des Invalides. A legacy of Louis XIV, this is one of Paris's grand open spaces, where avenues lined with lampposts and perfectly sculpted trees sweep from the gilt dome of the Hôtel des Invalides to the Seine River. Trying to get some perspective, I stared at the straightness and symmetry. It wasn't as if I had a life-threatening illness. At no point had Dr. G said it would be impossible to have children: *difficile* and *compliqué* were the words she'd used. As far as bad medical news goes, this was quite good. Everything was normal except this one result, a hormone apparently produced by the pituitary gland, a part of the body that rang a bell from human biology classes at school, though its precise location escaped me. Brain? Groin? I was healthy, I exercised, I ate well. I was neither a drug addict nor an alcoholic (and anyway, neither of those conditions precluded pregnancy, did they?).

It started to drizzle. The sky pressed lower, like the rain-beaten roof of a tent. The day was done with indecision and the heaviness overhead matched my own mood. My hands anchored themselves in my pockets. Later I would find comfort in Frédéric's valiant optimism. Having not heard the explanation from the horse's mouth, so to speak, he had more trouble believing how one high hormone reading could foil our plans. What was clear to us both from then on was that we wanted children dearly.

The search for a specialist began soon after and six months later Dr. B commenced treatment. I recall feeling relieved to be taking the step. Conscious that *il n'y a pas de temps à perdre,* we had try after try. When my spirits got low I repeated to myself the sort of platitudes I believed in back then. Everything happens for a reason; good things come to those who wait. At some point I began popping into church, which was ironic because Frédéric, a Roman Catholic, was the believer, not me.

"Don't forget the story of the other Sarah," he'd said once. "She had a baby at ninety."

"Ninety?" This beggared belief. "Sarah who?"

"Abraham's wife." From the casual way he said it, Abraham was a neighbor or an acquaintance. Frédéric raised his eyebrows at me in mock disbelief. Sometimes he couldn't credit my lack of religious education.

"The Bible, *banane.* Sarah and Abraham. They had a son called Isaac."

It was an appalling thought, a child at ninety, but the story pleased me, too, and I'd laughed. There was no harm in spreading hopes far and wide, from the pointy end of reproductive science to my pagan candle lighting to faith in a name. Months passed. Three more Paris winters came and went.

⌒⌒

Backs to the mountains, faces to the sea: on Mo'orea that was how we lived at first. Soon our attention would turn behind us, to the many trails that wound through valleys up to thin ridgelines with breathtaking views. But in terms of weekend pastimes our first priority was to learn to scuba dive. It had been something we'd discussed excitedly back in Paris, a little challenge we'd set ourselves. Perhaps because progress was slow on my other goals, achieving this smaller one became important.

After swimming in the lagoon for a few months I felt ready to venture beyond the coral reef. The aggro clownfish no longer made me splash in fright when it nipped. The stingrays cast a Pied Piper spell on me. When the pink whiprays flapped by, like a pair of friendly elephant ears, or a spotted eagle ray soared into the distant water-sky, I was overcome by curiosity and an urge to follow. Among the new friends we'd started to make on the island was a couple who was eager to learn to scuba dive, too. Daniel and Catherine lived *côté montagne*, next to Guite, in a house on stilts that backed onto a picturesque coconut grove. The pair had arrived on Mo'orea around the same time as us from southwest France, a region renowned for *magret de canard* and foie gras pâté. The theory about red wine and duck fat being good for you must be true, I thought, because they seemed so young at heart. Formerly a country vet, Daniel was stocky and down-to-earth and proudly claimed to be a "simple peasant"—albeit one with a taste for fine Bordeaux. One Sunday morning we popped over for a coffee that had turned into lunch that ended with us all heading back across the road to the lagoon, which is where the subject of diving came up.

Only after we'd agreed to start the course the next weekend did Catherine make an astonishing admission. Never in her life had she put her head underwater. No, not once. *Ever.* Her dry, springy curls jiggled earnestly as she shook her head. The claim was unfathomable to me—I could barely recall a family holiday in Australia that hadn't revolved around some or other body of water. Yet Catherine had lived nearly all her life at the foot of the Pyrenees. Holidays were spent snow skiing or, in summer, trekking through mountains whose low slopes were covered in wildflowers. "How on earth are you going to scuba dive?" I wanted to ask but didn't. Catherine was so thin she looked like she might get swept away in the gentlest of currents; it wasn't for me to shatter her confidence. Yet her next words revealed a bullish determination. "I've been practicing in the kitchen," she confided.

Daniel nodded. "I get home from work and there she is, head plunged in a big bowl of water," he explained.

Learning to scuba dive was a big deal for Frédéric, too. His childhood swimming teacher in Boulogne-sur-Mer had a lot to answer for in my opinion. "In you go, little monkeys," the coach would shout at the beginning of each lesson, shoving his charges into the deep end of the pool with a long baton. Frédéric's fascination for the sea was matched by his fear of it. In northern France in the middle of winter, he thought nothing of ripping off his clothes and plunging into the icy English Channel—a shifty soup if ever there was one. But his feet always remained firmly planted on the silty floor. On Mo'orea he preferred to jog in the muggy heat than swim laps. Even when he came with me, Frédéric experienced the lagoon differently. Having never properly learned freestyle, he swam breaststroke. Both of us were just brushing the surface but my gaze was directed within whereas his eyes never left land. He never came face-to-face with the stroppy clownfish or saw a spotted eagle ray.

The dive center at Cook's Bay was run by a group of tanned French guys with hair streaked blond, presumably from the sun, though you can never be sure these days. Unlike a few *popa'ā* we'd come across who appeared disillusioned with island life, these fellows positively glowed, as if they could scarcely believe their own good fortune. "Another day at the office," Nico fairly hummed one morning, waving admiringly at the painterly reflections of cloudless sky and green pinnacles across the bay. The atmosphere was professional but leavened by constant banter and teasing: someone's lack of luck with girls, another instructor's growing beer belly.

Our assigned instructor was friendly and professional, too, but with less larky charm. Christophe was stocky and powerfully built, all muscles and right angles, and looked and sounded very much like the ex-army sergeant he was.

There was theory to be memorized, written tests to be done, but it goes without saying that a good part of learning to scuba dive takes place underwater. The lagoon—like a giant, safe swimming pool—was the ideal environment in which to adapt to strange submarine sensations and amplifications. The hollow sucking sound followed by a gurgling exhalation made each breath sound like a last gasp. There was a lot to think about: keeping balance, not careening into coral, breathing not through your nose but through your mouth (the very opposite of what I'd practiced in yoga). A task as simple as kneeling on the sandy floor had us rolling around like circus clowns, pawing and clawing the water to keep upright. In the classroom we'd learned that holding your breath is about the most dangerous thing a scuba diver can do, especially on the ascent to the surface, when air in the lungs expands. The resulting condition, compression sickness, also known as "the bends," is potentially fatal. Yet strangely, underwater I needed to be reminded to do something I'd done quite naturally since birth. When my flow of bubbles petered out Christophe would make a circular motion with his finger.

Although we couldn't talk to each other below the surface, we had fun. Before the course, Catherine had graduated from the kitchen bowl to the lagoon; a couple of times from the house I'd watched as she submerged her head, first tentatively then with decisive splashes. During the first lesson there was a jubilant exchange of thumbs-up signals when she made it under, as if this three-meter descent was up there with walking on the moon. Once, watching Frédéric clumsily try to regain equilibrium, a rush of air bubbles shot from Daniel's mouth: through his mask his eyes were squinted up in laughter. In the shoals each exercise felt like a game: hand signals, equalizing our ears, removing our masks. We even mastered buddy breathing, which involved swimming along in pairs, sharing air supply by politely passing the regulator back and forth. The ultimate test of any marriage, I joked after. Back at the scuba center, we were offered pastis, and though I'd never much taken to its medicinal flavor, somehow after a dive it tasted okay.

Lesson four was the most instructive of all, though that was not how it seemed to me at the time. The morning was cloudy and the lagoon looked like a sheet of tin. Peering over the side of the boat into deeper water, none of us felt much like diving. Frédéric very nearly didn't. While the rest of us knelt below on the sandy floor, waiting, above us a pair of legs scissored wildly. To my eyes my dive buddy looked more skyborne than water-bound. There he remained at the surface, flapping with all the frustration of a flightless bird, unwittingly doing everything in his power to hinder descent. By the time he joined us on the bottom Frédéric looked thoroughly fed up.

Inexplicably, this time when it came to removing my mask, I balked. The previous week I'd had no qualms performing the exercise, which is one of the more vital scuba skills due to the high chance of getting kicked in the face by another diver's flipper. I'd imagined the deeper you descended into the submarine world, the freer you felt. But twelve meters below the surface, I felt encumbered, claustrophobic. There was *too much* water pressing in on me.

You okay? signaled Christophe, watching me intently. Like everything else underwater, panic appears amplified and my eyes must have been wide and fearful. But there was no hand sign to explain that removing my mask suddenly seemed counter to my most basic survival instincts. You see, Christophe, I might have tentatively explained on land, I do really want to scuba dive, only not in so much water. Instead I bit down hard on my regulator. In spite of myself, I okayed back. My left brain tried to assert itself with rational encouragement. *It's not hard. Breathe through your mouth, not your nose, you've done it before, everything will be fine.*

If keeping on breathing is the first safety rule of diving, the second is Never Panic. Yet as soon as I started coughing and choking, my only impulse was to reach the surface as fast as possible. Up I rocketed, as if someone had slapped a jet pack onto my back, providing my astonished fellow divers with a textbook illustration of scuba diving's golden no-no. Though what they may have thought was the least of my worries. I was out of there—or almost. Before I could burst through the surface, a strong hand grabbed my ankle, bringing me to a rude stop. My nose was pinched hard, and—hey, presto!—I could breathe underwater, through the regulator that had been in my mouth all along.

After, I was subdued. In deeper water my actions could have been very dangerous. The whole incident had been silly: if water had rushed up my nostrils, it was because I'd inhaled through my nose. Were my instincts not to be trusted? I was deep in contemplation, getting changed in the storeroom, when a conversation on the other side of the thin wall interrupted my brooding.

"They were all over the place today, *putain*, you should have seen them." It was Christophe and his voice was low and muffled, like he had his head in his hands. He went on despondently. "One wasted half the lesson descending. Then one shot to the surface because she thought she was drowning without her mask—never seen anyone move that quick underwater. Minutes later another floated away like a feather: one second she was there, the next gone—GONE! Found her sitting back in the boat." Frédéric, me, Catherine, I recognized. Only Daniel, as carefree in water as a dolphin, had completed the dive without incident.

A long splashing sound was followed by the clunk of something heavy landing back on the table. It struck me this pouring had been more generous than usual. And this time, it seemed, the pastis would not be shared.

"I had Americans," grumbled Nico, who didn't sound his jovial self either. No further explanation was offered; none was required: I'd already heard them joking about American tourists who turned up with high-tech gadgets but no dive skills.

Christophe grunted sympathetically. I couldn't help feeling guilty. We had grown quite fond of him, even if he had the manner and appearance of a marine commando. I pictured him on the other side of the thin wall, reduced to a sad heap of deflated muscle by the prospect of having to get us through this elementary course. Perhaps being a dive instructor in paradise wasn't so easy after all.

When Christophe spoke again, the anise flavor had already begun to numb his despair and he sounded in awe of us.

"Haven't had a group that hopeless in years," he mused, "not since I left Club Med."

⌐⌐

"Don't worry, no one fails the PADI Open Water level," Daniel assured us on the drive home when I repeated the exchange to the others.

"You mean no one's failed *yet*," chipped in Frédéric.

He seemed to have put his troubled start behind him. Later Frédéric would confide that the relief of knowing he had survived the dive always gave him a high afterward. Still, his difficulties today would only increase his apprehension about the final test of the course, when we all had to descend to 25 meters.

"I'm going to frame my certificate if I pass," he went on.

"Hang it in your office," joked Daniel. "With a *diplôme* like that you could increase your hourly fee." The pair of them chuckled; teasing each other was a sport.

Like me, Catherine was still reflecting on what had occurred underwater, and Christophe's comments. "We weren't that hopeless, surely," she said, sounding a bit indignant.

"*We?*" Daniel pointed out playfully. "What's with the we, *mon chouchou?*"

I didn't join in the banter but stared out the window, nervously contemplating the thin band of ultramarine beyond the breaking waves.

The boat skimmed across Mo'orea's glassy moat then headed through Taotoi Pass, one of twelve breaks in the island's reef. All of a sudden we were riding a dark denim swell, slapping down the sides of rolling humps. The last dive of the course is always in deep sea. We were already kitted up. Since I was helped into the equipment, I'd felt behind me three or four times and my air cylinder had not dropped off. The pressure gauge read more than 200 so the tank definitely had air in it. Inspired by Catherine, in the lagoon I'd practiced for hours removing my mask underwater, and in lesson five I managed to do it. I was as ready as I'd ever be.

After cruising parallel to the reef for a few minutes, the boat stopped to anchor. Combers rolled under us and continued on for another hundred meters, collapsing over the coral wall in a fantastic spray of beads and glitter that blew a salty mist back on our faces. One kilometer away, bathed in sunlight, Mo'orea's slopes looked as fresh as lettuce leaves. But for now my attention was on the water. Even with the sun pouring through the surface there was nothing to be seen of the ocean floor. Nothing but a few mottled shadows which may have been coral, though it looked to me like they were moving. I shivered. Sharks were one of the attractions for divers in these waters and the instructors often brought along tuna heads and tails to feed them. Apparently they weren't aggressive—so said Nico, who was covered in scars from mucking around too closely with them.

"Let's go, let's go," Christophe barked in his sergeant's voice. "*Un, deux, trois.*" The face of the driver, watching us; the boat; the sky: rolling backward off the edge of the boat, these were my last glimpses of the world as I knew it. In a lesser swell we might have regrouped on the surface but Christophe had told us to begin our descent straightaway. My heart thumped as the water closed like a lid over me. There was no accounting for the magnitude of human folly. I inhaled fearfully, amazed all over again to discover that this strange, astronautical arrangement of tank, straps and hoses contrived by Jacques Cousteau and Co. actually worked: I could breathe. Down, down we parachuted, not into darkness, as I'd feared, but through grainy, peacock-colored space to the outer banks of the reef.

The current on the bottom was strong, though there was something effortless about the way it held us back and propelled us forward, as if the ocean was expending no energy at all. To advance we used the sea's momentum by kicking on each surge. The visibility wasn't great and only when Christophe made a fin sign did I notice the three submarine-like shadows. As we hovered they circled closer. Lemon sharks, up to three and a half meters in length, Christophe would later inform us. I didn't much like the idea of shark feeding— feeding any wild creature seems like an interference. But now, with the predators so close I could count their random rows of teeth and see their scars, I thought tuna heads would have been a wise offering. Still, eye-to-eye with the sharks, the only scary thing about them was, in fact, their eyes, which were as still as marbles. The rest was exhilarating: their muscular grace; the powerful pendulum swing of their tails, driving them forward in a tacking motion.

Our time underwater was almost up when a large, corpulent fish bustled over, flapping ludicrously small pectoral fins, with lubber lips puckered up as if for a kiss. Its eyes, unlike the sharks' glassy gaze, swiveled over us anxiously, as if to convey its apologies for not making it over sooner. An exquisite pattern of scribbles and dots covered the fish's body, in blues and greens so electric the colors jostled and vibrated. A Napoléon wrasse, I found out later, so called because its bulging forehead is said to resemble the emperor's famous *bicorne* hat. It hovered at arm's length from me and we looked each other over then straight *at* each other, and in those seconds a lifetime of prejudices and perceptions fell away.

Practically the only fish I'd seen whole up 'til then were in a tank or grilled on a plate or washed up dead on a beach. In such circumstances a glazed and witless regard might be forgiven, yet fish had to my mind fallen into one of three categories: terrifying, tasty or merely decorative. Now here was something else: a finned hostess who neither flitted into the coral like all those small, blank-faced creatures nor hung about with blatant self-interest, like the lemon sharks. Maybe it's a sign of limited imagination, this need to project human qualities on animals to connect with them. Still, this was the first time a fish had looked me straight in the eye, the first time I'd had an impulse to *stroke* a fish, and a closed door in my mind was thrown open by the encounter.

SEVEN

A bare male back, as dark as the night; a flicking ponytail; a hand that seemed to swoop down on something—these were the few details I registered. When pressed for more, I put the guy's age somewhere between eighteen and thirty. "That narrows it down," the gendarme had remarked drily. He didn't bother filing a report or taking notes. The officer didn't say the words but we got the message: if he had a Pacific franc for every incident like this, he'd have bought a villa on the Côte d'Azur and retired.

The night of that first "visit" we had guests—invited ones. Earlier in the week, out of the blue, Frédéric had got a call from a cousin he hadn't seen in years. Patricia, an artist, was in Tahiti with a friend who had traveled from French Guiana to meet her. After an initial lunch in Pape'ete it was arranged for the pair to come and stay for the weekend.

We'd started with gin and tonics on the beach, moved on to a decent red with dinner and then resorted to a rough rosé. Toes burrowed in the still warm sand, we were all dreamily tipsy. "No resort could top this," Patricia sighed, gazing at the lagoon, onyx daubed with silver. A fog of stars arched across the sky. After so many evenings alone, Frédéric and I were delighted to open our home and to have company, and the four of us sat up late. The cousins were amazed to realize it had been almost three decades since they last saw each other, and as the evening wore on the exchange of family news grew more animated and open—illnesses, divorces, fortunes made and lost, the well-to-do uncles and their affairs. Isabelle, a strong and striking fifty-something, regaled us with stories of life in the heart of French Guiana's rainforest, where she ran a one-class school for Amazon Indians, two days' by canoe from the nearest settlement. Frédéric kept filling our glasses and we kept on chinking them.

It can't have been long after we went to bed that we were woken by Maddie barking. Since becoming an outside dog, she'd grown a bit nervy at night, and I'm sorry to say we didn't take her seriously. "A gecko's probably fallen off the wall onto her," grumbled Frédéric sleepily. (Months later this exact scenario would happen to him in bed: a big fat gecko landed, splat, on his face and I can confirm he yelped, too.) On Maddie yapped, furiously, insistently, hardly taking a breath. Perhaps she'd cornered one of the wild roosters that occasionally strayed into our yard. The floor tiles were cool beneath my soles as I padded to the bedroom door, which opened directly onto the encircling veranda. There wasn't much of a moon and with hindsight it would have been wise to have switched on the outside lights. As it was, the shrill scream cut through the darkness. Before I could take a step toward the spare bedroom, in front of my stunned eyes a shadow bolted around the porch. He took the steps to the garden in a single leap, swiping the balcony post as he went.

The house instantly came alive. Lights snapped on, Frédéric raced out from the bedroom: "What's happened, who screamed, is everyone okay?" Patricia tripped down from the mezzanine level, bleary-eyed and flushed from the heat upstairs; Maddie, proud of her star performance, ran in silly circles. And we all converged on Isabelle, poor shaken Isabelle, who had stumbled out of the spare bedroom. "I'm okay, I'm okay," she managed, breathlessly. "He ran off when I screamed."

Frédéric wanted to give chase but although I'd been standing less than eight meters away, I couldn't say whether the intruder had fled for the road or the beach. We'd heard Tahitians could move fast but this guy had simply dissolved into the darkness.

While I put the kettle on to make camomile tea, Isabelle told how she had been woken by a crackling sound, like a twig snapping. "He must have trod on my plastic bag by the door. When I opened my eyes, there he was standing at the foot of my bed."

"What a nightmare." I shuddered, filled with sympathy and also admiration, for Isabelle had already regained her composure. Perhaps after more than ten years living in the Amazon she was accustomed to dangers and intruders. Earlier in the evening she'd told of having to sleep in a hammock to avoid finding a deadly snake or spider as a bedfellow.

"I wonder whether he wanted to steal something," began Frédéric, "or—"

"What do they call that custom again?" Patricia interrupted.

"Motoro." For Isabelle's sake he explained the strange local practice of men creeping into houses at night and hopping into girls' beds in the hope of having sex. If the woman screamed or protested, the brazen opportunist ran off—so we'd been told. I didn't know what to make of it. People joked about it, as if no harm was intended, though I couldn't imagine feeling anything less than terrified if it happened to me.

"I didn't think to lock my door," Isabelle admitted.

"We should have told you," I pointed out. Careless as it now seemed, we rarely thought to lock our own bedroom at night. The layout of the house—three separate capsules linked together by the veranda and many doors—meant we usually only worried about the central kitchen and living area, which contained our wine, our stereo and television and my computer. Petty theft was endemic across the islands, the intrusions so common that even the gendarme politely referred to them as *visites.*

"He grabbed something as he ran off," I suddenly remembered, frowning. We all trooped onto the back porch with our tea. Under the bright lights the missing item was instantly conspicuous, at least to me. Hanging off the left post was the top of my new Eres bikini that had been a going-away gift from Alicia. "You *must* have one of these for Tahiti," she'd assured me. "It's the ultimate French bikini; they're so flattering." As soon as I'd tried it on I saw she was right. The bottoms and top did all the right things for your boobs and bum. It was such a thoughtful gift: a piece of Parisian chic for life on a tropical island. I'd worn it practically every day since we'd arrived.

But the half of it left to dry on the right-hand post— arguably the most essential half—was gone. "I don't believe it," I exclaimed, bewildered, crestfallen and furious all at once. "What would anyone want with my *bikini bottoms*?"

It was as if we'd flashed up on some radar, because there was a spate of brazen "visits" after that. We were *popa'ā*; well off compared to many islanders and irresistible targets. While being Polynesian was definitely no safeguard against burglars, pilfering from Europeans is a tradition that goes way back. The early encounters between white explorers and the curious and light-fingered Tahitians were enlivened by mysterious vanishings. Opera glasses, reading glasses and other trinkets were picked from pockets even as the foreigners were treated to ceremonious welcomes. Captain Cook's leg stockings, which he slept on as a precaution, were pinched right from under his head. At one point an islander managed to steal the carefully guarded astronomical quadrant that was vital for observing the Transit of Venus—the whole purpose of Cook's first visit to Tahiti. Most instances ended amicably but in 1777, spectacular Opunohu Bay on Mo'orea was the scene for terrible retribution. Livid at the loss of a small goat, Captain Cook went on a rampage, ordering his men to smash houses and canoes, kill pigs and dogs—tasks they performed with little enthusiasm.

Once, after driving to the island's post office at Maharepa, I returned home mid-morning to find the bedroom flyscreen cut, and fresh, sandy footprints on our pillowcases. My eyes took in the bedside table, which seemed curiously bare, though it took me a few moments to realize that Frédéric's watch had been lying there. Another time I got out of the lagoon after swimming to find our garden shower running at full blast. Wet footprints on our tiled porch led right up to our sliding door, which luckily had been locked. "Why leave the shower on?" I wondered to Frédéric later. Was the intruder sending us a message? Or did he really need a shower? "Maybe it's okay to steal but not with dirty feet," mused Frédéric, not entirely in jest. Tahitians were fastidious about cleanliness.

Clockwise or anticlockwise: when it's the only navigational decision you get to make, it gives cause for pause. At our gate I hesitated. It was raining again, though this surely must be the last of it before the dry season began. A little over a kilometer down the road to the right, Mo'orea's main supermarket nearly always had fresh milk. But that morning I drove a few kilometers in the opposite direction.

AFAREAITU. As the signpost came into view I practiced saying the name in my head. A-fa-re-ay-ee-too. Like a lot of local words it was a mouthful of vowels. Unlike the mellifluous flow of French, Tahitian—the most widely spoken Polynesian language in the territory—has a staccato rhythm.

You'd think it would make it easier, pronouncing each letter, but I found myself stuttering over simple words like Faa'a, the name of a suburb near Pape'ete.

A string of houses, churches and two small grocery stores was about all there was to the island's administrative head-quarters. Only the flags added an official touch: the dominant verticals of the French tricolor alongside the red and white bands of the territorial flag in a show of unity. The usual canine outcasts were lying under the eaves outside the grocery store, so deep in slumber they looked half dead. For a small store it had pretty much all the provisions you needed on a tropical island—mosquito coils and repellent, bottled water because you couldn't drink what came from the tap, lamb from New Zealand, tuna fresh off the fishing boats, as well as the imported staples of rice, pasta and corned beef. The fresh produce was top quality but in terms of supply it was the usual hit-and-miss story. We knew to stock up when the refrigerated counter was full, and would shrug when it was empty; it wasn't a big deal.

Like most of the corner stores on Tahiti and Mo'orea, this one was owned by an ethnic Chinese couple. The fortunes of the Chinese have vastly improved since they first came to Tahiti in the 1860s to work in the cotton plantations. These days the territory is proud of its melting-pot heritage, and ethnic Chinese are powerfully placed in business and politics. Still, old racial tensions may have increased the heat in a dispute that I witnessed one day in the store. "You pay tomorrow," the shopkeeper had cried, shaking her accounts book at a young Polynesian woman. "You pay tomorrow or it's finished!" In fairness, it can't have been easy running a small business on the old-fashioned credit system. In the past Polynesians used to settle debts by giving away portions of land but with property like gold now, such a solution is unthinkable.

On this morning, though, the only sounds were the rain hitting the roof and the soft slide of bare feet on concrete floors, as about half a dozen people trawled the aisles. The second delivery of baguettes hadn't come in but I managed to grab the last *pain au chocolat* and some fresh milk, which I badly wanted for my morning coffee. Outside, I stood a minute under the eaves watching the rain. A dog raised its head at me and another limped over unsteadily. It remained a mystery to me to whom they belonged or by whom they were fed. I'd been told that some of the island dogs had learned to fish for themselves, a piece of information that made a certain West Highland terrier seem somewhat lacking in resourcefulness. With their knobbly heads, bald patches and missing limbs, they reminded me of battle-scarred, happy-go-lucky pirates.

I thought about wet days in other places. In Paris you could always hole up in a bistro, a library or a museum. Whereas on Mo'orea, where life was made up of outdoor rituals, rain meant privations. I couldn't swim—and not only due to limited visibility and the risk of not being seen by a rare fishing boat. There was no sewerage plant on the island and when water poured down the steep slopes everything was washed into the lagoon. Ordinarily teal-blue bays turned a sickly orange with soil from the pineapple fields, regularly doused and sprayed with pollutants and pesticides.

On my way finally, the windshield wipers were waving briskly when a short distance from the shop an explosive impact sent the car careering across the road. When it came to a stop I was angled toward the lagoon. For a few moments everything was still and weirdly silent, except for a faint hissing, like sausages sizzling on a barbecue.

Only later, when the bruise and bump appeared, did I realize my forehead had struck the windshield, despite the airbag. Maddie, who'd been perched on the passenger's seat, must have launched straight into the dash. From the floor she looked at me wonderingly: if this were one of Frédéric's beloved *bandes dessinées* picture books there'd be stars orbiting her head. "Good girl, Mads, it's okay." The ringing in my ears was so loud I could hardly hear my own voice. A few moments passed before the chronology came back to me: milk; shop; a left turn across the road into a cul-de-sac to head home. Then bang.

The sizzling sound was coming from outside, I realized. It probably had something to do with the steam or smoke—something vaporish—pouring out from beneath the bonnet. This was my first-ever road accident and for want of real-life experience I took my cue from Hollywood action movies. *Get the hell out of the car; any second now it might burst into flames*, screamed a voice in my head. I might have rolled Bruce Willis–like out the door but it wouldn't open: the left flank was completely smashed in. In panic I scrambled out the passenger side, scooping up Maddie in my arms. There was no blood on my legs or arms or anywhere.

Standing in the rain some twenty meters away, two people were examining a sedan that a few moments before must have looked quite respectable. Though bigger than our small Clio, it had definitely come off second best: the entire front end had been punched in, creating a cartoonish disproportion that in different circumstances might have appeared comical. Viewed from a safe distance it seemed unlikely either vehicle would burst into flames. "Are you all right?" I thought to call out finally. My voice was still tremulous but I could feel the first flush of relief. They both appeared unscathed, perfectly fine.

A guy and a girl. Brother and sister, cousins, girlfriend and boyfriend, ex-girlfriend and boyfriend, young parents—the fluid, extended nature of Polynesian families allowed for myriad possibilities. It was only later that I would ponder their relationship. Now I had to concentrate. The fellow was speaking, screaming in fact, though my brain was still addled from shock and it took a few seconds to realize the abuse was directed at me.

"Whatdoyouthinkyou'redoing? That's not how we drive here. You'll see how we deal with *farani* like you, I'll show you. Go back to fucking France. Who do you think you are anyway, coming here stealing our jobs, our houses, our land?"

It would require capitals and bold, blown-up font, not to mention an unseemly number of exclamation marks, to convey his fury on paper. The tirade must have lasted no more than a couple of minutes but to me it seemed interminable. For my benefit possibly, he spoke in French, though even I understood the scattering of Tahitian insults. At a guess he wasn't much older than twenty-five. He had a stringy, strong physique: slim waist, square shoulders, knotty arms. Possibly he competed in the outrigger canoe races that many island men were passionate about. Anger made him uncoil. He'd stepped right up close and now I could smell something fruity, maybe his shampoo. *He's going to hit me.* The thought was more of a question than a certainty, and even as it crossed my mind it was too surreal to be frightening. On the other side of the road, a few bystanders had gathered under the eaves of another small shop. Their presence was reassuring, though after I wondered whether anyone would have intervened. I'm sure they would have. Probably. You never know.

At last I found my tongue. "Calm down, please calm down," I implored him. My heart thumped. "You saw me indicate, didn't you?"

The girl, who had been hanging back near the car, approached. Shocked by the young man's aggressive anger, I was glad for the presence of another woman—even if from the tight zip of her mouth she, too, could barely contain her rage. Though her next words were flung not at me but at her companion. "I told you not to overtake!" she snapped.

An approaching truck followed by a long line of traffic saved us or her from whatever might have happened next. From the side of the road an onlooker bellowed common-sense instructions: "You're blocking the road; move your cars." Thankfully both vehicles started immediately and we were able to shift them to a side street. But the accusing words of the young woman had zapped the air with electricity. Her companion had wheeled around, fist balled and raised, I was sure. "Are you saying it was my fault?" he'd snarled, before we were interrupted.

By the time he got out of the car again he'd calmed down. Perhaps his passenger, who'd wisely decided to stay out of the rain, had given him an earful. From her grim expression she'd been more inflamed than intimidated by any threat of violence. It might have also been her who'd pointed out his anti-French tirade was wasted on me, for he seemed suddenly aware of my accent. "Where are you from?" If the inquiry wasn't exactly friendly, some of the aggression had gone out of his tone. My answer seemed to mollify him further and for a second or two he regarded me curiously, though he didn't ask what had brought me to the island and it didn't seem wise to explain. Better to keep quiet about my French connections. Being Australian, at least I wasn't viewed as a colonizer.

The gendarmerie was about twenty kilometers away, amid a stretch of houses hidden behind high fences at the lip of Cook's Bay. The driver had seemed anxious to reach the station first, peeling away quickly so that I soon lost sight of the car. By the time I got there, the pair was already behind closed doors, giving their version of the accident. Only after about forty-five minutes did a policeman come out and invite me into the office. Solid, amiable, Polynesian, he was not the same gendarme we'd seen about the intruder. Judging from the familiar rapport between the two men, he was on friendly terms with the other driver. "This won't take a minute." He handed me a piece of paper on which someone had drawn a diagram of the accident, with arrows showing the direction our cars were traveling in. "You just need to sign here."

Every culture has its own code of communication. When Polynesian pupils flick their eyebrows in answer to questions, what they mean is "yes"—though the gesture often vexes teachers straight from *la métropole*. For Westerners eye contact is important, whereas to show respect Aboriginal people look away when addressing their elders. What was the Tahitian rule? In the circumstances I couldn't help wishing someone would meet my gaze. "I indicated," I said, looking at the girl, who instantly found something to examine on the wall. "He overtook me in the middle of Afareaitu," I told the policeman. "Isn't there a double line?"

"You shouldn't have turned left there," the gendarme told me flatly. "It's not permitted. There's a sign." These last words were so mumbled it was possible I misheard.

Confused, I called Frédéric on my mobile but his voicemail message clicked on straightaway. Truth was, I was keen to have this business over and done with, too, no longer craving coffee but a soothing cup of weak tea. If we got a move along, Nelly would still be there when I got home, which was a comforting thought. Though I wouldn't tell her all the things the young man had called me. This was her country and she would shake her head sorrowfully and feel personally responsible. I felt oddly embarrassed, too, as if I'd turned up at a function uninvited and made a spectacle of myself. Given that the accident occurred right near the shop, probably half the island already knew about it.

Around us, officers got on with police duties: several talked on telephones; another tapped with two fingers on an antiquated typewriter; someone else read a newspaper. From inside, the gendarmerie could have been anywhere in France. It had the same 1950s ambience of the police stations I knew in Paris—though at least here no one was playing cards. Most of the employees were white mainlanders. Mo'orea, with its petty theft and illicit *paka* plantations tucked away in verdant valleys, must be a sweet reward after Montfermeil or Saint-Denis or any of the riot-ridden suburbs around Paris. There was nothing smart about the building or offices but the location was sensational, right on the edge of the world-renowned bay.

The impression of business as usual was reassuring. The gendarme must know the road rules. Cursing myself for my carelessness, apologizing profusely, I added my signature to the accident report, then weakly drove home.

Several nights later, sitting on our back porch, Frédéric and I were still arguing about it.

"The other guy was in the wrong. It's clearly marked; you're not allowed to overtake there," he insisted heatedly. Returning to the scene of the accident, we'd found there was no sign prohibiting my turn, which was permitted by a break in the double line.

We'd been over this already. "It was my fault, too," I said. In the rain, my focus had been on the road ahead and foolishly I hadn't checked what was behind me. Although my indicator said otherwise, the young man must have assumed I was pulling off the road.

"The driver abused you; the gendarme misled you," Frédéric argued. On the rare occasions he talked like a lawyer at home it always seemed out of character but neither of us was in a frame of mind to tease. "We should lodge a complaint with the *procureur de la République* in Pape'ete," he went on.

"We're new here, we should just drop it."

"His insurance should cover our claim."

"His car probably isn't insured. It probably wasn't even his car."

"They must be cousins or in-laws," Frédéric muttered furiously, meaning the driver and the policeman.

"No one was hurt at least," I reminded him, adding truthfully, "it's been a good lesson." Tahiti had one of the highest accident rates per head of population of anywhere in the world, I'd read in a local newspaper. The claim had sounded far-fetched—how dangerous could it be, driving on a tropical island? But now I saw there might be some truth to it. On Mo'orea, where there were no overtaking lanes, impatient drivers often passed recklessly on blind bends.

My eyes flicked to the wall behind Frédéric, where a large, fat gecko was slyly stalking a smaller one. "And the driver knows our address; it was on the accident report," I went on. Having witnessed the young man's flaring anger, I didn't wish to inflame it again. Perhaps the break-ins had made me paranoid. In e-mails and phone calls to family and friends, I played them down: things always seem far worse from a distance and I think they pictured me locked in the house in a state of fear. They're not scary burglars, they're not armed or anything, I pointed out. I'd be a lot more frightened of intruders in Paris or Sydney; I can always run over to Alain or Guite if there's any trouble.

Yet being an impressionable newcomer, privately I was unsettled by the incidents. Someone had watched and waited for me to go for my swim, before taking a shower in our garden then trying the back door. Somewhere on the island, a guy with a ponytail was keeping my best bikini bottoms as a trophy. The lure of the exotic works every which way. Just as some Western men lusted after Polynesian women, white women were a source of sexual fascination for some Polynesian men.

After a few months the *visites* stopped, as though they'd been part of a strange and elaborate initiation. The tirade of abuse that followed the car crash turned out to be a one-off experience. Still, it became a habit to count my underwear when I pegged them on the clothesline, to be sure none went missing. Around the island I drove like a Polynesian *mamie* or *papi*, nose to the windshield, never exceeding 60 kilometers an hour, one eye always on the rearview mirror.

EIGHT

It was Alain's wife, Aima, who invited us to help pollinate vanilla flowers on her stepfather's farm—though "help" is perhaps overstating our clumsy ministrations, and "farm" does not convey the tangle of vines and fruit trees nestled at the base of the crater walls that rose in front of us, magnificently fluted with dark green shadow. For the moment, though, our heads were bent down and all eyes were on plant parts so tiny the effort of seeing them made us squint. With a thumb as blunt as the head of a hammer, Clement delicately peeled back a curly flap. "You take this, see? And then scrape here." Aima translated for us into French while her stepfather demonstrated. Using what looked like a toothpick he collected the pollen from the stamen and gently deposited it in the round opening of the pistil, which wasn't much bigger than a pinhead.

We'd met Clement once already at a lunch, though conversation between us was hampered by our lack of Tahitian and his limited French. Still, you don't need language to see the goodness in someone. A stocky Polynesian with a smile of crooked teeth, a tatty straw hat and a rocking gait, he reminded me of an old fishing boat—a bit ramshackle and seaworn but the sort of sturdy vessel you'd trust in any storm. Most of what was grown on these slopes overlooking Paopao valley he gave away. Avocados, mangoes, limes, grapefruit, papayas and bananas were distributed among family and friends and, through the local church, to those in need; the occasional bag was deposited by our front door too. It all tasted marvelous. The vanilla he sold, simply to cover the high cost of cultivating the labor-intensive crop. His stubbornly low prices meant we'd begun using Clement's vanilla to flavor all sorts of things: rum cocktails, fruit salad, coffee, as well as a range of experimental savory sauces and salsas. Guite had popped over to show me how to make her banana beignets. "Half your red bowl of flour," she instructed, pausing for me to write this down. "One and a bit cups of milk— this chipped blue cup. A bit more again. *Encore, encore.* You don't want it too thick but you don't want it too runny either." The secret was the generous quantities of banana and vanilla, sliced lengthways and then in half so that the beans stuck out of the fritters like twigs.

This would be only the second season his vines produced pods but Clement's calloused fingers worked nimbly, careful not to crush the tiny plant organs as he pinched and extracted. Nature couldn't be relied on to do the job, apparently. Apart from an elusive bee in Mexico, pollination was carried out by human hand—hence the high retail cost of vanilla beans. After a few demonstrations Clement peered at us through some of the thickest lenses I'd ever seen. His next words in Tahitian, accompanied by an encouraging nod, needed no translating: your turn.

It was the sort of day you praise the gods for being alive—a stunning dry-season morning. Earlier when I went for my swim, across the strait Tahiti had stood out like a cut-out against the palely luminous sky. By the time we began spreading out among the rows of vines, the sun was well up in the sky and I was glad for my wide-brimmed straw hat. It was a different kind of heat from a few months before, not as muggy. Around April, the dense, milky quality to the air had given way to a startling clarity. We were midway through "winter," as Alain jokingly called the dry season. The daily highs were only a few degrees lower, yet having to don a cotton cardigan at night or sleep under a light doona felt like a novelty.

Although in Paris it had never occurred to me to wonder which way the wind was blowing, living on the ocean's edge brings the elements right into your face. The smooth surface of the lagoon was like a canvas on which the prevailing winds made patterns with little dabs or sweeping brush-strokes. At the onset of the dry season the northeasterly had swung to a fresh southeaster known as the *maramu*. Its grip on the water was firmer and the tiny waves, which occasionally had teeth, rolled into shore at a new angle—at two rather than ten o'clock. Instead of depositing coconuts and seaweed and a dispiriting range of plastic items—bags and fishing floats, old buckets and boating sandals—the *maramu* was a conscientious housekeeper, constantly sweeping our beach clean.

The clouds that clustered around the peaks of the main island looked different, too, not as bruised or as swollen. My diary was peppered with new observations. "Snow on Tahiti! Lovely creamy dollops covered the peaks this morning when I went for my swim." Knee-deep in the lagoon, I'd watched the snow morph and melt until it had stretched into elastic bands across the top of the island. "My cloud friends were up to their usual tricks," I'd written cheerfully.

It was exceptionally fiddly but pleasant work, shuffling from one waxy, pale green flower to the next. They looked a lot like orchids. "They *are* a type of orchid," corrected Aima, who knew her plants. Come nightfall, these fresh morning blooms would shrivel and die, which meant the window of opportunity for pollination was extremely narrow. Clement proudly told us that last harvest, well over half his flowers produced beans—an impressive success rate for a novice. Still, vanilla is not a crop that rushes to deliver rewards. Nine months: that's how long it took for the beans to mature on the vine. "*Comme un bébé*," he'd chuckled in French.

A perfect morning; a few innocent words. And now that stabbing feeling in my core, that inner space below my navel.

Paris felt very far away from this tropical valley, but as I prized and scraped the vanilla flower, my thoughts traveled back to our own experiences with reproductive science. How many goes we had at IVF I wasn't exactly sure. Only six of our attempts went right through to the end. But added to that were the countless times we went through weeks of treatment only to discover my body hadn't responded to the hormones. No point harvesting unless there were enough eggs, basically. It is a common outcome for women with high FSH, whose ovaries often won't be stimulated by the drugs. These unsuccessful strikes were a great frustration and after each one I'd hurry ahead with the next try. "You need to give your body a rest this month," my doctor had to say more than once.

Over time the process came to seem like a marathon— something that could be won by will and stamina. If we just plod on, we'll get there in the end, ran my reasoning. Surely the more goes we had, the greater the odds of success? The awakening came with our fifth try, and as is often the way with awakenings, it was rude but instructive. The lesson I learned had to do with failure—more precisely, repetitive failure and its brutal, cumulative impact. I had news for Nietzsche: just because something doesn't kill you it doesn't necessarily make you stronger.

The final step in an IVF cycle is always the clincher, though in that penultimate attempt its ramifications would be more far-reaching. Earlier that day I'd had a blood test to determine whether or not I was pregnant. As usual I'd steeled myself for disappointment before getting the result. But then as someone would later point out, you wouldn't go through the long, involved process without *hoping*. At the same time as telling myself it wouldn't work, I was also making mental preparations for twins. Fond as we were of our newly renovated apartment, we'd have to move. That tiny spare room could barely fit one cot let alone two.

When the phone rang in my office I knew who it was. Dr. B's secretary always called punctually at 2.30 pm.

"I'm sorry," she said straightaway, "the test is negative."

There was nothing different about the message or the soft, apologetic way it was delivered. What was new this time was my heartbreak. I, who had always checked my emotions and rationalized that there were worse things in life than a failed IVF attempt, was overcome on this occasion by a choking sense of loss. How? Why? Are you sure? I might have begged answers from Dr. B's secretary but all that came out was a muted "Oh," followed eventually by "I see," then another pause before a whispered, "*Merci, au revoir.*" The avalanche of tears fell as soon as the receiver clicked down. I cried for myself and also for Frédéric, who for as long as I'd known him had expressed a desire for three children. Perhaps some primal instinct would drive him to leave me, to spread his seed in younger, more fertile pastures, and this thought unleashed the sort of loud hiccupping sobs that inevitably sound put on. Reason and rationale abandoned me; nothing made sense. Fourteen days before, when the two embryos had been inserted inside me, they were alive. Perhaps one of them had briefly implanted; for a few hours or maybe days I might have been pregnant. Yet the test was negative. In other words, those microscopic beginnings of life had died in my womb. In the emotional flood I couldn't rule out self-pity, and certainly anger was there: with a bit more *effort* surely one of those embryos might have hung on. I sobbed for them, too, our little lost ones, they who would never grow into our children. Probably the embryos got swept away in my imminent menstrual tide but the image that came to mind was of dust motes settling on a shelf. Grow they wouldn't but carry them with me I would, my precious fragments of a crumbling dream.

Despite vowing "never again," I ended up returning to my specialist for one last attempt. But that unexpected, plunging despair had made me realize I couldn't keep doing IVF indefinitely. When Frédéric's job prospect came up, it was not such a blow to learn from Dr. B that French Polynesia had no facilities for infertility treatment. It was another sign, we said. In moving across the world we were not relinquishing hope, simply transferring it. Because my hormonal anomaly had been picked up early, we'd spent hardly any time trying to get pregnant unassisted. It was time to turn our backs on science and put our faith in Mother Nature.

Amid the vanilla vines I straightened, filling that space below my navel with a few deep breaths. Around me, the scenery stretched and soared as if to vindicate our reasons for moving here. No wonder the first white explorers went on about the Garden of Eden. The island must have been a tantalizing sight to sea-worn eyes—and not only for its fertile landscape offering fresh water and food. Back then, Tahitians were devoted to 'Oro, god of war and also fertility, and his worship brought new emphasis on sex and permissiveness, as well as more fighting. With their rotting teeth and scurvy wounds, the sailors can't have made attractive bedfellows, and the island girls made sure to get something in return. Sex was offered in exchange for coats, gold buttons and, most valuable of all, carpenters' nails, which Tahitians shaped into fish hooks or planted in the hope they'd grow. So many nails were pulled from the *Dolphin* that its commander, Samuel Wallis, was forced to introduce harsh punishment to prevent the ship from falling apart.

But it was Louis Antoine de Bougainville's visit in 1768, nine months later, that would propel Tahiti in European imaginations from mere place to an ideal. A charming, witty courtier, he called it New Cythera, after the birthplace of Aphrodite, and while the name didn't stick, the association with the Greek goddess of love did. "The mildness of the climate, the beauty of the scenery, the fertility of the soil everywhere watered by rivers and cascades, everything inspires sensual pleasure," he raved. Prone as the Frenchman was to poetics, from where I stood in the valley at Paopao his words didn't seem an overstatement. In such a place surely you'd only need to spit out your pips for something to sprout.

Part of me wished I hadn't read the book on natural conception that I'd thought to buy in Paris at the last minute. There is something to be said for ignorance. It had brought me no comfort to know how ridiculously hard it can be for even a perfectly healthy woman with no issues and normal hormone levels to get pregnant. It was a process almost as labyrinthine and dependent on precision timing as IVF, it seemed to me. Myriad factors could get in the way of conception. There was an inexplicable inequity, too. While men are prolific producers, able to summon sperm on a whim throughout their lives, girls are born complete with their life's stock of eggs. The numbers sound impressive—between one and two million at birth—but the vast majority of these follicles, or egg cells,

degenerate and die. Each month during ovulation, one fol-
licle bursts open and releases its egg. The ovum lives for only
twenty-four hours. Even trigger-happy men have their design
flaws. Of the hundreds of millions of sperm fired off in a
single ejaculation, most of them die within an hour. Only the
strongest, most determined swimmer will make its way
through the female floods and tides of mucus to the ovum in
one of the fallopian tubes.

I'd do as well to enlist 'Oro to my cause, I thought despondently, after reading the book. Though it was unlikely the
god of fertility, whom Tahitians had worshipped with ecstatic
dances that culminated in group masturbation, would be
aroused by prim candles and prayers.

In my diary, scribbled numbers tracked my cycle and days
11 to 15, when ovulation occurred, were lit up with pink or
yellow highlighter. Increasingly the fluoro markings were
about the raciest aspect of these occasions, which invariably
were tainted by a sense of duty. At the slightest suggestion of
postponement from Frédéric, I morphed into a version of a
pitiless school sports mistress of old, who on frosty mornings
used to cajole us into cross-country runs. "Righto, off you go,"
she'd bellow to a class of shivering girls, ludicrously under-
dressed for the Canberra winter in T-shirts and cotton bloom-
ers. "The sooner you make a start, the sooner it will be over."
I never voiced those words, of course, but conveyed my
thoughts through a brisk lack of sympathy. There are worse
things, Fred. Buck up.

A couple of times my period had come later than usual,
and simply writing the numbers 29 then 30 in my diary had
prompted a rush of interrogation. Could it have worked this

time? Was I . . . ? But if life on Mo'orea was different in almost every way from the one we led in Paris, a pattern had emerged that was unexpectedly familiar. Each month began with fresh hope and ended in failure.

And so there was a hint of something more somber that joyous morning spent pollinating vanilla—anxiety, doubt, longing? Back in Paris it had been easier to put names to feelings. Now it was harder to distinguish; it just felt like emptiness. Whatever it was, the feeling had expanded on the island, nourished no doubt by my solitude and lack of busyness. The same sensation had begun to gnaw at me when I sat down to write. It seemed possible that anything might disappear into this black space, not just dreams of book or baby but whole days. If every Eden must have a serpent, then this was one I'd brought with me. Its presence was nothing new yet now for the first time it began to rise between us.

"Sarah from the Bible, remember her?" It may have been the night of our vanilla-bean operations, or days later. Frédéric meant to cheer me up over dinner, in the least draw a sort of indulgent, fond smile: you and your religion. But I was no longer in the mood for crazy fables and instead he got a withering look. "My name's not a good luck charm," I snapped. Although it had been only six months since we left Paris, my days of reading miracles on church walls were over. "I want a child now not in fifty years' time."

In a way that seemed perfectly logical at the time, this led to an unfortunate reeling off of associated disenchantments.

I was tired of being the keeper of the calendar, fed up with writing down those niggly numbers. "*You* can keep track of my cycle from now on," I huffed. Frédéric's look of bewilderment, possibly not unjustified, was tinder to my fire. And while we were on the subject, why was it that precisely when we *had* to make love he was most unenthusiastic? "You're not making enough effort."

"It's not supposed to be an *effort*," he retorted.

The release I'd felt in firing off my angry accusations quickly dissipated once they lay like spent firecrackers on the floor. All that was left was a hollow feeling, into which soon trickled remorse. I wished he'd fought back instead of stomping off wordlessly to bed. I sought out Maddie on the back porch, who beat her tail on the tiles lethargically then deigned to raise her head off the tiles to eye me—a little too inquiringly for my liking. It was day 13; I was probably ovulating. "You always have to pick fights when we're supposed to be making love," Frédéric had pointed out in an injured tone.

I've always marveled at couples who claim to be able to channel anger into desire, to move seamlessly from accusations to passionate sex, although privately I have trouble believing them. That night in bed we practiced strenuous avoidance: any further apart and one of us would have fallen onto the floor. As surely as one of our beach hermit crabs, Frédéric had withdrawn into his shell. On my side of the invisible partition, I lay stewing. Was it for me to swallow my pride and make a conciliatory move? Had I spoken too harshly? Tentatively I touched his shoulder. It rose and fell gently, in time with peaceful breaths, then vibrated as a contented snore put paid to any hope of reconciliation. There was always the morning; I would be extra sweet. But lying there in the dark I couldn't help fretting that tomorrow would be too late. Silently I bade farewell to another precious egg from one of my two tired baskets before it blasted off into oblivion.

NINE

A little over an hour after the plane had flown northeast from Pape'ete, I saw my first atoll. Nothing had prepared me for the strange reality. On the vast Pacific plain, Tikehau looked like a smoke ring—so fragile and fine it might blow away in an eye blink. "The world contains certain patterns of beauty that impress the mind forever," wrote James A. Michener, who claimed that coral atolls were one of these incomparable images. On we flew over more islands in the Tuamotu group, one of five archipelagos that make up French Polynesia. I didn't know whether to laugh or cry. How foolishly vulnerable they seemed in the face of cyclones, tsunamis and rising sea levels. How marvelously courageous.

I couldn't recall ever being as moved by a landscape— though "landscape" was hardly the right word for them, there was so little land to speak of. The islands were like long strings of beads—most of which were too tiny for human life. Between the islets or *motu*, as Tahitians call them, were shallow, limpid sections where the sandbar was submerged, as well as the odd deep channel. "UNBELIEVABLE COLOR," I scribbled excitedly in my notepad from my window seat. Along the ocean shorelines it was pretty much a direct descent into sapphire. But lagoon-side there was one hue after another, sharp delineations and rainbow-like segueing, as the sandy floor of the coral-dotted shoals slid to radiant depths. "Mushroom pink, yellow, honeydew melon, beryl, turquoise, cobalt!" I wrote.

The playful patterns and brilliance must have had a mesmerizing effect because after some initial exclamations Frédéric and I both got lost in our own thoughts. I couldn't help wondering why on earth the ancient Polynesians settled in the Tuamotus in the first place. Did their hearts sink when they sailed here in their catamarans in about 700 AD? Had they hoped for a continent? Or did the interminable ocean make them grateful for any land, however insubstantial? Two hours after leaving Pape'ete we came to another sandy contour encircling a lagoon so vast it resembled an interior sea. Its satiny surface was spotted with cloud reflections as fleecy and distinct as the real things and for a moment I felt completely disoriented. Where was up and where was down? Was that sky below or ocean? What a shame Henri Matisse hadn't seen Fakarava from the air. What fun he would have had in his old age, when the painter had turned to his paper cutouts, sitting in bed with his scissors and brightly painted paper, effortlessly cutting out embryonic atoll forms.

Until recently, the only world-famous artist I'd known of who had any connection with Tahiti was Paul Gauguin. To many Polynesians he might have been an irrelevance or even a nuisance, yet reminders of his role as mythmaker were everywhere. His paintings of solemn Tahitian women were printed on place mats, bottles of *monoi* coconut oil and calendars, which were eagerly snapped up by mostly American passengers of the *Paul Gauguin* cruise ship. In downtown Pape'ete, Rue Gauguin passes near the central market, where the artist used to pick up prostitutes.

By contrast, there were no Matisse souvenirs or eponymous sites and streets. It wasn't until I came across a slim book in Pape'ete one day that I learned of his visit to the islands. *Matisse, Le Voyage en Polynésie,* by Paule Laudon, turned out to be a fascinating account of the artist's three-month stay. Unlike his compatriot some thirty years earlier, he never intended to settle there. While Gauguin had undoubtedly influenced the Frenchman's choice of destination, Henri Matisse was not interested in perpetuating a myth. He didn't sail across the world in pursuit of primitivism or dusky-skinned *vahine*—during his stay he wrote daily to his wife, Amélie, back in France. Nor did he share Gauguin's fascination for Polynesian culture and language. Abandoning his customary pith hat for a casual pandanus sun hat was about as far as Matisse went toward going native.

But Tahiti was no random destination either. The long sea journey via America was not something done on a whim. Like Paul Gauguin—like almost everyone, including us—he came to French Polynesia seeking renewal. Travel, wrote his biographer, Hilary Spurling, had always been the artist's solution to creative crises; Matisse himself explained it was a way of forcing one part of the brain to switch off while releasing another part. The legendary southern light would unleash new inspiration, he hoped. In art galleries I had often admired Matisse's paintings of peaceful interior scenes and his audacious use of color—in which, incidentally, he was greatly influenced by Gauguin. But if the artist came to resonate in my own island life it was because of his transformative trip to Fakarava.

⌒⌒

When Henri Matisse arrived on the RMS *Tahiti* in 1930, he was sixty years old and already famous. The French overseas territory, too, was enjoying renewed celebrity. If the end of the eighteenth century had brought waves of European explorers to Tahiti, the late nineteenth and early twentieth centuries saw an influx of artists, writers and adventurers, among them Herman Melville, Jack London and Robert Louis Stevenson. Somerset Maugham had already come sniffing out Gauguin's trail and the subsequent novel, *The Moon and Sixpence*, had been a bestseller.

Bespectacled, bearded and portly, Matisse must have looked the quintessential respectable European gentleman (unlike Gauguin who arrived in a felt hat like a cowboy's, with hair to his shoulders, though he cut it after Polynesians laughed and called him a *mahu*, the old term for men who live as women). In the days immediately following his arrival in Tahiti, the artist marveled at everything from the black glossy seeds of a sliced papaya to the decorative shape of breadfruit. Fascinated with the exotic forms and feral fecundity of the place, he sketched plants and trees. But after a few weeks Matisse grew disillusioned with Pape'ete. The combination of promiscuity and prudishness, encouraged by the missionaries, confounded him: while sex could be had at a whim, no Polynesian woman was willing to sit for him, clothed or unclothed. He stopped sketching. To avoid the nightlife and flirting, the depressing sight of middle-aged European men pairing off with local girls half their age, he ate early, alone. Nor was he enthusiastic about official soirées at the French governor's residence, where during his three-month stay the famous artist was a sought-after guest. In their white tropical uniforms and rounded hats, the colonial administrators reminded Matisse of painted skittles. "You instinctively look for a ball to knock them down," he grumbled in one letter to his wife.

Inspired by Gauguin, no doubt, the artist had planned a side trip to the Marquesas, the northernmost archipelago, where his compatriot spent the last two years of his rather tormented life. When arrangements fell through, Matisse despaired. Desperate to salvage the voyage on which he'd pinned his creative hopes, he seized the next opportunity to escape that came along: a place on a government supply schooner bound for the Tuamotu atolls of Apataki and Fakarava.

For a man of his age and epoch, the two-day journey across rough seas in a leaky boat must have been a remarkable adventure. Even our seamless two-hour flight felt like a journey into the unknown. Fakarava itself was barely wider than a runway, and as the plane prepared to touch down, its wingtips seemed to hang over the water. I always found it weird when passengers broke into applause on safely landing, as if arriving alive were an unexpected bonus. But clap we did on this occasion, quite spontaneously, because touching down on a sand bar in this ocean wilderness seemed nothing short of miraculous.

⌒⌒

Lord, the light. Even with dark glasses on, even with my eyes half-closed, the next morning the glare was almost painful as the boat sped across the lagoon. The sun beat down, making us sweat in our black wetsuits; rays streamed through the shoals then bounced high-spiritedly off the white sandy floor like it were a trampoline. "Perfect conditions for scuba diving," the instructor had said. "The visibility couldn't be better." The only thing was that due to the full moon the current in Garuae Pass, the island's main gateway, would be pretty strong. At this piece of information Frédéric and I exchanged nervous glances. It was our first drift dive, we reminded the instructor, a French fellow who had the deep suntan and laid-back demeanor you'd expect of someone who lived on an atoll. As if to highlight our inexperience the three other divers pulled out sleek wetsuits and their own buoyancy vests. But the instructor reassured us, "You'll be fine, I'll be right by you, just stick close." He spent the next few minutes talking us through the dive. Garuae Pass was 800 meters wide, a real giant, he enthused. At our point of entry it would be bottomless blue, though we'd stop our descent at 25 meters. The current would swiftly carry us through a "wall" of several hundred sharks and into the neck of the channel and from there we'd coast on into the lagoon.

"You don't drift, you *fly*:" that was how an Italian tourist we'd met on Mo'orea described drift diving in Fakarava's other, smaller, channel. His hand planed through the air, then with a sheepish smile the diver had said, "I met God in that pass." Since getting our basic PADI qualification we'd had some marvelous experiences on Mo'orea, where we regularly dived with reef sharks as well as lemon sharks, moray eels and all sorts of smaller fish whose names I was still learning. But, with respect, unless God was a fat, friendly Napoléon wrasse, I had not met Him underwater. Nor did Mo'orea's coral bed—or what I'd seen of it—have the ethereal beauty and high color associated with many reefs. Much of it was broken and bleached, the damage caused by a combination of factors including warm water temperatures, possibly pesticide run-off, as well as anchors dropped carelessly by fishing or even dive boats. To hear the Italian, pristine Fakarava was a mecca for scuba divers. It was obvious we were missing out on a higher—or deeper—experience. I didn't say this to anyone; it wasn't even a conscious thought. But I think that was what I was hoping for that morning in Garuae Pass: an encounter or experience of a more spiritual nature.

I would like to be able to report whom I met in that seething rush but once we bombed off the boat everything happened so fast. In the first instances underwater I recall scanning below in panic for the ocean floor. *Le grand bleu* might sound poetic but plunging into those abyssal depths was terrifying. My thoughts should have been on my dive buddy, who often experienced ear squeeze and had to descend slowly, pegging his nose and blowing constantly to try to relieve the pressure. Instead I held hands fast with the instructor—gripped on to him for dear life, grateful for something firm on which to focus. Garuae really was a giant, just like he'd said. One intent on swallowing us alive.

The combination of our tentative descent and the current meant we missed seeing the shark wall altogether. We sailed straight over it apparently, though this didn't even register until we were back on land. The floor rose and it was then, as coral brains and blossoms flashed beneath me, that I got a measure on how fast we were traveling. The current wasn't strong, it was supersonic. My mask shook and my regulator rattled and I had to use both hands to clamp them tight to prevent them from being ripped from my face and mouth. Stick together, the dive monitor had said, as if we might casually steer. The five of us had spread out and Frédéric, perhaps caught in a rogue jet stream, had somehow veered off to the left.

At least we were riding the lagoon-bound current and there was no risk of losing him in open sea or seeing him taken away by a fatal downward current. Traveling on the inflow is one of the golden rules of diving in ocean passes. Still, the growing distance between us was worrying and now my attention *was* on my buddy. As I watched, Frédéric managed to grab on to a coral head. I clung to a huge cauliflower. Touching the flora and fauna underwater is a diving no-no but there was no alternative. Slowly Frédéric began to crawl back, pulling cross-current from one floret to another. Up ahead I saw the instructor, anchored to something himself, waiting. It was all he could do: there was no hope of him reaching us. *You okay?* I signaled to Frédéric when he'd completed the 20-meter marathon. Behind his mask, his eyes were like golf balls. He made a wan loop with his fingers in reply.

Finally the current eased and we were poured into a giant bowl in the lagoon floor, filled to the brim with fish. Aladdin's Cave, I think they called it, though nothing about that dive is sure. Normally I made mental notes of species of sea life but I was too dazed to do anything but kick about mindlessly. Later, back on land, the others would avidly compare notes on the highlights Frédéric and I had missed: the hammerhead shark lurking in the deep, the school of flashing barracuda and, sadly, a glimpse of a manta ray. Our inexperience had allowed little time to smell the roses—not that I'd have gone sniffing around a hammerhead. For once I felt exactly like Frédéric, simply happy to have survived the dive.

"Let's do an easier one tomorrow," I suggested after we hauled ourselves back on the boat.

"The snorkeling is supposed to be great in front of the hotel," he replied wryly, not yet recovered from the rollicking ride.

That was exactly how Henri Matisse spent his four days on Fakarava: head down, bum up in the lagoon, peering through the wooden-framed swimming goggles fashioned on the atoll. In my mind's eye I pictured the elderly artist as a playful seal pup, diving down to explore, then surfacing for breath only to go under again. The ephemeral webs of refracted sunlight fascinated him, as did the crystalline clarity of the water. "Pure light, pure air, pure color: diamond, sapphire, emerald, turquoise," he raved in a letter home. "Stupendous fish." Having read Robert Louis Stevenson's descriptions of Fakarava—of fish "stained and striped, and even beaked like

parrots" and of coral that "branched and blossomed"—
Matisse wasn't disappointed. These were sights he claimed no
visitor to French Polynesia should miss.

Like a sponge absorbs water: that was how the artist described the incremental way he processed what he saw. Interestingly, many years would pass before these memories would
bubble into his art, producing exactly the creative climax he
had sought. Following a bout of illness that left him bedridden and unable to paint, Matisse changed his method of
work to what he called his *découpages*, or cut-outs. At seventy-
six his sight was diminished yet the swiftness and facility with
which he cut out form after form, swiveling scissors as if in a
trance, dumbfounded visitors. Pinned on backgrounds of euphoric blue, the pale shapes floated, darted and swooped:
coral, sponges, fish, sea birds and jellyfish. "At an age when
most artists are either dead or repeating themselves," wrote
Robert Hughes, "Matisse had re-entered the avant-garde and
redefined it."

More than the submarine world, which had flashed by too
fast, it was the atoll itself that marked me on that first trip to
Fakarava. The island's village and virtually its entire population of roughly 750 people, as well as the hotel where we
lodged, were all located on the main islet. In preparation for
a visit by Jacques Chirac in 2003, the *motu*'s only road had
been tarred and, incongruously, Parisian-style street lamps
were erected along a short strip. In the end the French president didn't come and islanders were left with the souvenir
lights which provided a touch of Champs-Elysées pomp to
the low-key atoll. It was pretty in a sparse, overexposed way.
Beside the limpid lagoon, pirogues painted blue and pink

and yellow lay beached on the shore and fishing nets were spread out to dry in the sun. Apart from coconut and pandanus palms and scrappy-looking shrubs, there was little in the way of vegetation and almost nothing in the way of shade. Winds blew straight over these sand bars without releasing any of their moisture but the harsh conditions seemed to suit the bougainvilleas, whose flamboyant colors blazed against the glare of blues behind.

Michener, who sold millions of books about the South Pacific, wrote movingly of these thread-like islands as symbols of security for men in a wilderness of ocean. "This is the wonder of an atoll, that you are safe within the lagoon while outside the tempest rages." On Fakarava the tempest—or threat of one—is never far away. Even as you wade into the calm lagoon, you can hear the Pacific Ocean pounding the other side. The dimensions are delirious: just 3.5 meters above sea level at its highest point, the atoll is rarely more than 300 meters wide. Walking to the other side takes only a minute or two, as we found out on an after-dinner stroll. Compared with the lagoon, which around the hotel was lit up like a swimming pool with spotlights, the ocean side felt different, dangerous. The waves swooshed and rattled over the rocks. Instead of a caressing sea breeze, the wind felt a little wild, as if it wasn't accustomed to meeting land and people. "This must be the purest air in the world," I said, inhaling deeply, as we lay down on the lumpy limestone bed to admire the night sky.

The stars looked like holes pricked in a black quilt, through which shone a wondrous, blazing world on the other side. How puny we felt! We must have still been on a narcotic high after the hurtling pass dive, judging from the discussion that followed. How many stars were there, how many planets and galaxies? Could there be more than one universe? Was the atoll *drifting*? At one point Frédéric solemnly quoted the seventeenth-century French philosopher and mathematician Blaise Pascal: "The eternal silence of these infinite spaces frightens me."

"It's incredible to think that Fakarava used to look as high and green as Mo'orea," I said aloud. It was almost impossible to picture. How inconsequential our own lifespans were compared with the aeons it took to create this coral causeway— once the fringing reef for one or more mighty volcanoes. Over millions of years, a combination of erosion and sinking caused all the peaks to slip beneath the water. Now, only Fakarava's immense lagoon gave an indication of the size of the former high island. Two centuries had passed since Darwin solved the mystery of atoll evolution yet still his theory seemed as much a leap of imagination as of science.

With a total of seventy-seven islands, the Tuamotu archipelago is the world's largest chain of atolls. Unlike people on more vulnerable Pacific islands such as Tuvalu, French Polynesians have not had to resort to desperate measures to hold back rising sea levels caused by global warming. Not yet. Scientists didn't agree on the time frame—I've read estimates ranging from 50 to 150 years before the atolls become uninhabitable. "I suppose they'll be moved to Tahiti," I said, of the 15,000 or so inhabitants of the Tuamotus. Frédéric was silent for a moment. "It's sad to think our grandchildren probably won't have this experience," he said. "They might not even get to see an atoll."

I felt a rush of love for him then. When I'd first met Frédéric he'd just gone through a divorce and his mood was reflected in portentous pen sketches—usually a dark forest with a melancholy figure mooching between the trees. He credited me with encouraging him to experiment with gouache paints and vibrant color, with showing him the joy in life with my energy and enthusiasm. Now I found myself wondering if he wasn't the more positive of the two of us. His statement about the disappearance of atolls didn't strike me as pessimistic but mildly optimistic.

"Grandchildren?"

TEN

Nelly didn't come that first week after our return from Fakarava. Nor did she appear the second Wednesday. Frédéric was perfectly capable of ironing his own business shirts and it wasn't as if we couldn't clean the house ourselves, but her absence made me realize how I'd come to rely on her weekly visits. I missed her company, her happy humming in the garden, the *tiare* buds on our pillows, the ephemeral flower towers. Her influence could be seen in other ways around the house, which was unmistakably more colorful than it had been. Recently I'd brought home from Pape'ete some hibiscus-embroidered cushion covers in shades of greens and oranges and pinks that previously would have struck me as florid. Made in Bali though they were, they added a distinctly Tahitian flavor and Nelly had lit up in delight and approval, "*Ils sont jolis!*" Brash color seemed entirely natural on the island, where even the exotic flowers that grew wild along the roadside seemed like experiments in complements and inversions. "It was so simple to paint things as I saw them," Gauguin wrote of the rich palette he developed in Tahiti, "to put without special calculation a red close to a blue."

It wasn't until the third Wednesday passed without a word that I started to worry. In the past there'd been occasional absences, mainly due to rain. But three weeks in a row when there hadn't been a drop? Perhaps one of her children was sick? Alain or Guite would surely have told us if anything serious had happened but I resolved to pop across the road the next day to check.

However, that very morning, a Thursday, there was a familiar rattle of a rusty bike outside. It was followed by an uncustomary pause and some shuffling, as though the visitor was plucking up courage before calling out. "Sah–rah, Sah–rah." From where I sat at my desk, the rolled Tahitian "r" merged with the soft rumble of waves breaking out on the reef. When I stepped outside, there was Nelly, white *tiare* laced through her black hair, not looking unwell or injured at all but decidedly sheepish. She handed me a plastic bag of bananas from her sister's garden, hanging her head like she expected to be ticked off. "I've just made coffee," I said, resisting the urge to hug her.

"*J'étais fiu*": that was the simple explanation offered for her three-week absence. Locals often intermingle the territory's main languages and the first two words were French while the last one, "*fiu*," was Tahitian. Pronounced "phew," everyone on these islands knew exactly what it meant. She was fed up/tired/flat/over it/over everything. What had caused Nelly to feel this way she didn't say: there could have been one reason or many or none easily identifiable. The expression refers to a state of mind that might account for a decision to spend the day in bed or to walk out on a husband or wife or simply to disappear for a while, perhaps to an outer island to stay with relatives. A local psychiatrist who studied the condition likened it to depression. Importantly, instead of denying it or maintaining appearances, Polynesians allow themselves to succumb to it. Just like the wet-season rains, feeling *fiu* is considered a normal part of the life cycle and it is understood it will pass eventually.

In the same way that in Australia the Aboriginal tendency to go walkabout exasperated and mystified white people, in French Polynesia the colonial perception was that *fiu* was a sign of native laziness. But Maco Tevane—who heads the Tahitian Academy, responsible for promoting and documenting the territory's *ma-'ohi* languages—has asserted that this ability to switch off and withdraw may go way back. For the first Polynesians, long ocean voyages were as much a mental challenge as a physical one. As well as dangers and frenzied activity, they had to cope with extended periods of drifting and boredom. Tevane has also written that these biorhythmic lows may be a natural way of coping with intense remoteness and being surrounded by ocean and emptiness. Yet modern Western life, with its high value on efficiency and productivity, doesn't allow for the doldrums. Even in Tahiti feeling *fiu* was becoming less acceptable as an excuse.

We sat on the front steps sipping coffee, Nelly's sweet and black, mine white. This was my opportunity to lecture about responsibility and commitment—in the very least to point out that it'd be nice to know in advance if she didn't intend coming. Though given she didn't have a telephone at home this would require getting out of bed and leaving the house, which surely defeated the purpose. Behind the rounded peak straight ahead, another sharper peak rose from the island's interior and for a moment I stared at it. Inexplicably, a lump formed in my throat. "*Moi aussi*," I said finally. "I'm *fiu*, too." Saying it aloud, my voice had cracked, as if that dear little word tapped into a deeper fissure, though when Nelly glanced at me anxiously I simply patted her knee and looked away.

The idea of remote islands as pressure cookers has been around almost as long as the idea of islands as paradise. In the short time we'd been in the territory Frédéric and I had witnessed several marriages implode soon after the couples had arrived from France. Perhaps the tropical glare throws clarity on irreconcilable differences or maybe in the fertile volcanic soil problems grow at an alarming rate. While a similar potential might exist in any remote community, from a snowed-in alpine village to a sun-scorched outback town, a barrier of empty ocean thousands of kilometers wide makes for a profound sense of isolation. It was this geographical reality—at once beautiful and fearful—that made your skin prickle right from page one of *Lord of the Flies*. Though, of course, in William Golding's classic tale of shipwrecked schoolchildren, as in real life, the true menace lay within. You come face-to-face with yourself on an island: this remark had been repeated to me many times since we'd arrived.

After Nelly left, I sat for a moment on the front steps scratching Maddie behind the ears until she was almost hypnotized, eyes half-closed. She was looking pretty again, having recently been trimmed and groomed; the fellow who worked for the *Aremiti* ferry had received another bag of snipped fur to use to catch bait fish. *"C'est bien, c'est beaucoup,"* he'd nodded, pleased. It was nice to think that some part of Maddie was playing a small, useful role in the island's food chain. Eventually, when I could procrastinate no longer, I went back to my desk. Recently I'd said yes to contributing an essay for an anthology of travel writing. After floundering in the obscurity of fiction, I was back on terra firma. It can be about anywhere, the editor had said. Having read up on history, I had decided to write about Tahiti and the paradise myth.

I frowned at the computer screen. The jottings I'd made before Nelly arrived seemed to have been written by someone else. "Bougainville—metaphysical crises—*Lord of the Flies*": where this enigmatic arrow of thought had been heading I could only guess. A mosquito hummed. They were beginning to come back again; the dry season was drawing to an end. Once it started, that high-pitched irritation was all I heard. Slap. Slap. I'd become quite skilled at this slaughter and pretty soon the little pest was humming no longer.

I blinked at my screen, which was the same pearl-gray of a wintry Paris sky. Now, where was I?

Squeeze, squeeze, squeeze: just recalling Frédéric's wasabi-tube analogy for writer's block put me in good mind to go and squeeze the fiery paste all over his pillow. I'd been sitting at this desk, squeezing and pushing for months. For me writing had always been a lot of hard slog lifted by exhilarating moments when it seemed my words might have captured a small truth. It had been a very long time between highs. My heart went out to my poor Bretons who had grown more stodgy and lifeless by the day. Why am I doing this? I began to wonder. It was clear that prolonged and painful effort wasn't achieving anything. When finally I put my "novel" into the metaphorical bottom drawer, it was with more relief than regret.

Henri Matisse likened the creative act to slitting an abscess with a penknife. The joyous color and tranquillity in his paintings of rooms with pretty balconies and vases of flowers belied inner turbulence and fearful labor. But struggling to produce an artistic or literary masterpiece was one thing. My struggle with a simple 5000-word essay—which could be about Paris or Tahiti or *any* travel experience of my choice—was harder to justify. For all the talk about creative inspiration and the mysterious powers of the subconscious, writing is not greatly different from building a house. Word by word, sentence by sentence, paragraph by paragraph, page by page: that is how it is done. So what was wrong with me? What had happened to my building blocks? Where had all my words gone?

My mind wandered from the travel essay I was supposed to be writing to the possible excuses I might give the editor for failing to deliver it. Sorry, I squeezed really hard but nothing came out. Apologies, I'm just too empty. I could call and weep and tell her I was having a nervous breakdown. But no, that was too unoriginal: writers were always breaking down before deadlines. Then it came to me, that wee word richly endowed with the wisdom of the ancient Polynesians. This was surely one excuse she had not yet heard. Dear Fiona, terribly sorry but I am *fiu*.

It's possible that around this time my grip on reality had loosened. There was the incident at the Maharepa shops on Mo'orea when I'd tried to drive off in someone else's car—not an isolated incident I have to confess. The car was small and white like ours. But not a Clio, as it turned out, not even a different model Renault. Cursing, I'd tried to force the key into the ignition until slowly—too slowly—it dawned on me there was something different about it. Interestingly, it wasn't the upholstery that registered first, which was blue, not gray like ours. It wasn't the different dashboard straight in front of me, nor the thicker steering wheel in my hands. Instead it was the smell: an artificial apple scent that was nothing like our car's earthy, wet-dog pong. It registered then that not only was Maddie's odor absent but Maddie herself. Looking up, I saw three middle-aged Polynesian men standing on the curb ahead, watching me with wide eyes. "*Pas grave*, it's not a problem," the owner of the car said affably when I leaped out, apologizing profusely.

Then there were my pleasant interior monologues, which according to Frédéric were becoming increasingly animated. "Mind if I interrupt?" he teased one afternoon after joining me on the ferry. I'd been looking out the window, smiling, moving my lips, waving my hand for emphasis, deep in conversation with the flying fish or the ocean, so he said. On occasion, unbeknownst to me, random snippets would pop out of my mouth, prompting bemusement from Frédéric, who hadn't been privy to the rest of the conversation.

"Pardon?" he'd inquire patiently. Usually I returned a blank look. "What you just said, Sarah, it didn't make sense."

"I didn't say anything."

"Yes you did. You just said: 'and I think that's what we should do.'"

A look of pure astonishment would blow across my face: my husband the mind reader! Then comprehension would worm in and I would have to mumble apologetically. "Oh, sorry, sorry, I didn't know I said it aloud."

On a rare evening alone I grew inexplicably weepy watching television. Frédéric had stayed over in Pape'ete for a dinner with his boss. It was not unusual for me to feel moved by a tragedy on the world news but a nature documentary on the African dung beetle? On safari in the Serengeti years before, I was so busy spotting giraffes, elephants and wildebeest I hadn't spared a thought for the tiny creatures that cleared away their dung. Now the sight of the female sitting atop that perfectly rolled elephant manure being pushed along by her mate touched an emotional nerve. They looked so fervent and full of purpose, heading off to build a burrow for their lovely sphere of poo into which Mrs. Beetle would lay her eggs.

"Get your thoughts down on paper," Alicia urged over the phone from Paris. Her ability to read my emotional state remained undiminished by the distance. "Write just for you, whatever comes into your head. If nothing else it might give you some release." It was difficult to explain to her that this would be like trying to squeeze sap from dried-up driftwood. Words had fled my creative source that, whatever scientists said, was not in my head or right brain but in the vital space where breath and life come from. Even in the private pages of my diary there were no confessions, no unburdening. I stuck to safe subjects: what we had for dinner at Alain and

Aima's place, the feisty clownfish in the lagoon, the spaghetti threads of refracted light underwater. Fetishist descriptions of clouds filled paragraph after paragraph—pavlovas, snow-falls, frangipanis, *tiare*, ribbons, fortresses. Though perhaps my diary was more revealing than I thought. If what we don't say is just as telling as what is said then perhaps silences, gaps and omissions are an eloquent expression of inner empti-ness.

⌒⌒

Can one form of barrenness lead to another? It would be disingenuous—delusional—to pretend my novel was floun-dering simply because I couldn't get pregnant, wouldn't it? If every woman needed a child to write there would have been no Virginia Woolf, no Simone de Beauvoir, no Hilary Mantel; Mexican artist Frida Kahlo used her loss and anguish as a powerful source of inspiration. Still, a couple of years from then, a few paragraphs in a book would grab my attention— or rather trigger such a powerful sense of recognition that reading the words gave me goose bumps. "Pregnancy has al-ways been a visible statement and proof of fertility and virility for both men and women," wrote psychoanalyst Juliet Miller in *Inconceivable Conceptions.* "When a woman is unable to make this happen, the lack of concrete expression of her pro-creativity can feel like an attack on her capacity to trust in any other of her creative acts. It may confirm a sense of being empty inside and having nothing to draw on."

In my copy of the book, a slim but dense volume that ex-amines the impact of unwanted childlessness on the creative impulse, many lines are highlighted. "Failure to conceive may imprison women in a state of permanent failure" is one of them, along with a few dramatic Jung quotations. "For a woman there is no longer any way out; if she cannot have children, she falls into hellfire because all her creativeness turns back to herself, she begins to eat herself," he wrote some eighty years ago.

⌒⌒

While I sank deeper into myself, Frédéric seemed to be thriving. After a slow start, business had picked up and by the end of the year he'd taken on a couple of other lawyers, which meant my "city bureau" was no longer mine. That there was an unhealthy disparity between our situations was obvious each evening as we debriefed by the lagoon. Frédéric would talk about lunches with colleagues and clients, the latest political gossip gleaned from Pape'ete, and tell funny stories from the local courts. I, on the other hand, often felt I had little to recount at all. I might have looked for a job except my French residency visa didn't allow me to work in the territory and it wouldn't have looked good had the wife of the new Paris lawyer been found to be working illegally. Apart from his concern for me, Frédéric seemed more relaxed than ever. It had been a while since he threatened to dye his hair—even if, to be honest, he was now a shade grayer than George Clooney. His desire for children was undiminished but it was not visceral like mine. His pain was not as deep. Or so I thought. And then one day a little creature unexpectedly dropped into our garden.

"A heron," he'd declared, picking it up very gently off the grass. "It's definitely a heron. You can tell by its long neck."

I looked at the tiny bundle in his hands, its feathers stuck together with flecks of mud and dirt. With its wings folded and beak tucked into its chest it looked to my inexpert eye like any number of spindly, pathetic creatures. It hadn't even looked like a living thing when I'd gone outside to see what Maddie was barking about. Lying beneath our tamanu tree, from a distance it might have been one of its fallen nuts, from which was extracted the precious pungent green oil that was supposedly a miraculous balm for the skin. During the night there'd been heavy rain and high winds. The chick must have fallen out of the tree, though we couldn't spot a nest on the ground or in the branches overhead. Rapid breaths pumped its tiny rib cage as Frédéric gently stroked its back, which might easily have broken with a push of his thumb.

"Maybe we should leave it there," I suggested. "That way the mother might come back for it." Vaguely I recalled having read something about human contact ruining the chance of mother birds reclaiming their young. I scanned the trees to see if we were being watched. Though now that Frédéric had gone and picked it up the damage might well be done.

"We can't do that, the rats will eat it. Maddie might hurt it," he objected. But our intrepid hunter had already ambled off, and as if to make her disdain for the twig creature plain, she raised her rump high in the air, burrowing into the hole of a mud crab.

I was about to remind him of the laws of the jungle, survival of the fittest and so on. But then he lifted the bird until it was level with his face and eyed it squarely. It blinked back;

in the warm bowl of Frédéric's hands it started to breathe easier.

"I'll look after you, I promise," I heard him say softly.

At the risk of sounding callous, my nurturing instincts were not stirred by this beaky find. It had nothing on the noble beauties and characters I'd grown up with in Australia: sulfur-crested cockatoos, kookaburras and king parrots to name a few. It was likely an Indian myna—sadly one of the few bird species on the island that was flourishing. A family of these mean-spirited colonizers had recently moved into our front garden, and as they've done across the Pacific, immediately set about chasing every other living thing away from their new territory. Whenever we ventured to the gate or tried to hop in the car, the mynas bleated lividly and swooped on us in pairs. It had been tempting when Clet, a good-natured Polynesian fellow who helped Guite in her garden, offered to get rid of them for us. With a grin that revealed many gaps, he'd made his hand into a gun and fired: paf! Death by drowning would have been more seemly, I thought, more traditional—wasn't that how islanders had always got rid of unwanted animals? Shooting was too raucous, too much like sport. We'd all want a go. Regretfully I declined.

Frédéric made a home for the bird using a small box that he padded, without asking, with one of my torn but favorite sarongs. During the day he left it on the kitchen bench; at night he sat it on the small table right beside his pillow. After checking with Daniel, our neighbor the former vet, he began feeding it tiny amounts of water through a syringe and trying to entice it with crumbs of milk-soaked bread. His life-saving efforts didn't flag even when Daniel broke the news that our ugly duckling would not grow into a graceful, long-necked water bird at all. "A *pigeon?*" Daniel nodded, his amused expression inviting me to view the heron story—a ruse to get me to play mother hen to the chick, I now suspected—as one of my husband's charming quirks. Frédéric carried on mashing up something to be sucked up in the syringe, as if he hadn't heard. "At least it isn't an Indian myna," I allowed peevishly.

On one level Frédéric's actions were not surprising; he'd always been a softie. While many of his childhood friends from northern France were enthusiastic recreational hunters, he had always shunned the tradition. Relishing a baked woodcock caught by one of his *chasseur* mates was one thing but the thought of pulling the trigger made him shudder. Still, it seemed to me his determination to save the little bird was a bit obsessive. Even when Daniel had said it would probably die, even as the bird appeared to me halfway to heaven, Frédéric hung on to the hope of coaxing it back to life.

Five or six days after we had found it helpless beneath the tamanu tree we awoke to find the baby pigeon huddled and still in the box. For what seemed like ages Frédéric sat on the edge of the bed, stroking the still-warm form, which in death resembled a downy egg. "*Pauvre petite bête*, poor little thing," he whispered over and over. Morning sun flooded through the red curtains, casting a ripe radiance over the bedroom at odds with the somber mood. I watched, feeling deeply sad, though not especially for the pigeon. Something about the slump of Frédéric's shoulders, the curve of his spine, indicated a greater defeat. His inability to save the small creature had brought to the surface a deeper sense of impotence and bewilderment.

"*La vie, l'amour, la mort,*" he replied with a wry smile when later I asked what he had been thinking as he cradled the bird. Life. Love. Death. Frédéric let out a heavy sigh. "Soon I'll be fifty."

"Not soon," I protested. "Not for another couple of years!"

But it wasn't difficult to follow his thinking. Even an optimist could see it was getting a little late in the day for three children. Perhaps this was his Proustian moment of realizing how life had diverged from his dream. My hopes had been diminishing for a while but this was the first time I'd glimpsed despair in Frédéric.

ELEVEN

When Christmas arrived I wondered where the year had gone. The impression of time flying was ironic, given the limping pace of many of my days on the island. But then time is a magician: it can drip by or fly like an arrow, as the French say. It can't stop but it may *run out*. Early on we'd made the decision to remain on Mo'orea for Christmas. Frédéric didn't have much leave left and it wasn't that long since we'd seen our families: my parents had come to stay for a couple of weeks in June, and in August the two of us had returned to France for a holiday, along with practically every other *popa'ā* in the territory. Still, on our own, Christmas Day might have been a bit subdued were it not for the invitation from Alain and Aima to celebrate it with them.

By now the customs were familiar to us and arriving at their house the first thing Frédéric and I did was slip out of our sandals, which we left on the grass at the bottom of the steps. The long table on the shaded terrace overlooking the garden was covered in bright tablecloths and festooned with flowers. Knives and forks had been laid for us, though given this was to be a traditional Tahitian feast, nearly everyone else would eat the old way, with fingers. In a delightful contrast to a formal French dinner, there was no particular order to dishes. Sweet and savory could be piled on the one plate, raw tuna salad heaped next to slabs of roasted pork and baked taro, all swimming in the sweet juices of papaya *po'e*, a pudding baked in fresh coconut milk.

Each of us had contributed a dish but it was Clement, Aima's stepfather, who had got up at 4 am to put the suckling pig into the earth oven—a hole in the ground lined with hot rocks and covered with banana leaves to keep in the heat. Alain's brother had made the bread; Alain had made his raw tuna salad which to my mind was the tastiest *poisson cru* in the territory. Guite had made her rum punch, floating with vanilla batons from Clement's last harvest, and together with her daughter Moetu had made garlands for all the women— fragrant *tiare* interspersed with sprays of orange and mauve bougainvillea and mint leaves. We brought wine and I made the chocolate cake that had been greeted with so much enthusiasm the first time, it had become my staple offering. "We don't normally like *popa'ā* cakes," Guite had confided. "They're not sweet enough; there's never enough icing." But somehow this rich cake with its mousse-like center pleased everyone.

Friendship can take many different forms, especially when another culture is thrown in the mix. Ours had unfolded over the year, built not on shared history or family ties but simple moments in the present. Sunday mornings we often bobbed about in the lagoon, chatting about politics or the weather or encouraging Aima, who worked at Mo'orea's dispensary and was contemplating studying to become a nurse. She worried her written French might not be good enough for the exams. With her quiet intelligence and passionate concern for others, it was obvious to the rest of us that Aima would make a brilliant nurse, though when we told her so she'd give one of her tinkling, embarrassed laughs. Alain often dropped by our house with bags of fruit grown by Clement. We cooked for each other; we swapped recipes. Our different ways and habits seemed to amuse them. Every morning, when Frédéric roared off on his motorbike, they glanced at their watches, betting whether today would be the day he missed the ferry. Guite said she always waited for the two good-bye beeps he gave me. *Au revoir, mon amour,* she'd chuckle to herself.

Perhaps it was not hard for them to accept us when their own families—*demis*, as mixed race people are known—had already absorbed so much diversity. Among Alain's relatives was a French grandfather who as a gendarme was responsible for upholding the colonial administration. Yet Alain's uncle, John Teariki, was a highly respected Polynesian politician who back in the late 1960s boldly challenged President de Gaulle by opposing the French nuclear tests. That Christmas I looked at the people seated around the table, unable to imagine our life on the island without them.

The men sat at one end, the women at the other. The separation occurred as naturally as a stream parting around a rock and it was only after I'd witnessed it several times that it struck me the arrangement wasn't accidental. Frédéric and I ended up in the middle, which meant we could participate in conversations on both sides. The women talked about *les jeunes* and the growing problem of petty theft. The other day Aima's mother had made a big platter of raw tuna salad, only to return to the kitchen and find it had disappeared.

"For pity's sake!"

"In broad daylight."

"In our day we never locked anything up," Guite said.

"Do you have any idea who it was?" I wanted to know.

Aima shrugged. "There's much more poverty these days. *Ça fait pitié.*"

Her mother nodded. A devout woman, she was kindness itself, just like her husband, Clement. "It was a good *poisson cru*, too. At least someone got to enjoy it."

The men talked politics and soon everyone joined in. It had turned out to be a tumultuous year, beginning with the astonishing ousting of Gaston Flosse in the territorial elections back in May. No one had thought Oscar Temaru stood a chance of winning—least of all his arch rival. The result triggered a contagion of celebration. Streams of pickup trucks drove around the islands, packed with Polynesians beating drums and waving blue banners for Temaru's political party, Tavini Huiraatira. The massive voter swing seemed less about support for independence than a widespread feeling of *fiu* for the territory's longtime leader, who'd taken his excesses too far, everyone said. But then after a brief and some said none too impressive stint as president, Temaru himself was now out: Flosse had wrested back power with a no-confidence motion. It was the beginning of a cat-and-mouse game between the two men that would play out for years. For now, though, around our Christmas table the talk was hopeful. If only Flosse would exit the stage and let someone else take the spotlight; if only Temaru would stop harping on about independence and start addressing problems like jobs and education.

Eventually, when the mosquitoes started biting and we'd had a laugh about solving the world's problems, Frédéric and I walked home.

On the front porch, Maddie stood eagerly to attention as we came through the gate. Then her tail went off, batting from side to side like a needle of an old metal detector that had struck gold. With her sweet round face, black button nose and that mechanical wag, she looked like a wind-up toy. We made a fuss of her: it was Christmas after all. There was an unmistakable fishy stink as she leaped up to lick my ear. "Have you been rolling in crab carcasses again? Pooh, Mads, you're disgusting!" My nose wrinkled but I pulled her close and thumped her rump, which set her tail going again.

Since moving to Mo'orea the three of us relied on each other more than ever. If there were downsides to this dependency—the odd disagreement, Maddie's feral odors— there was also no denying we were a close-knit unit. Families come in all shapes and sizes these days; all that's required is a whole lot of love. Who's to say a family couldn't be a couple with a dog?

One overcast afternoon a few weeks later the three of us sat on the beach. Dark gray clouds often brought out the luminescent greens of the lagoon, but on this day both sky and sea looked pewter. Not that we were there to admire the view. This was a planning meeting. A notepad rested on my knee. "Hobbies" I'd written down already. My pen hovered.

"We'll just have to fill our lives with other interests," I said. "We can *create* things other than children." I paused, trying to think what I was good at. On weekends Frédéric and I sometimes packed a picnic and headed off together to paint. Sitting on low slopes silver with pineapple plants, we'd try to capture the dramatic volcanic interior. That my Mount Rotui always turned out purple and rather fearsome might say something about my frame of mind. While I loved spreading thick strokes of color across virgin paper, I was no artist.

"You have your painting," I said. "Why don't we both learn to play a musical instrument?"

Frédéric smiled or maybe it was a grimace. Loving music was one thing, playing an instrument quite another. "What do you want to do—learn the ukulele?"

Ignoring him, I wrote down "musical instruments." Briefly I considered pottery, though there was hardly anything in the way of craft courses, even on Tahiti. "We can lead an alternate life, visit places you wouldn't go to with young kids." I added "travel" to my list of headings. "Where would you like to go?" I asked, like a life coach determined to draw out deep ambitions and desires.

During our nine years together I'd written many lists and plans of action. Every now and then something came from one of them—for instance Maddie had first appeared on a notepad among solutions for home-office loneliness. Usually the lists were written then promptly lost or forgotten. The impulse wasn't the sign of an orderly mind but rather the opposite. Somehow these little ceremonies, the neat columns of pros and cons, the time management schedules, gave me the illusion of being a planner. Part of me still wanted to be the kind of person with a two- or five- or ten-year plan.

Perhaps it was seeing Frédéric so upset over his heron-pigeon. Or the emergence of frankly counterproductive tensions on those highlighted days of my cycle. Thoughts that in the past had only flitted across my mind had lately begun to circle persistently. There was more to life than having children. Indeed, there were compelling reasons *not* to have them. Didn't kids bring constant worries and sacrifice on the part of parents? Couldn't a difficult child ruin parents' lives? Is it possible I'd overestimated my maternal instinct, which hadn't been much stirred by the baby bird? I'd already told Frédéric all about the book *We Need to Talk about Kevin*, the story of the monster child. Imagine having a Kevin! Doesn't research show that couples without children are actually *happier* than those who are parents? Had we been brainwashed by societal expectation? We were doing our bit for the planet by *not* having babies, given overpopulation and everything. Childfree, not child*less*.

As I waxed lyrical about future trips into the Amazon and to visit friends in war-torn Congo, Frédéric remained silent. He did not contribute a single instrument or travel destination, not one bullet point. It wasn't the theme he disagreed with, he explained much later: among our friends were numerous couples without children who led happy, fulfilled lives, as did a number of my parents' friends. But underpinning his obstinacy was a cultural difference as much as a personal one. "I found it delusional," he told me, "the way you tried to present being childless as an *opportunity*. It's such an Anglo-Saxon *maladie*, the need to find a positive in everything."

As the attempt to recalibrate our lives fizzled, I turned my attention to the lid of cloud, where a pale fork of light now glowed. With each second the fissure grew more definite and more brilliant until it resembled not sunshine but an electrical current. My list morphed into a wordy description of the sky. Maybe Frédéric was right. I'd become obsessed with finding the silver lining in everything.

⌒⌒

It is likely that this discussion was prompted by one of my sessions in the spearmint room. Once a week I went to Pape'ete to talk through my stew of thoughts and emotions with a psychotherapist. It may seem odd I hadn't sought out professional help earlier but there hadn't seemed much point: if I couldn't express my feelings and thoughts in my diary, however would I voice them to a complete stranger? I went at the urging of Alicia, who though she was thousands of kilometers away, seemed to have a more clear-eyed view of the situation than I did. This was my first experience with a counselor of any sort and for the first appointments I had blathered on nervously about how wonderful everything was—my husband, my family, my friends. You may well laugh, but I am a rather private person. "Do you realize," Dr. M later pointed out somewhat wearily, "that it took five sessions before you talked about wanting a child?" At times I was tempted to invent a fabulous surrealist dream from the night before just to fill a silence. Often I felt like a hapless spectator forced to sit through my own dull ramblings. At other moments it seemed we were actors in a poorly scripted television drama, such as when Dr. M came out with a line straight out of a therapy manual: "You have to come to terms with your mortality."

Yet tentatively, as the weeks passed, my guard dropped. I told him about the prayer candles I used to light despite considering myself an agnostic. This opened up a discussion about religion and how diminished belief in God had heightened people's existential dilemmas: in passing on our genes we are at least assured a measure of immortality. I spoke about the little girl who had skipped into my imagination years ago, as I walked past a smart children's boutique in Paris. Her fair curls jiggled with life. Together we splashed through puddles and read *The Magic Faraway Tree* and *Charlotte's Web*. Like old memories, these scenes were at once sharp and elusive, and if I tried to grab hold of them they shyly melted away. "She's just an illusion," I thought aloud in one session. "Maybe I have to let her go."

Dr. M's attentive gaze turned up a notch then, which was significant in this room where everything—the pale walls, his habitual white shirts—was mild and quiet. The clock that he must surely have kept an eye on because, believe it or not, psychotherapists were much in demand on Tahiti, was hidden from view.

"*Il faut faire le deuil*," he replied with a nod.

To my ears it's one of the most poetic expressions in the French language: *faire le deuil*. It means "to mourn." But unlike the forlorn-sounding English term, the words in French are like a gentle arc. Not a complete circle but something with a beginning and an end point, conveying a sense of passage from one phase to the next, as well as the possibility of closure. The French use it a lot. Nevertheless I was startled to hear I needed to go through the mourning process. Mourning was what you did when a loved one died. I'd read many books which dealt with loss and grief, both novels and non-fiction, without ever making a conscious connection to my own situation. None of them had offered insights on how to mourn a person who never existed, an imaginary child, a baby with no name.

⌒⌒

Travel is often a solution for creative crises—it was for Henri Matisse and also for Paul Gauguin before him. It was an idea that made perfect sense to me—though procreative crisis was perhaps a better name for my problem. Early in the New Year I came up with a plan to get away. In the past I'd traveled a lot on my own, as a backpacker around Europe and then later as a freelance journalist. It was time to get on with life, to revive my spirit of adventure. And so off I set one morning early in March, bound for the territory's northernmost archipelago, one of the world's most remote and mysterious destinations.

"I'll write a travel piece about my trip, on spec," I had enthused to Frédéric. Didn't writers always return with legendary tales from the Marquesas? Certainly the likes of Melville, London and Robert Louis Stevenson had. Frédéric remained unconvinced. "Wouldn't it do you good to go to Sydney or San

Francisco?" he'd suggested. "Somewhere with cafés and cinemas. Don't you need a city fix?"

He may have had a point. Yet faraway places have a gravi-
tational pull, not unlike the attraction of deep water for some
scuba divers, who describe an urge to go deeper, further. No
sooner had we got to Mo'orea than both Frédéric and I
yearned to visit islands that were more remote. At one point
during the year I'd even raised the idea of moving to an atoll
and working on a pearl farm—a mad suggestion from someone still adapting to island life, though Frédéric had not
laughed. "But we don't know anything about pearls," he'd finally said, as if this were the only flaw in the plan. Part of the
appeal is simply the desire for intense experience. Then
there's the idea that such places are good for the soul, that
raw nature has the power to heal—not a modern belief but
one that has acquired more resonance as our planet grows
more crowded, more polluted, more packaged. In Australia
we send troubled teenagers into the bush in the hope that
wilderness might straighten out what parents and teachers
and counselors or even jail could not.

My first thought when we stopped over at Nuku Hiva was
not that I might find myself on these rugged islands but that
I might lose myself completely. Even from the air, looking
right down on it, the island appeared inscrutable. The single
dirt road was obliged to coil around craggy peaks and spiny
ridgelines; it squiggled so much there was no way of telling
where it ended up. Little wonder the island was chosen by the
American reality TV show *Survivor* as the location for its
fourth series. Three hours of uninterrupted northbound flying had brought us within 10 degrees of the equator yet the

island didn't look at all tropical. The black cliffs and rocky coves evoked Scotland; the bald, dry mountains Wales; pine forests conjured up I don't know where—Bavaria or Canberra maybe. A waterfall splashed down a vertiginous cliff to a pocket-sized pool far below. With a population of 2500, Nuku Hiva was the archipelago's main island and administrative center but I couldn't see much sign of human life.

It was quite a relief not to be disembarking. From my seat I watched as eskies filled with fresh food were unloaded, along with the latest purchases from Tahiti—televisions perhaps or freezers, judging from the heavy-looking boxes. Roughly half the passengers got off. Minus their body weight and cargo—both of which appeared substantial—the plane seemed to get airborne less effortfully than it had earlier. Thirty-five minutes later we flew low over another formidable, frowning island, albeit slightly greener than the last.

Part of the mystique of the Marquesas is the people. With their own language and culture, Marquesans are said to have more in common with New Zealand's Maoris than Tahitians. Proud, reserved, melancholy, heavily tattooed: such was the stereotype. The bouncy, bubbly woman who met me at the airport did not fit it at all. Tania ran a guesthouse which had been recommended to me by a friend, and on the drive to Atuona, the main village of Hiva Oa, she chattered away, pausing only to exchange toots and warm waves with passing vehicles. When I expressed surprise at her sunny, outgoing demeanor she chuckled. "I was sent to Tahiti to get an education," Tania explained. "My parents didn't want me to spend my life growing copra, I was lucky."

"But you came back," I prompted.

Her lovely almond-shaped eyes roved over the landscape. "This island is my *fenua*," she said, using the heartfelt Tahitian word for homeland, which refers to the place where one's placenta is buried. "Besides," she boasted, "it has everything."

⌒

It was the wet season and there were hardly any tourists on the island; I was the only guest. After breakfast Tania often joined me at the table outside, on a pretty terrace laced with bougainvillea, facing the ocean. Her mother popped by a few times, too. Vito was a dynamic sixty-something who still worked as a social worker. Conversation skipped from problems such as obesity to Vito's concern about the growing dependence on welfare. "In some homes I find kids as young as nine or ten smoking *paka* in front of the telly, watching a show from Australia or America," she said. "It's a way of running away from reality: they know they can't go there." Like many Marquesans, mother and daughter supported the idea of splitting from French Polynesia and depending directly on France. "The territorial government does nothing for us," grumbled Tania. "They don't market us to tourists; it's all Tahiti, Bora Bora and Mo'orea." Her mouth formed an arch. "We're out of mind, out of sight."

"But you do get more tourists than any other island in the Marquesas," I said.

She nodded brightly. "We can thank Gauguin and Brel for that."

⌒

The cemetery above Atuona where both the artist and the much-loved Belgian singer are buried is the island's most accessible tourist attraction. I had not chosen Hiva Oa for either Gauguin or Jacques Brel—not consciously anyway. The fact is, only two out of the six inhabited Marquesan islands were serviced by regular flights from Tahiti. Yet that morning meandering among the crosses that cascade dazzlingly down the steep hill was one of the highlights of my trip. There was the magisterial scenery: mountains rose like ramparts 1000 meters above the harbor, where corrugated green roofs were strung along the shoreline. No big hotels or overwater bungalows—no lagoon or fringing reef either for that matter. Amid the high theater, the cemetery felt like a human-sized oasis, surrounded by papaya and coconut palms, wild hibiscus and mango trees. I doubted I could live in a place such as Hiva Oa but this remote hillside seemed a most pleasant place to lie in rest. It was the wish of Brel, who died in France while being treated for lung cancer, that his body be brought back and buried on the island, which had been his home for the final years of his life.

Gauguin's grave was quite humble for one considered a pioneer of modern art but given the artist's love of the primitive, its rough-hewn allure would no doubt have pleased him. Sunlight streamed through the branches of a frangipani tree, falling in buttery blobs that drifted across the reddish slab of volcanic stone. Simply painted in white on the headstone was the inscription PAUL GAUGUIN 1903. About the only adornment was a replica of one of his sculptures, *Oriri* ("The Wild One" or "Savage"), of a woman with a dead wolf at her feet. A strange piece, perhaps, but then Gauguin was always harping on about being *un sauvage*.

In his own words, the artist had sought to reignite his creativity on Hiva Oa after his second period on Tahiti ended in disillusionment. Gauguin's friends revealed another reason for seeking fresh pastures: no Tahitian women would sleep with him anymore. It seems he hoped that on an island of fewer refinements the women would be less squeamish about the weeping, syphilitic sores that by then covered his legs. Whatever his motives, the artist never found his Polynesian paradise; the whalers had taken care of that. Since the early nineteenth century, when European and American boats began making frequent stopovers for supplies and pleasure, Marquesan culture had been in tragic decline. By the time Gauguin arrived, smallpox and other imported diseases had all but wiped out the population. In little over a century, the estimated number of inhabitants across the entire archipelago had plummeted catastrophically, from 80,000 when Cook first charted the islands to just 3500. Gauguin was perpetually searching, he never fully belonged anywhere—tensions that undoubtedly fueled his creative energies.

While his paintings from Hiva Oa grew darker, by all accounts the artist was happier there than he'd ever been. His contrarian nature found a cause when he took on the colonial authorities and transformed himself into a crusader for the rights and culture of Marquesans. In the tiny settlement of 500 people, of which a mere handful was European, the ailing artist relished provocation: he hobbled around the settlement with a walking cane whose handle was carved in the shape of an erect penis. Pornographic pictures covered the walls of the home he named *Maison de Jouir* (House of Pleasure), where at night the generous flow of claret and rum ensured a regular crowd. In the journal he wrote on Hiva Oa, *Avant et Après,* he concluded: "If you hang up a little indecency on your door, you will always get rid of the honest people, the most intolerable people God ever created."

"Oof!" Tania chortled when I asked what locals had thought of Gauguin. "From what I've been told people laughed at him a bit, at his paintings. But he didn't bother anyone except the authorities. Here as long as you do your own thing you're accepted."

"But his 'thing' happened to be thirteen-year-old island girls," I pointed out.

She shrugged. "Things were different back then. My grandmother had my mother at thirteen and that was with a Marquesan."

Like numerous other discussions I had on the island, this one wound back to geographical isolation and the fear of being forgotten.

"You can say what you like," she insisted firmly, "he put us on the map."

Until then I'd felt little empathy for Paul Gauguin, who on many levels seemed to me a cliché. There was the older man's obsession with girls, the misfit's search for paradise, the exile's bitterness. Truly great artists rarely make the women in their lives happy, it seems, but one senses that Matisse, say, tried hard. Gauguin, on the other hand, showed blithe disregard for the health of island girls (though whether he knew for certain that syphilis was sexually transmitted is open to discussion). Whereas Matisse made me smile with his dry, grumpy observations of colonial officialdom and his child-like wonder for the islands' natural world, I plodded through *Noa Noa*, Gauguin's sweetened account of his first stay on Tahiti. His letters home paint a less idyllic picture but even his misery did not move me. I felt sorrier for his estranged wife and friends, who surely opened them with trepidation: when he wasn't begging for money Gauguin was lambasting them for not sending enough. Reservations about the man had also overshadowed any feeling I had for his art. Seemingly I had forgotten the jewel-like colors that had stunned me at the Grand Palais in Paris. Or that by incorporating a muddle of Polynesian and Maori motifs in his paintings, the artist forced the world to see the artifacts of "primitive" cultures not as mere curiosities but as art.

Perhaps Tania's pragmatic views softened me. Not that I felt sentimental. But something did shift as I sat on the hillside where in 1903 Gauguin was buried without fanfare, aged fifty-four, by the gloating local bishop, his archenemy. Sitting on a soft padding of frangipanis, for the first time I considered the artist's courage. If Hiva Oa felt like the end of the earth now, what must it have seemed like a century ago, when a steamer from Tahiti was the only link with the outside world? It struck me I might have brought a flower or two to leave on his grave—something to replace the rotting garland of *parohiti*, a decorative fruit that resembled marble-sized oranges. Twenty or so meters away, someone had left a bouquet of white roses by Jacques Brel's headstone. Could English roses be bought in the Marquesas or had an ardent fan gone to the trouble of bringing them on a plane?

Gazing at the unimpeded view of the sea, my thoughts drifted to a young lone sailor. Maud Fontenoy was somewhere out there right now, in her small red and white boat, rowing of all things. The entire territory and much of France was following her attempt to become the first woman to complete the so-called Kon-Tiki route, retracing Thor Heyerdahl's 1947 voyage from Peru to Hiva Oa, across one of the world's loneliest stretches of ocean. Articulate, with a radiant smile, Fontenoy had captured the people's hearts and there was feverish celebration on Hiva Oa when she made landfall after seventy-three days at sea. By then I was back home and watched the scenes on television. Unable to walk after so long sitting down, Fontenoy had to be carried to shore by a couple of Marquesan strongmen, handsome and proud in traditional palm leaf skirts, necklaces and crowns. Islanders, young and old, reached to embrace her. There was nothing reserved about the welcome they gave to this lover of the ocean who, like their own ancestors, was a true navigator, a survivor.

It may have been that my awe for Fontenoy's epic journey and my new respect for Gauguin were heightened by an awareness of my own sense of diminished courage. If I'd come to the Marquesas to find myself, it was the old me I wanted to find. Not the writer who'd run out of words or the nutter who climbed into the wrong car. Not the woman who grew weepy watching dung beetles but the confident, capable Sarah who had headed off with a backpack to Europe and as a journalist ventured to some dubious destinations.

So much for rekindling my adventurous spirit. I'm embarrassed to say I felt a bit homesick during my five days on the island. I found myself wishing that Frédéric was with me to

share in the experience—how he would love the raw rugged-
ness of the island. Maybe he'd been right about Sydney or
San Francisco. I felt small and far away—and not in a dreamy,
exciting way like that night lying on Fakarava with the universe glittering above me. Writer Larry McMurtry, who
cruised around the Marquesas on a freight boat, found himself contemplating the peculiar quality of farness of these islands, which he claimed went beyond geography or the lack
of big hotels. "It has more to do with landscape and aloneness," he wrote in *Paradise*. "The sea is so vast, the mountains
so high, the settlements so tiny." And the ocean so black, I
might have added. The coastline appeared to have been
hacked by a giant ax so dramatically did land plunge into sea.
I longed for something more tapered. I missed the lagoon.

Mostly, I stuck close to Atuona. I talked with people kindly
introduced to me by Tania; I took notes; I wandered around
the Paul Gauguin Cultural Center, which included a replica
of the house the artist built and lived in. Because of the rugged terrain, exploring the island required hiring a capable
vehicle and a driver familiar with the hairy dirt roads. When
my planned excursion to the island's northern coast was can-
celed due to bad weather, I felt relief more than disappointment. True, even Paul Theroux—a man not easily
impressed—had raved about the impressive tiki monuments
at Puama'u. But the last thing I wanted was to be stranded in
a far corner of this remote island.

It seemed to me something of the essence of the Marquesas was summed up in an encounter on my last night, which I
spent on the principal island, Nuku Hiva. On an evening
stroll from my pension, I stopped for a drink at the small re-

sort hotel on a hill overlooking the village of Taiohae. There were plenty of empty tables and so when a Marquesan woman and her child asked to join me I assumed it was to chat. But after some preliminaries, during which it was revealed her husband was one of the musicians, Maeva sat back in her chair. Above the mellow strumming and vocal harmonies I kept up a run of polite inquiries. Would you like a drink? I asked finally, thinking that might help. But Maeva smiled and shook her head. When I left an hour and a half later we had exchanged no more than five minutes of conversation, and grumpily I wondered why, if they intended to sit like stone ti-kis, mother and son hadn't sat somewhere else. Tellingly, I found the silence awkward yet later it occurred to me that Maeva had appeared perfectly content. It was then that I re-called Aboriginal communities in Australia where as an eager young journalist I'd been baffled by the same ease with sitting silently. Perhaps it is a skill white people have lost, though Frédéric thought it was a peculiarly Anglo condition. In the past he had professed to feeling exhausted by the frenetic, friendly chitchat of English speakers, including myself, "as if a slight gap in conversation represents some kind of social failure," he'd mused.

Flying back to Tahiti, it seemed years not days since I'd left. At Pape'ete, in the tiny one-room terminal that operated connecting flights to Mo'orea, I felt like hugging my fellow commuters. How reassuring it was to be back on familiar ground amid the bustle of strangers! It takes a total of seven minutes to fly between the two islands and no sooner had we taken off than the sixteen-seater aircraft began descending. Floating in the sky like lovely tentacles, Mo'orea's peaks appeared to wave at me. How finished the island looked with its waistband of blond beach and billowing, silver lagoon hemmed with a white frill. The afternoon ferries from Pape'ete had just come in and somewhere amid the stream of vehicles below, Frédéric was zooming home on his motorbike.

Tania's jolliness aside, the Marquesas had seemed to me austere and melancholy. Yet how much of that was me and how much of that was the place I cannot fairly judge. When I look now at the photos I took from the cemetery, the ocean looks not ominously dark but a velvety ultramarine. While my memories are of massive mountains, Hiva Oa's highest peak is roughly the same height as Mount Tohiea on Mo'orea, which stands at 1207 meters. Perhaps my impressions were colored by a sad truth about the Marquesas: in the end extreme isolation was no protection from the brutal impact of the outside world. Social problems were, if anything, exacerbated by the remoteness. My inner emptiness had grown there, too. It was no longer a confined feeling. Like a gas, it had seeped into the air, tainting everything.

That is what, in my halting way, I was trying to explain in the spearmint room a few days later. I prepared myself for the usual silence, vowing this time to sit it out. Maybe I'd come to the end of the road; there was nothing more to be said. But to my surprise the psychotherapist spoke up straightaway. His reply bounced to my side of the table, not a statement but a question—one that, given everything we'd discussed in this room, completely floored me.

"Have you thought of having one last try?"

TWELVE

For a moment all I could do was blink. The meaning of "one more try" was perfectly clear to me but perhaps because I looked so astonished Dr. M felt the need to spell it out.

"Have you considered giving IVF another go?"

I hesitated, unsure how to answer. "Well, yes . . . *enfin, non.* Not really." Family and a few close friends occasionally dropped hints about "very good clinics in Australia." But coming from this impartial professional the suggestion seemed nothing short of subversive. What of his talk about repetitive failure and the need to break the cycle? "You need to fix an end point to *trying*," he'd advised more than once.

"We spent four years giving IVF a go," I reminded him. Wasn't I supposed to be coming to terms with my mortality? Going through the mourning process?

Like me, Dr. M was fond of the expression *faire le deuil.* But when I came out with it this time there was no nod of agreement or approval. Instead, my reply met with a subtle facial ripple that began with a tautening around the mouth then shifted up through his cheeks and ended with a slight upward flick of the eyebrows. In this room of carefully modulated responses it was about as close to theater as you got: a put-on expression of surprise. Counselors and psychiatrists must spend years perfecting it.

"But *are* you going through the mourning process?" His tone was as mild as ever but his steady gaze bore into me.

The air-conditioning hummed loudly. "Well I think so," I started. "I mean, I'm trying." My voice faltered. "What do you think?" I asked finally.

The answer came swiftly, as if it had been in some holding pen, waiting for the right moment to be let loose. "I think you're frightened of risking another failure."

"But I thought the whole idea was to move on!" I protested.

"But you're not moving forward," Dr. M pointed out patiently. "You're not even going backward. You won't have another try but you can't let go of your dream. You're stuck."

Never before had he offered his opinion so bluntly. Perhaps he'd given up waiting for me to reach my own conclusions. His next words were uttered more gently, though perhaps this is just how my memory replays them. "It's not a crime to hope, you know."

It is probably not possible to explain why one simple sentence should provoke an epiphany. Words, however they might elude me at my computer, had lost none of their power. Over recent years certain statements had lodged in my head—sometimes to my detriment. *There's no time to lose*, Dr. G had warned all those years ago. And now: *It's not a crime to hope*. The message blazed through my mind like a comet, leaving in its wake a glorious clarity. For the first time in oh so long, I knew precisely what we should do.

In the clammy heat I ran back to Frédéric's office, where the groundbreaking exchange in the green room was relayed breathlessly. "I think we need to have one last go, to get unstuck, going backward beats not moving at all," I jabbered. "It's not a crime to hope, you know, so what do you think?" Frédéric's face registered confusion and amusement then finally excitement.

For couples in French Polynesia wanting to undergo IVF treatment, the options are either to return to *la métropole* or to travel to a "close" neighbor such as New Zealand or Australia. Faced with these options, Australia seemed the natural choice. It was a world leader in infertility research; even my Paris specialist, Dr. B, had told me that. Geographically it was much closer than France. I had friends and family in Sydney. Australia was my country, after all, even if all told I'd spent more of my life outside of it.

Throughout my childhood my family had moved every two or three years, to Singapore, Malaysia, America and England. My father's job as an air force pilot had meant regular postings. But between stints overseas we went back to orderly, landlocked Canberra. With its bike paths and man-made lake it is the only place in Australia where gum trees grow in rows, a family friend liked to joke. Whatever its shortfalls, for kids it offered precious freedoms. Carefree and careless in shorts and thongs, my brother and I would scamper into the long, dry grass behind our house, with Mom's cry chasing us up the hill, "WATCH OUT FOR SNAKES!" In summer we went on camping holidays to Myall Lakes, where entire days were spent in the water. Joys were simple: cooking spaghetti toasties over the fire; seeing who could peel off the longest ribbon of sunburned skin; building labyrinthine palaces for ungrateful ants.

What these childhood memories had to do with where we did IVF I can't really say. But somehow home sounded a propitious place for our final try at having a child.

Once we put the word out, family and close friends rallied. They seemed relieved, delighted by our decision. My bravado about moving on hadn't fooled them, apparently. Mom sent me articles on IVF centers in Sydney; friends offered spare bedrooms and couches should we need to stay close to the city. But it was Sarah, an old friend who with her husband had done many years of IVF before finally giving birth to a baby girl, who helped us on the medical front. Through her uncle, an anesthetist, we were put in touch with a top Sydney specialist who agreed to take us on from afar.

It was mid-afternoon on a Wednesday in Tahiti when we had the first consultation via telephone. Outside my window the sun was still high; in Sydney it had set. It was already Thursday in Australia, ten hours away by direct flight but twenty-one hours ahead in time. The specialist went over the past results I'd faxed him, and unsurprisingly one hormone in particular caught his attention. "Sixteen point five, eighteen, *nineteen point eight . . .*" His voice trailed off dubiously as he read out my previous levels of follicle-stimulating hormone. Poor egg quality, low egg stock: that was what the figures told him. My heart sank. From his tone the conversation about me coming to Sydney for treatment was about to derail.

The problem had been explained to me many times before but in my mother tongue the explanation had an unmistakable clarity. The issue in French was not one of comprehension but my interpretation. If certain words had set off alarm bells—*stérile*, stamped on my medical papers, had a particularly dire ring I thought—speaking in a foreign language had also allowed me to minimize the situation. At times I'd wondered if Dr. G wasn't exaggerating the sense of urgency; the French have a tendency to look on the bleak side. But in English there was no glossing over meanings, no putting anything down to cultural nuances. "High levels of FSH are more than *complicated*," corrected the Sydney specialist, Dr. L, after asking me what I understood about the issue. "For all the technical advances, one thing we can't do is improve the quality of someone's eggs."

He paused. "I have to be honest. With your history, the chances of you getting pregnant are very remote." (Later, recounting the conversation to Frédéric, I would pick over his words: had he said "very, very remote" or just "very remote"?) "The first step is to have another blood test to determine your FSH level now," Dr. L continued. Then came the crucial condition that dashed my hopes. I'd never heard of clinics setting FSH cut-off limits for clients—though as it turned out most do. "If your level is higher than fourteen then I'm afraid that we can't help you."

It was a subdued end-of-day debriefing that took place on the beach that evening. Darkness had already dropped over the island. We'd pulled our plastic armchairs to the edge of the lagoon so that our toes were in the water—not that you could tell, because the temperature was no different from the air. The Milky Way spread lavishly across the moonless sky but my eyes stared fixedly at the lagoon, as broody and black as an oil spill.

"The decision to have another try had felt so right," I sighed.

"FSH levels can fluctuate, can't they? You never know, it might come down." Though Frédéric sounded glum too.

"I've been over all my old medical records, scores and scores of blood test results," I said dully. "Only one time was it lower than fourteen—and that was five years ago." It wasn't necessary to explain that in women the hormone level gets higher with age; he knew that already.

Not for the first time I found myself wishing for a problem I could picture. A diagnosis of blocked tubes, for example, would be devastating but for the layman, quite visual. There was something nebulous about this unseen "level," which on its steady climb up the ladder of infertility might briefly slip a few rungs, offering, inexplicably, a window of opportunity. In my failure to fully comprehend the biology, I had at first privately harbored some naive hopes. Surely, if the human body and brain was one big cocktail of hormones and other chemicals, there existed a drug or magic potion to bring down this troublesome *ef es arsh*, as Dr. G had called it. When the levels were wrong in a drink, for example, you simply added more gin or more tonic.

Another thought crossed my mind that night, though it didn't bear thinking about. According to the Sydney clinic's criteria, only once in the past, when my hormone level dropped, had I had any chance of getting pregnant. Were all those tests and procedures in Paris a waste of time? Had our efforts been in vain?

⌒⌒

On May 17, I caught the early ferry to Pape'ete to go to the pathology clinic. I know this because "BLOOD TEST" are the only words written under that day in my diary. FSH levels are tested at the beginning of the follicular phase, when follicles—which is to say the little sacs containing eggs—mature in the ovaries. A few days later I returned to the main island, having opted to collect the results in person rather than wait for them to be mailed. Frédéric accompanied me. So much hinged on just one number.

We had thought to go somewhere private to read the result. But there were no parks in Pape'ete, few shaded benches or quiet spots. When the receptionist at the clinic handed me the envelope, we found a couple of plastic chairs in the central covered courtyard—which was less charming than it might sound. Despite efforts to freshen up the interior with greenery and shrubs the place looked tired. The marks and smudges might have been permanent but it looked like the floor needed a thorough mopping.

A few meters away sat two local women. The younger one, who might have been in her late teens, was pregnant and her stomach was a tight brown drum between her shorts and T-shirt. The older lady must have been her mother—then quickly I checked my assumption. Given the fluid nature of extended families here, she could just as easily have been an auntie, a grandmother, a stepmother or perhaps a sister-in-law whose brother had since fled the relationship. They must have been waiting to see an obstetrician but in the typical Tahitian way they didn't appear to be waiting for anything. Their expressions were neither happy nor discontented, neither bored nor curious. They didn't fidget impatiently; they didn't talk. They sat with their hands folded in their laps, solid as two rocks, while we perched on the edge of our seats like jittery seagulls liable to take flight at any moment.

"Let's just get it over with," I said.

It is a mystery to me why critical medical results are written in such tiny print, as though we all carry magnifying glasses in our pockets expressly for the purpose of reading them. We bent over the sheet of letters and numbers. Once upon a time, before all this started, they would have been meaningless to me. I was still a bit vague. LH was another hormone produced by the pituitary gland, which I knew now was located in the brain, not the groin. Oestradiol might be related to estrogen and must have some vital function, too. But these normal levels were of no interest to me. The one thing I could tell at a glance was a good FSH result from a bad one.

I drew a line with my finger across the page to ensure I landed on the right figure. My heart quickened. That couldn't be right. Using the cover letter as a ruler, I checked again. And again. With breathless incredulity, I repeated the result to Frédéric, who was impatiently peering through my hair, trying to see. *Seven point eight?* Looking up, my eyes met the gaze of the *mamie* sitting nearby. She nodded at me kindly, in the way of one who knew a thing or two about life and its quotidian mysteries. Perhaps she thought we'd just learned I was pregnant, because we hugged and kissed and then simply sat back on the hard seat, stunned. After a few minutes the gynecologist who had seen me before the blood test came over. In my excitement I forgot that I had not liked him. I waved the paper in the air. "*Sept virgule huit!* Looks like I'll be going to Sydney after all!"

"You don't think there's been a mix-up, do you?" Frédéric queried anxiously. The doctor assured us, huffily, that the clinic had not made a mistake. The question, combined with our undisguised joy, seemed to annoy him.

"No sense in getting carried away," he said sourly.

It might have been this dampener that made me mull over the wording of my fax to the Sydney specialist that afternoon. Dr. L had promised to act quickly if the result was acceptable: the idea was to have a try before my level had time to spike up again. "Unbelievable news," I wrote, then pressed delete. "I am thrilled to tell you," I began again, before toning it down more: "My FSH was lower than expected." There was no telling how long it would stay down. By the time I got to Sydney the capricious hormone level may have soared again. Yet a door had cracked open. It was only a ruler of light but it was unmistakably light.

For a long time after, I would ponder the mysterious plunge and what prompted it. Could our move from Paris to Mo'orea have helped in some way? Had my swimming been a factor; the clean air? Eating fish four or five times a week? I still drank most nights, moderately but needfully, one or two glasses of wine. My stress levels were surely no lower than they had been in Paris. Specialists seem at a loss to explain the high levels of FSH increasingly seen in young women. Once, Dr. B had cited French research pointing to environmental factors, including toxins, pesticides and industrial pollution. He had been quick to suggest other factors, too, though I'd never smoked and my family history did not point to any problems: my mother was thirty-nine when she had my sister. If aspects of modern life, including increasingly modified foods and industrialized processing, could contribute to the sharp rise in cancers, for example, then it seemed logical to me that they might also be one cause of infertility.

For the moment, though, all that counted was the magical number. Sevenpointeight. Sevenpointeight. Sevenpointeight. *Septvirgulehuit.* A blissfully normal result for a woman my age, for days it bugled in my ears like a world record.

⌣

The next few weeks were spent preparing for an extended stay in Australia. Assuming we got through all the steps in the treatment, right up to the final blood test to determine pregnancy, I'd need to be there seven weeks. Frédéric would arrive in Sydney a few days after me, in time to do the required tests and sign the paperwork before supplying a fresh specimen of his finest swimmers. There was the question of where to stay because, as it turned out, my parents were between houses themselves. Luckily for us, friends were going overseas and had offered us their apartment for a month. I threw myself into making arrangements, glad for a sense of purpose. There was no time to dwell on the likelihood—or near certainty rather—that this whole costly exercise would amount to nothing.

A chance conversation in Pape'ete was a timely reminder that the lengths we were going to weren't extreme. "Enjoy your holiday," the newsagent had said, after a polite exchange about my trip to Australia. "I'm not really going for a holiday," I replied, then hesitated. She was practically a total stranger but what the hell? "We're going back to do IVF," I blurted.

"Oh," she nodded. "I'm off to Athens in a fortnight." With a small, complicit smile, she added: "Not exactly for a holiday either." In Greece, where laws allow for egg donors to be paid, a stranger's egg would be implanted inside her. This would be her third and final trip—"I'm forty-six now," she sighed. The other two attempts had ended in miscarriages. Lowering her voice so as not to be heard by other customers, she confided, "I was very, very down after the last one. I told my husband no more, this is it."

"I said that, too!" I exclaimed. It felt good to laugh with someone about the ups and downs of infertility treatment.

"Apparently you can do it in Spain too," I said that night, relaying the conversation to Frédéric. Using an anonymous egg donor was a course of action we hadn't examined, though we did seriously consider my sister's generous offer. After carrying out her own research, Anna, who lived in London and was nine years younger than me, had urged us to proceed. But friends and family who have not yet had their own babies are not considered ideal egg donors. What if my sister and her partner were for some reason unable to have children? There was the risk, however slight, that one of the eggs she gave away might turn out to be her only child, and who knew how she'd feel then? Frédéric and I had both agreed it was unwise to go ahead.

⌒

A few days before my departure, I sat on our front steps with Nelly. She knew the reason for our trip, as did our neighbors. "Don't worry," she said to me, stubbing out her cigarette. "If it doesn't work, Mo'e and I will make you a baby." It was said casually yet some years before, Nelly and her husband had done just that: given their sixth child at birth to a French couple wanting to adopt. The daughter, who now lived in France with her adoptive family, returned to French Polynesia for holidays every few years.

When I asked if this separation made her sad, Nelly admitted at the hospital she'd cried and cried. Her husband held firm, convinced it was the best thing for everyone. "But now I'm happy," she told me. "My daughter's happy. They send me letters and photos. It's better this way." Nelly waved a hand dismissively, "*Laisse, laisse*." Said in her unhurried way the word rolled lightly through the air: *Laaaïsse*. In French it means "to allow" or "to let" but as with many things that came from somewhere else, Polynesians have made the expression their own and given it other layers of meaning. Don't worry about it, she might have meant. Let life take its natural course. You can't look back, only forward.

It's not every day that someone offers to make you a baby. Touched, I patted Nelly's smooth knee. But adoption was one avenue Frédéric and I had never wished to pursue. The process had always struck me as long and fraught—more so than doing IVF. In most places we were already too old to be adoptive parents but in French Polynesia the situation was somewhat looser. In the past it was common particularly for a first born to be given to grandparents or other relatives, though this did not preclude close ties with the biological parents. But not all traditions translate easily into modern life. Arrangements that had been so clearly understood within the parameters of the old culture became more complicated when Europeans started adopting Polynesian children and removing them from their *fenua*. A French doctor we knew told us he stopped facilitating these adoptions after seeing the potential for confusion and heartbreak on both sides.

"Besides," I teased Nelly, who was only a year older than me, "you're a grandmother now. You're too old."

"Nahhh," she laughed, slapping her sturdy thighs. "It's easy for me, I'm strong!"

It was our second year on the island and I would be away for a good part of the dry season. I would miss the pleasant evenings when it was possible to sit outside after dark without the relentless attack of mosquitoes. And those high-definition mornings when Tahiti stood out so prominently against the shimmer that to my still sleepy eyes the island looked like a new creation. Before I left, the wind changed. The *maramu* ruffled the lagoon, teasing up waves. From the beach I watched little whitecaps scutter to shore. The air on my face was fresh. Fingers crossed, it was a lucky wind blowing from the south.

THIRTEEN

From the ferry, the skyscrapers jostled competitively, like children standing straight to see who was tallest. After Mo'orea's tapered, natural heights, the geometric towers were startling, yet this view of Sydney Harbour with the city's skyline ahead and the Opera House over to the left and the bridge over to the right had always thrilled me. It was bold, it had verve. Frédéric loved it, too, though as the controversial Toaster building came into view his expression darkened and it wasn't difficult to read his thoughts. "Why build something so big and *square* right next door to the Opera House?" he asked as we admired the latter's shining "sails"—surely the world's most lyrical roofline. To his European eyes, a lot of modern architecture in Australia appeared pretty lackluster. As we disembarked the ferry there was muttering, thankfully in French, about suitable punishments for unsightly developments: public flogging or the guillotine.

I'd forgotten the onshore wind, the way it funneled up the

city's canyon-like streets. Turning up Loftus Street, damp, cold air blasted our backs. This was Frédéric's first experience of a Sydney winter and before leaving Mo'orea's 86-degree heat, he'd hesitated over whether to pack his heavy Paris coat. Luckily for him he had. I, former resident, had not shown the same foresight, though if anything this proved I was still a Sydneysider at heart. Night after night for several months on end, the city's population huddles around tiny bar heaters, convincing themselves that winter lasts only a couple of weeks, as wicked drafts blow through gaps and cracks around doors and windows. From Paris, trips back at Christmastime had only reinforced my impression of Sydney as a perennially summery place of beaches, barbecues and chilled white wine—which is exactly how the city likes to be seen. But this time I wouldn't be drinking much at all. For the first time in years we hadn't come for a holiday.

There'd been a last-minute panic on the way over in the plane. The trip had been planned, dates fixed and appointments made in Sydney based on my calculations of my bodily cycle. Because of work commitments Frédéric was booked to come twice to Australia: once to sign consent forms and undergo mandatory tests, and then again for later procedures, assuming we made it to the end of treatment. Timing was everything and getting my period early would blow the entire effort, yet to my dismay, somewhere between Pape'ete and Auckland cramping pains started squeezing my abdomen. As the aircraft winged its way across the Pacific, I alternately berated, cajoled and implored my body. *Come on, you did so well with that winning FSH result! Don't. You. Dare.*

But after that midair false alarm, the first week had gone

smoothly, beginning with the initial appointment with our Sydney doctor. The moment I walked through the door I had a strong sense of being in the right place. Dark wood and gold-framed qualifications and honors provided the necessary venerable effects, without appearing stuffy. A tall, straight-backed man ushered us into his office, where after some brief chitchat about Tahiti he opened our medical folder and started scribbling indecipherable notes and figures. "Your last FSH result was a pleasant surprise, wasn't it?" He glanced down at my fax. "Seven point eight—yes, a good result." In a measured tone he went on to explain that IVF was our best bet because it enabled them to intervene at exactly the right moments. It occurred to me this faint encouragement might have been offered out of kindly consideration for the distance we had come.

The now familiar mention of statistics made my mind drift, and my eyes traveled around the room. Here was an interesting new line of research: how many IVF specialists own collections of fertility statues? Standing on a nearby table, scores of potbellied sculptures similar to the African statues in Dr. B's office fixed us with bulgy eyes. Many were from Asia or Papua New Guinea, apparently. I felt heartened by the sight: maybe this South Pacific cheer squad would bring us better luck. Dr. L was talking about putting me on a flare cycle—the same treatment I'd undergone in Paris, shorter than a typical cycle and designed for women whose ovaries are difficult to stimulate with hormone drugs. "But of course," he reiterated, "this is subject to your blood test. Let's hope your FSH stays down."

When the blood test was carried out two days later my

level had bobbed up. Nine: I'd never thought of it as a lucky number. But it was still lower than any result in Paris and well below the clinic's cut-off of fourteen. A nurse patiently demonstrated how to inject myself with hormones using the latest pen-like needles. Like all my tests and checkups from then on, that appointment took place not at Dr. L's consulting rooms but a few city blocks away, at the Sydney IVF clinic.

It looked like any other anonymous city building. I must have walked by it many times in the past but there was no way of knowing that inside something special was going on: not just the usual board meetings and business presentations but the mysterious science of creating new life. Unlike Clinique de la Muette, where we used to go for procedures in Paris, there was nothing hospital-like about the place at all. With its harbor views, plush waiting area and expensive art, it might have been a city law firm, only with more clients. To answer the many calls, the receptionist spoke into a microphone that hovered like an insect in front of her mouth. I stared at the device; this small symbol of the onward march of technology made me feel like the fabled country mouse in the city. Headsets hadn't been in wide use in Paris when we left and in Tahiti the only standard accessory worn by receptionists was a *tiare* bud.

All the seats in the waiting room were taken up by women who, like me, had come in for one of the routine blood tests used to monitor the body's response to the hormones. Frédéric, accompanying me for the last time before returning to Tahiti, was one of only a handful of men. Every few minutes a nurse popped out and called a name and we soon got to sit down. Flicking through a glossy food magazine, I kept stealing glances at the people around me. It was the first time I'd been in the same room as so many women with stories similar to my own. Here we were, the Officially Infertile, the Involuntarily Childless. It wasn't a select club. One in five Australian couples seeks medical assistance to get pregnant, I read somewhere.

With everyone dressed for work, I felt conspicuous in my casual jeans and running shoes—the only covered shoes that had not grown a blue mold on Mo'orea. Opposite, scanning the *Financial Review,* sat a woman in navy, from her jacket to her stockings and court shoes. It looked like a uniform but she might have been a banker or maybe an accountant. Next to her was a publishing type—black turtleneck, chunky beads, spectacles that made a statement. Each woman had a different story, I knew from my own circle of friends. Multiple miscarriages, bad eggs, endometriosis or the cruelly opaque "unexplained infertility"—the diagnoses differed, along with the number of attempts each couple had made. Some of the women at the clinic were likely not in couples at all. In France a friend who had tired of waiting for Monsieur Right had recently taken the brave decision to use a sperm donor and do IVF alone.

You might expect the air in the waiting room to be quivering with hope and sorrow but it was an unemotional place. Deep inner emptiness is a hard thing to share and express, so I'd found. There was no sense of sorority; no knowing, sympathetic glances. Eyes were fixed on books or laptops or the perky morning-show hosts animating the flat screen televisions. In a strange way we were competitors. For all the media reports about IVF success stories and "take home babies," most of us in the waiting room would take home only a high bill. Who among us would get pregnant? The younger ones were the safest bet, of course. But appearances can be deceptive. I was younger than the woman in the navy suit by a few years, I'd have guessed. And yet her two trusty baskets might be overflowing with fabulous eggs, you just couldn't tell.

"Hello Sarah, hello Frédéric." After a fifteen-minute wait a friendly nurse ushered us into a small room. "How are you feeling, Sarah?" she inquired, running an expert finger over my inner elbow. The sharp smell of alcohol permeated the room as she wiped the pale skin with a swab. "Make a fist, that's right, clench it for me, Sarah. Take a breath, just a little prick . . ." My fine veins had a habit of rolling and moving, and in the past blood tests had sometimes involved prolonged poking. But this test was fast and painless.

Afterward, sheltering from rain in a city café, Frédéric and I sat reminiscing. The Sydney clinic was triggering memories of doing IVF in Paris and it was hard not to compare. The science of the process might be the same, give or take variations and new techniques, but experiences could differ from country to country, from clinic to clinic no doubt.

"Do you remember the way that dragon at the admissions office at la Muette used to greet us?" Frédéric asked. He raised his voice to a sharp, authoritative pitch: "You have your papers, have you? *Tous?*"

"Where's your *entente préalable?*" I mimicked. "I'll have to cancel this cycle if you can't find it, *vous comprenez.*"

It felt good to take a vengeful poke at the dragon lady. She'd made me dread that preliminary visit to the hospital before each attempt. To this day I didn't understand the importance of the *entente préalable,* the sort of flimsy document that is the cornerstone of the French administration. The more impatient she grew, the more I fumbled anxiously to find that damn piece of tracing paper in my medical file. Presented with it at last, she would scrutinize it like an airport control officer suspecting a fake passport. Helpful and kind she wasn't but no one could fault her thoroughness.

There were many wonderful things about the French system—fine doctors plus the advantage that infertility treatment was almost entirely state funded, making it far more accessible than it was in Australia. But now I couldn't help recalling remarks made by my Paris specialist, the kindly Dr. B. Some of the Australian IVF clinics are doing great things, he'd told me once. When I'd asked in what ways, he'd mentioned impressive success rates and also advances in the "psychological support" for patients.

I couldn't vouch for the science side—and besides, success rates, even laudable ones, depend not only on medical skill but also on how selective clinics are in the clients they take on. But what I could say was that, psychologically, it felt better to be smiled at than barked at. It felt better—safer—walking into a specialized center rather than a maternity hospital teeming with happy families visiting new mothers and babies. After my sessions with the psychotherapist in Pape'ete I didn't feel the need to see the clinic's counselors but it was nice to know they were there. At times of vulnerability, small things can be meaningful. Frédéric was touched by a simple cultural difference. In France, *Madame* and *Monsieur* were as familiar as it got, whereas the nurses in Sydney naturally used our first names. At the chemist where I bought the IVF drugs, the pharmacist handed over the hormones with the warm words: "My daughter went through this. I hope it works for you."

⌣

You return home to find nothing has changed: that's the accepted view about living abroad. As if everything ground to a standstill when you left the country, you find that coming back is like slipping on an old sock. Everyone's just doing the same old, same old; you haven't missed out on a thing. It isn't like that at all, I can tell you. Inconsiderately perhaps, your loved ones get on with their lives. Some of my friends had moved overseas, others had changed cities. Those who remained in Sydney had started families and taken more high-powered jobs. Seeing their progression on trips home was often a bit unsettling. If my own life felt real enough to me in Paris, on holidays back home it often seemed a bit make-believe—a way of evading reality, which was what I came back to in Sydney.

On this trip it was my parents who were on the brink of a bold new change. Aged sixty-nine both of them and only recently retired, they were about to head off to France— "goodness, who knows, perhaps forever," my mother responded excitedly when asked for how long they were going.

I suppose I'd assumed they would just keep talking about the idea, as they had been doing for a few years now. When my parents came to Mo'orea on holiday, we'd spread out the map of France on the outside table and pored over the different regions. Provence was too expensive, we decided; Burgundy was too far north; Dordogne had too many English, ruled Frédéric. The upshot of those discussions was that a large ring was drawn in pink highlighter around the area of interest, roughly a quarter of the country, France's southwest.

It was a shock to come home and see the plan in action, though. To begin with there was no "home." The house where my parents had lived and where the family had spent many happy Christmases—the one true home in the long succession of houses we'd known—had been sold. Temporarily my parents were renting a studio; in less than two months they would be gone. All their belongings had been put in boxes in storage. "Oh, I think we sold them at our garage sale," Mom answered vaguely to inquiries about heirlooms like my old treadle sewing machine and antique chair—"your present to me for my eighteenth," I pointed out, miffed. But after a shared lifetime of moving, my parents had an unsentimental approach to belongings. Ridding themselves of possessions they'd stored on behalf of their children seemed to have been liberating and my indignation met with hilarity. "What did the chair go for, Murray, can you remember? She's saying it was her eighteenth birthday present!"

"Forty dollars," Dad said, making a show of delving into his wallet. "Here, honey—but let's see. How much shall we charge for ten years' storage, Jan?" They both hooted at that.

While my siblings, Mark and Anna, embraced the move unreservedly, my enthusiasm was muted by a sense of responsibility. Indirectly it was me and Frédéric who got my parents into this. The idea had formed during numerous holidays together in the French countryside, where Mom had marveled at the village markets and their rich array of produce—not just the cheeses but the different varieties of strawberries, the *saucissons*, the vegetables that seemed to have been pulled straight from the field. Dad had pondered the lovely stone houses and envisaged days spent rebuilding garden walls and trawling the aisles of hardware superstores. But the plan to move to the other side of the world only really gained momentum after a bruising professional experience. Following his years in the air force Dad had set up a flying school for a large company, the success of which prompted him to launch his own. My father is a gentle, honorable man, ill-suited perhaps to cutthroat private enterprise. When this venture went under after years of struggling and stress, he paid his creditors and they sold the house. The money that was left they decided to invest in an adventure that would help them look forward not back, and encourage them to count their gains rather than losses. Every move, it seems, is a search for rejuvenation.

Admirable though their positive outlook was, part of me suspected, superiorly, that they had no idea what they were getting themselves into. On this trip, more than others, my position was curiously ambivalent: I swung from being the vulnerable child again, needy as ever of parental love and support, to feeling, frankly, more sensible and mature than my parents. It was one thing to love visiting France but living there full-time was another matter. Perhaps Tahiti and its history had made me wary of romantic dreams. What would they do if they didn't find the right house—or, more likely, couldn't afford it when they did? How would they get by when they could barely string a sentence together in French? I recalled friends who had moved to a village in the Drôme only to find that country life was not as quaint as it appeared: five years later they were still regarded with suspicion as *les Parisiens*. And they were French.

This anecdote I kept to myself, though I did raise other concerns as we sat one afternoon in their rented granny flat, looking out at dashes of ocean between scribbly gums. Dad had just poured two glasses of wine; I was sipping mineral water.

"You're not to worry about your old parents," Mom scolded. My mother has never allowed anyone to piddle on her fire, so to speak. Once her enthusiasm caught alight, there was no dampening it. "It's not like we haven't lived abroad."

"Yeah, but you've only ever lived in places where English was spoken," I pointed out, as diplomatically as I could. "This is different."

"Darling, our French is coming along just fine. *Je vais, tu vas, il va*," she recited. Dad joined in then and they chanted in unison, conjugating the verb "to go" in heavily accented French, delighted to show just how ready they were for their adventure. *"Nous allons, vous allez, ils vont!"* They beamed at me.

Naturally we also discussed the purpose of my visit. Mom, who'd been so thrilled by our decision to have another try, regularly asked how I was feeling, how it was going. Fine, I answered curtly a few times. The hormones seemed to have made me snappy. Sometimes I was grateful to talk but mostly it was a relief to turn my mind to other matters. In the end I let myself get swept up in their excitement.

⌐⌐

This was the longest period of time I'd spent in my own country since leaving Australia some twelve years before, and as the weeks passed I pondered the changes. Since when had the city—perhaps the entire country—switched to sauvignon blanc, for example? When we took a bottle of chardonnay to a dinner with friends it was passed over as if it was poison. Panna cotta was clearly in, because every restaurant listed it on their dessert menu. At times it was hard to know whether the place had really changed or if I had simply forgotten how it was. Had Australians become louder? "It was like the whole place was shouting," Frédéric reported after a night at a very busy, popular new restaurant. "I couldn't follow any conversation."

"I couldn't either," I consoled him.

Was there a harder edge to Sydney? On arrival at the international airport we'd been confronted by the longest customs queue I'd ever seen there. It coiled and wrapped around the hall, as inclined to movement as a lizard sunbathing on a rock. Standing in line were several couples with young babies who looked worn out after long flights; an elderly man seemed to teeter. I pointed them out to a uniformed airport official. "Couldn't you take those people to the front of the line?" I asked. "We're going to be here forever." In an even, steely tone he gave me a warped version of Aussie egalitarianism: "If we bend the rules for a few, we'll have to bend them for everyone. No one jumps to the front of the queue."

Another incident made me question Australians' reputation for being famously easygoing. After dropping me at the Cremorne Point ferry stop, Frédéric ran after me waving my wallet, leaving the car running in a bus zone. Unfortunately a bus arrived to drop commuters for the boat, and was unable to complete its turning circle. The driver went apoplectic, swearing and beating the steering wheel. Too scared to move,

I left it to Frédéric to run and shift our car. As I waited, the bus passengers walked by. "People like you should be locked up," spat one woman. "Good on ya," snarled another fellow. In self-righteous fury, they stomped down to the wharf, where it would be another couple of minutes before the good ferry even rounded the point. "And I thought Parisians were supposed to be uptight," exclaimed Frédéric, who'd copped an earful from the bus driver when he went to apologize. "Australians *are* mostly easygoing," he theorized later, "except when it comes to petty rules and regulations. Then you turn into the Swiss of the Pacific."

Harvest day; it's odd that I should remember so little about what is arguably the most important step in the treatment process. But then it wasn't a memory I especially wanted to revisit. I do recall Frédéric rejoining me before the procedure, having just carried out a crucial procedure himself. I was sipping tea, rather enjoying the fuss the nurses were making of me after my confession about feeling "very nervous." He looked pleased with himself. "*Oui, oui, aucun problème,*" he'd nodded—"too easy." The sperm were in the bag or rather in the dish; none spilled or spurted onto the floor as had happened to a poor friend of ours who, fearing that carpet fuzz would obstruct his swimmers, had rushed to get the nurse, practically in tears. At the clinic in Paris, Frédéric had been offered tatty magazines of very buxom blondes; once, on a particularly busy day when all the rooms were taken he'd had to do the job in the toilet. Perhaps French men are expected to have more imagination. But here the experience had been five star. "There was a minibar," Frédéric raved. "I poured myself a whisky and watched a porn movie."

I possibly responded with insufficient enthusiasm. After all, no sperm, no embryo, no baby. But my thoughts were on the imminent "egg collection," a deceptively sweet term evocative of collecting seashells or searching for freshly laid eggs in a garden. In fact the procedure involves something very long and very pointy inserted between the legs, through the wall of the vagina right on up into the poor unsuspecting ovary, from which eggs would be extracted by draining the liquid from the follicles. In the past I'd always been happily unconscious for it. This time it would be performed with only a local anesthetic and mild pain relief. My specialist had given me all sorts of sensible reasons as to why this method was preferable but still I remained nervous. Besides, he was a man, what did he know? Somewhere between period cramps and labor contractions on the pain scale, according to the nurses. It's not that bad, offered one friend, before going on to compare it with chewing on barbed wire.

My palms sweated and my knees trembled a bit. Frédéric held one hand, a nurse the other. But it was all over in about fifteen minutes and actually the pain wasn't as bad as I'd expected. It was a relief to have the procedure out of the way but afterward there wasn't a mood of great optimism. It had been a modest harvest.

Earlier ultrasound tests had shown up four follicles but first one had disappeared off the radar and then another. According to the blue book the clinic gave us, the two remaining "oocytes," or egg cells, were then placed in separate dishes with approximately 100,000 of Frédéric's sperm. You'd think given the proximity and such numbers, fertilization was sure to occur but this is not the case. There was no way to improve egg quality, Dr. L had explained during that first phone call. The printed summary we were given after the collection procedure bore out the truth of his words, detailing our diminishing chances step by step:

Oocytes collected 2
Oocytes inseminated 2
Oocytes normally fertilized 1
Embryos transferred 1
Embryos frozen 0
Embryos not suitable to freeze 0

The hopes that had been lifted by my unexpectedly good FSH levels came crashing down. The result was a bitter disappointment: all that for one measly embryo. Were it not for the fact we'd traveled from Tahiti, Dr. L would have advised canceling the invasive collection procedure, he admitted.

"At least we'll be able to say we did everything we could," I sighed later to Frédéric, trying to be philosophical.

Several days later we were back for the next crucial step, the transfer, when the fertilized egg or eggs are implanted in the uterus. In the darkened, windowless room there was my specialist, an assisting nurse, the embryologist, Frédéric and me. Images of our embryo, magnified zillions of times over, illuminated a screen on the opposite wall. The embryologist stood next to it, pointing. "It's doing everything it should be doing at this stage," she said. "See, it has already divided into eight cells."

The shape on the screen looked to me like a four-leaf clover, only with six petal-shaped leaves. Where the eight cells were I didn't know. This was the first time we'd seen images of our very own embryo and I might have been curious. Instead I left it to Frédéric to ask questions while I turned my head to the side, the way Maddie does when punished: a gesture of submission, resignation. Dear little Mads, at least we had her. She was probably being thoroughly spoiled back on Mo'orea by our neighbors, Daniel and Catherine. The blank wall, though not particularly interesting, was more soothing than staring at the screen. The embryo may have looked more plant than human but it was undeniable proof of life. I couldn't bear to see those interlacing circles, didn't want their imprint on my mind, this fragile, three-day beginning of a baby that I would never get to name or hold in my arms.

This was our final attempt, we'd been adamant. That was the understanding from the outset; Dr. L had concurred. But having already written off this go, my mind raced ahead. "Will you take us on for another try?" I asked in a small, pleading voice.

"How about we talk about that later," suggested Dr. L, kindly but firmly. "Let's give this one a chance first, shall we?" His response drew me back to where I needed to be—in the present. Consequently I was paying attention when the embryologist spoke. Standing next to the screen, she pointed at the image. "There's no fragmentation. Nice clean edges. All the cells are evenly sized." In her white coat and glasses, she appeared the quintessential scientist so it was touching to detect a note of wonderment in her next words.

"It's a lovely embryo," she said.

It is known as the "two-week wait," though even the clinic's upbeat blue book conceded that to many couples it's the terrible two-week wait or the dreaded two-week wait. In the interests of accuracy, the blood test for pregnancy is carried out sixteen days after the embryo transfer. For many this "protracted period of uncertainty" after so much "forward activity" is the most stressful part of the IVF process. A phase of drifting and waiting on the heels of action: it was a less extreme version of the contrasting conditions the Polynesian seafarers had to cope with at sea. We could have returned to Tahiti and had the pregnancy test done in Pape'ete but it wouldn't have felt right. Having begun in Sydney, the process had to end there. Yet we couldn't just hang about brooding.

Despite his many trips, Frédéric had seen little of Australia beyond Sydney. Annual holidays had always been about spending time with my family and friends. The vast southern continent might well have been a skinny atoll for all he'd seen of the interior. Being here in winter, the ideal season to visit the desert, gave us a rare opportunity. Immediately we thought of close friends who were now living in Alice Springs. Back in Paris we'd spent many fun nights with Vinnie and Gen, who were both Australian, but it had been several years since we'd been in contact. Over the phone, Vinnie immediately dispelled any awkwardness. "Yeah, yeah, fantastic, of course you gotta come. Stay as long as you want!" As his enthusiasm and warmth surged down the line, I couldn't help thinking that these qualities were the real gold in our land. Since this trip was a first for both me and Frédéric, we decided to stop on the way to see Uluru. And so two days after the embryo transfer we were flying over the tangerine crust of Central Australia.

There was a moment—a prolonged one, if I'm honest—after picking up our rental car and driving from the airport to Yulara, the resort complex, when the destination seemed a mistake. Peak season meant lots of tourists, of course, yet at the Outback Pioneer Hotel it was a shock to see the long ranks of coaches lining the car park, and converging tour groups. At the reception, we waited to check in behind a busload of jolly middle-aged European visitors, dressed as if for safari in khaki shorts and walking boots. By the time we got our room key it was early afternoon and we stopped to order lunch at the outdoor barbecue grill. The atmosphere was boisterously cheerful and, despite the Slim Dusty CD playing in the background, vaguely American I thought, though this impression may have come from the oversized hamburgers and steaks. In the middle was a pool table where several local Aboriginal people were having a game. To our horror a few people started taking photos of them, as if they were a tourist attraction, too. We watched tensely, half-hoping for a scene: a cue, perhaps, thrown spear-like, at one or two cameras. Finally one of the pool players gruffly but politely asked the snappers to stop. The game resumed as if such interruptions were not unusual.

"Let's go see the rock," suggested Frédéric as soon as we'd dumped our bags in the room.

From a distance it looked exactly like it had in the Qantas in-flight video: like a gargantuan paperweight pinning down planet Earth. Up close it didn't look quite so smooth or inert; its flanks appeared to ripple and waver as we followed the path around the rock's base. "What are the colors now?" Frédéric kept asking as the afternoon wore on and the sandstone began to shimmer like sari silk. The rich, shifting hues, which melted from pink to orange to mauve, were hard for him to see. Color-blind or not, he was awed by Uluru. "It does feel sacred," he said quietly. As we watched tourists slowly inch back down the slippery sides, he added, "You can understand why Aboriginal people don't like people climbing it."

It was the center's other natural monument, Kata Tjuta, some fifty kilometers west, that affected me more—the Olgas, as it was known when I was growing up. Here there was no monolith but thirty-six domes that rose voluptuously from the earth. Meandering among the undulating rock, soaking up its mammalian warmth, unconsciously I pressed a breast: no tenderness or swelling, nothing.

A hard-bitten outback town with a pretty name: that had long been my perception of Alice Springs. During the five-hour drive northeast from Yulara, across monotonous, featureless country, I shared with Frédéric what I knew from television, newspapers and books. It was the kind of rough, redneck place that turned people, both Aboriginal and white, to drink, though this common interest did little to unite them. A town built on the banks of a river so dry the drunks bedded in it each night. The sort of place you watched your bag and didn't go wandering after dark.

Whether the view we got was truer or simply telescoped was hard to say. Perhaps the town had changed. During our week in Alice we hung out with our hosts and sometimes their friends, a collection of teachers, health workers, psychologists and art coordinators who mostly worked with Aboriginal communities and in their spare time painted or wrote books, poetry and songs. When we'd last seen Vinnie and Gen they were running a restaurant in Paris and living behind the Musée d'Orsay in a grand apartment with high ceilings and patterned parquet. Now they had swapped their view of man-made monuments for the rugged beauty of the bush: home was an old railway cottage set amid coolibah trees, mulgas and kangaroos, at the base of a rocky escarpment ten kilometers from the center of town. At night we built bonfires in the backyard while Gen, who sang beautifully, would strum and sing. Their home reverberated with desert color; rooms were painted crimson, pink and orange. Pinned to the walls and free of frames, artworks by their children and local Aboriginal artists added to the effulgence. I was reminded of something I'd read about Matisse, who used to talk of the healing properties of color—"beneficent radiation" he called it—and prop his paintings "like sunlamps at the bedside of sick friends."

Stuff it, I thought on my fourth night when Vinnie, who knew his wines, opened a bottle of his favorite Aussie red. Might as well enjoy myself. Alcohol was not recommended during the wait period and so far I'd been good, but ten days had passed since the embryo had been implanted and whatever anyone said about it being too early to tell, I knew it hadn't worked. Frédéric confessed he felt the same. Yet somehow this deep conviction didn't spoil our holiday. Time was suspended in Alice. Stimulated by a landscape new to us and interesting people, we pushed our own reality aside.

We drove several hours northwest of town to the Aboriginal community of Yuendumu, which was holding its annual

Sports Weekend. "No matter what you do, it won't fall out!" That was what the blue book had to say about the likelihood of an embryo being dislodged. Still, jouncing along the dirt road I did wonder if the safety tests had included outback corrugations. "Faster, you've got to go faster, otherwise you feel every bump," I urged Frédéric, repeating the instructions we'd been given by Gen, whose four-wheel drive was way ahead. For a minute or two we sped along seamlessly until our wheels seemed to leave the ground. "Jesus," I cried in alarm. "Slow down!"

Naturally Frédéric and I fantasized about moving to Alice, just as on those past holidays we had got excited about living in Marrakech or Sarajevo or Istanbul. I saw myself crocheting and linking up the squares to make technicolor blankets. I would knit beanies with side plaits, woven with sparkling thread and painted beads, mad creations that would be sent as gifts to baffled family members and friends who'd wonder whether the desert sun had done something to my head. I might take up the ukulele after all, to strum along with Gen around bonfires. Frédéric dreamed of taking off into the distant gaps and malachite-green gorges of the MacDonnell Ranges with his paintbrushes and a billy can.

The spell broke on the flight back to Sydney. Part of me was impatient to get the final step over and done with, to have the blood test confirm what in my heart I already knew. But mostly as the olive and pink land finally gave way to indigo hills then to the comparative lushness of the coast, I dreaded the dreaded wait coming to an end.

FOURTEEN

"Press down firmly. That's it." The nurse wheeled her chair back to reach for a Band-Aid while I held the cotton-wool ball to the inner crease of my arm where the needle had left a purple dot of blood. "You'll get a call between two and three in the afternoon with the result," she said, sticking down the plaster. Alison, I think her name was, patted my back sympathetically. "Do something nice," she advised.

Compared to the many intense weeks that had already been consumed by this IVF attempt, seven hours wasn't much of a wait. Yet after my early morning blood test Frédéric and I stood outside the clinic wondering what to do. It was Saturday, just before eight; there was no one about. Shaded by tall buildings, the narrow city streets looked empty and gloomy. I had a sudden urge to be out in the open, in brassy sunlight, surrounded by people.

"Let's go to Bondi," I said, on impulse.

In the past I'd often wondered what the fuss was about. It

was just a beach, a built-up one at that, hardly Sydney's finest: as far as I was concerned the British backpackers could have it. But when we got there I was glad to see the long, familiar arc of sand, grateful for the way it smiled at us, not begrudging my prejudices. In this season, at this early hour, there were no tourists along the esplanade, only a passing parade of power walkers and joggers, some of whom ran pushing the latest in aerodynamic strollers. Below on the beach, a small group of people obeyed a trainer in fancy fitness gear, sprinting on command across the soft sand. On the still water surfers sat astride boards doing what surfers do best: bobbing and waiting. The ocean temperature couldn't have been more than 14 or 15 degrees yet there were a few swimmers, too, their arms wheeling out of the water like spokes, backlit by sun. They made me think of Mo'orea. I'd need my therapeutic swims when I got back.

After a walk and coffees and flipping distractedly through the weekend newspapers, it was still only ten o'clock. Time was displaying its uncanny ability to do exactly the opposite of what we wished, not flying or marching but *oozing*, as if gelatine powder had been added to the mix. "Five hours to go," Frédéric announced a bit grimly, after checking his watch. Since returning from Alice Springs we'd moved into my brother's place on the northern beaches, so at least the drive home would chew up another hour. He and his wife were away, we had the place to ourselves and I wanted to take the phone call there, in privacy, not in town on my mobile. We had plenty of time yet I was anxious to get on our way. "If we head back now we can stop at that art gallery," I suggested. "Just to have a look."

A friend told us about this place, which specialized in Aboriginal art. But we weren't in the right mood for browsing. Somehow all the dot paintings only added to our jitters. We were heading for the door when a canvas hung high on the far wall caught my eye and I stopped. It was olive and pink, mustard and crimson, soft gray and burnt orange, and it reminded me of the desert we'd just visited, which was no coincidence because the artist lived near Alice, as it turned out. The dots were very small, very precise. I usually prefer vigorous, untidy brushstrokes but still I couldn't take my eyes off the painting. "What do you think of that one?" I asked Frédéric, swallowing.

Seemingly transfixed, too, after a moment he said: "Let's see how much it is."

Our show of interest incited an animated explanation from the gallery manager of the symbols and meaning of the painting. The artist, Nora Watson Nangala, was depicting her country during the wet season. The wavy hourglass contours represented water running after rains; the circular forms were rock pools; the parallel lines were lightning. Et cetera et cetera. I was only half listening.

Like the landscapes they represented, to my inexpert eye Aboriginal dot paintings were about color and pattern— open to interpretation, in other words. To me the rock pools looked like eggs or embryos. To Frédéric the running water evoked a curving, feminine form. The artist's representation of country looked to both of us like a fertility symbol. But this discussion only took place later. When we left with our purchase, barely ten minutes after we'd stepped inside the gallery, we were unaware that the other had seen it in the same

way. Voicing the thought might break the magic. The painting was a talisman, an offering. A last plea to God or the gods
to be kind.

On the way back we brooded on the issue of who would
take the phone call. In Paris it had always been me. But in the
car I felt sick with dread. The remove we'd felt during our trip
to Central Australia had vanished. Now that the moment of
truth was imminent, our grand self-deception was exposed:
we were not reconciled to another failure at all. No one goes
through IVF without dreaming and hoping it will work.

"I can't do it," I said flatly. I didn't want to hear the words.
"You take the call."

Unlike the pale, suffused light of a Paris winter, in Sydney
the July sun is a powerful force. Low in the sky, it aims straight
into windows, fading carpets, curtains and upholstery. My
brother's west-facing house was radiantly lit when we got
back. It was a shack, really—one whose lovely Pittwater views
more than made up for its small size. When the phone rang
between two and three, Frédéric sprang to his feet, picked up
the cordless receiver and strode onto the deck outside, as I'd
requested. I hovered inside only a few meters away, on the
other side of a sliding glass door that didn't quite shut, unable to tear my eyes away.

"Yes, it's Frédéric," I heard him confirm. I suppose the
nurses had to make sure they had the right person. There
was a pause as he listened. A look of confusion blew across his
face. "Sorry? What's that?" Slowly, very slowly, his expression
seemed to clear a bit. "Really? Do you mean— " And that's all
he had time to say before I wrenched the phone from his
hand.

"Hello, hello, this is Sarah," I said breathlessly, though I'd only sprinted a few meters.

"Hello, Sarah. It's Kate."

She wasn't the nurse who took my blood earlier. I couldn't picture her face but her voice was familiar, as gently comforting as toast and tea. Perhaps Kate had just had to deliver unhappy outcomes to other couples. She would have had to find the right words, strike that delicate balance between telling the truth and providing comfort. Weary, she might have saved us for last, planning to end the day on a high note.

"I was just telling Frédéric the wonderful news. The blood test is positive."

A flock of sulfur-crested cockatoos exploded from a nearby spotted gum, screeching over some trifle like pigs about to be slaughtered. Angel-white and magnificent though they were, I could have happily shot the lot of them for their poor sense of timing. There was an urgent need for confirmation, to know I hadn't misheard. "Sorry, can you . . . ?" Kate repeated her words. I had to check again. "Are you sure?" I recall feeling charged—so electrically alert it made the rest of my life look like one long slumber. It was then that Kate uttered the phrase I'd waited almost six years to hear, the words I'd heard so clearly in my imaginings: "You're pregnant." Though my reaction in real life was very different from the scene in my head. There was no gushing gratitude, no shrieks of joy, no disbelieving omigods, no exclamation marks. If Kate's tone was buoyant, mine was tense, sharp. Sound by sound, frame by frame, I shut out the world: the mischievous cockatoos, the neighbor's ringing telephone, even Frédéric. I didn't rush to embrace him, didn't even look at him. Gravely—fiercely, he later said—I stared unseeingly into the cinematic sunbeams, every cell in my body wrapped up in the effort of absorbing the news. An onlooker might have thought I was trying to digest news of the death of a loved one.

Indeed the feeling that launched from the tender place below my ribs must have been grief. Bottled up for so long, it now traveled up inside me, expanding as it rose, rather like the air bubbles we made when scuba diving. The speed of it made me choke. Whether I coughed or gulped or made a sound Kate heard, I can't say, though it's possible my heartbeat was audible.

"Hello? Sarah?"

Later, I learned my reaction was not unusual. Tears, hysterical laughter, stunned silence, disbelief—the nurses have heard it all. Upon learning of the long-awaited pregnancy, some patients need to talk while others are unable to string two words together. In the past I'd always been measured, unfailingly polite: *je vous remercie*, I'd say upon hearing the unhappy news, thank you so much for the call. *Bonne journée, au revoir.* But now I forgot my manners completely. Kate, the sweet voice on the end of the phone, the messenger of the miracle, probably understood when, without warning or so much as a good-bye, the line went dead.

It was an intensely private moment and there was only one other person with whom it could be shared. Interestingly, the person in question was looking calm and pleased, the way he did after a productive day's work or a satisfying run. Only after I'd got hold of myself did Frédéric start to process the full enormity of the news. From the kitchen, as I fetched some water, I watched him abruptly sit down at the faded teak table, as if his legs had folded beneath him. The force of gravity suddenly seemed too much for him: his spine sagged and his head dropped heavily into his hands. His shoulders shook ever so slightly. It was hard to say, watching through the kitchen window, whether he was sad or happy, laughing or crying.

Men and women experience infertility differently: all the literature tells you that. On a practical level the focus must be on the women undergoing treatment, who unlike their partners are central to every step in the process. A brochure from the clinic stated that men are far more reluctant to seek counseling, too. If there was any remaining doubt as to the toll these years had taken on Frédéric, the truth was laid bare that afternoon. He spent most of it bowed over the table. Several times he got up to move, only to sink back into the chair. Having played the role of supportive partner for so long, his well of suppressed emotion ran deeper than mine. I stroked, I held but mostly I let him grieve: for the scrawny baby pigeon he'd fought so hard to save, for all the follicles that didn't mature, the eggs that failed to fertilize, the countless embryos that never became our children. For the hope that had grown so thin we could almost believe at times it no longer mattered whether or not we had a child, until another failure exposed our self-deception.

A little while later, Frédéric fetched the box of watercolor paints he'd brought with him from Tahiti and settled on the deck overlooking a small bay. It was late afternoon, the sky was turning coral pink, and yolky sunshine fell through the branches of backlit gums. I don't recall Frédéric ever painting anything with such assurance. Without sketching, he applied color directly to paper. The trees in the foreground were rendered in slim strokes, like calligraphy. But the real subject was the background radiance, which was blocked in first with a thick brush. There was more light in that small watercolor than any sunset could ever produce. It was as though the countless candles I'd lit in dark churches had, all these years, been quietly burning and now they'd come together on the page to celebrate our lovely embryo, that microscopic cluster of interlacing bubbles. To think it had got its footing and was actually growing inside me. To think that all over the world, at that very moment, millions of four- or six- or eight-leaf clovers were doing exactly the same thing. Now I understood why the humble circle was the symbol of life.

More than my words, it is the paintings that best tell the story of that day. The Aboriginal canvas bought out of desperation and superstition. And then Frédéric's small watercolor, awash in yellow, the universal color of hope.

FIFTEEN

The sound of humming floated up from the beach to where I lay reading on the back veranda. La-di-da . . . da-di-dum. It sounded like a parody of someone humming, a theater actor overplaying a private, happy moment. "Cut, cut, you're over-doing it!" a stage director might have interrupted from over near the coconut palms. But in real life the sound continued. It reminded me of my father-in-law in one of his charming good humors. On days when the northern European sun shone unexpectedly and the hydrangeas in his garden bobbed like balloons, he would tra and la and di-da. No words, just a series of improvised notes sung in celebration of an ordinary pleasure: sunshine, family, a winning streak in golf, the bird that was browning in the oven, the tasty sauce simmering on the stove to accompany it, which at the table would provoke the customary proclamation, only half in jest: "*Je suis un grand saucier*," I am a great sauce maker.

Now his son—soon to be a father himself—was humming,

too. I watched Frédéric trailing along the sand below. With his nut-brown back and battered straw hat and one of my sarongs slung around his waist, he bore little resemblance to the former Parisian lawyer who liked his smart suits and silk ties. Utterly absorbed in beachcombing, he bent to pick up something—a knob of coral perhaps or a shell. Its whiteness glinted in the sunshine. Strange, perhaps, that this everyday scene should stand out in my memory. Pregnancy is a series of milestones, trimesters and ultrasounds and, due to my age, a nerve-racking amniocentesis. But when I look back on those months what comes to mind are small moments and sensory details.

⌐⌐

By the time I got back to Tahiti it was mid-September and the cooler, drier days were coming to an end. For peace of mind I'd ended up staying on in Sydney another month—long enough to pass an initial milestone. It was at my first appointment after the momentous phone call from the nurse that Dr. L had mentioned the seven-week ultrasound. Still flying high from the news, I'd rehearsed a heartfelt speech of gratitude, thinking I'd be heading back to Tahiti in a couple of days. "An excellent outcome," Dr. L had said, by way of greeting. "Quite unexpected." Positive words but not celebratory. The note of circumspection raised the dark specter of miscarriage—another risk that increases as women age. We were not out of the woods yet, his tone said. "With the advances in ultrasound technology, now at seven weeks we can get a very accurate idea of how the pregnancy is progressing," he had continued. Along with other factors, a strong heartbeat at that point meant the chances of giving birth to a healthy baby were extremely high. The important test may well have been done in Tahiti, but unable to bear the idea of flying back not knowing, I made a snap decision to stay on.

When the day arrived, our six-leaf clover was nowhere to be seen. In the darkened room the screen was a fuzzy swirl of currents. My eye was drawn to a calm black lagoon, within which a white bean pumped and blinked. "That's a very strong heartbeat," the ultrasound technician announced approvingly—words that caused my own heart to leap. One week away from officially being considered a fetus, the "lovely embryo" had come along nicely and had grown to the size of a grape. Some women report a rush of maternal love at this first ultrasound test but all I felt was a surging relief that made my legs almost buckle when I stood up.

⌒⌒

The untidy path of seaweed, shells and jetsam was a sign the wind direction was swinging around to the northeast: the *maramu* was no longer sweeping the beach clean. Our third wet season was about to commence. As I watched from the veranda Frédéric examined his newfound treasure, admiring its texture or shape. Obviously it was a keeper. Poor Nelly— how she despaired with our sea-worn finds. "Mo'e will polish up those shells for you, give them a coat of varnish," she regularly offered, perplexed when I explained we liked their rough, pocked texture which reminded us of old stones. Even from a distance I could read Frédéric's thoughts, we'd spoken them aloud often enough. What a remarkable journey this little ocean gift had made. If only it could talk. How wonderful the tides and moon, the wind and currents, and the grace of God conspired to bring it to this very beach. Where there's a will there's a way, people say, but will did not deliver the shell to us. Our own modest energies count for little without some grander intervention. Luck and chance, chance and luck: we thought about them a lot these days.

We'd told our families, of course, plus a couple of close friends in Australia who'd followed the process every step of the way. Back on Mo'orea, Frédéric had blurted out the happy news to Daniel and Catherine after an arduous climb to the top of Mouaputa, the mountain with the eyehole. They had called me in Sydney from the summit. *"C'est sublime!"* Frédéric had shouted down his mobile. Presumably he meant the view but he was too euphoric to make much sense. A cork popped in the background—a reckless sound to my ears, coming from a razor-thin ledge. They weren't off Mouaputa yet: there was still the treacherous descent and most guides came casually equipped with nothing but a few frayed ropes. With my fear of heights it was one island mountain I had no desire to tackle, pregnant or otherwise. "Was that a cork again?" I asked worriedly, at the sound of another whup in the background. *"t'inquiete pas, tout va bien."* Frédéric's gay bellow was taken up by the others. There seemed to be quite a party up there.

Apart from the impromptu announcement to Daniel and Catherine, we decided to keep the pregnancy a secret for a few more weeks. It felt deceitful not telling our neighbors, who had become like family to us on Mo'orea, not telling Alicia in Paris, or even the psychotherapist in Pape'ete. But neither of us wanted to risk jinxing our good luck by broadcasting it prematurely. Delicate inquiries met with ambiguous replies: Sydney was fine thanks; um yes, well I guess we may try again at some stage. Our neighbors showed exemplary discretion, asking after my parents and family in Sydney and leaving it at that.

But behind the bright floral curtains, *radio cocotier,* the word-of-mouth island news network, was fully operational. I should have known there would be no hiding anything from Nelly, a woman who'd had six babies, after all, and knew a thing or two about pregnancy. By week 8 the evidence was beginning to pile up: packets of crackers by my bed and pyramids of glass yogurt pots by the sink, empty and washed. "You probably won't show for ages," a Sydney friend had knowingly advised. "With all that swimming your stomach muscles must be really good." But pregnant at long last, my body was eager to show off its achievement. My waist quickly vanished, thanks to a firm belt of flesh around my hips and lower back. By week 9 I had a pronounced frontal bulge. Buttons had to be left undone, zips at half-mast. For comfort I started wearing maternity pants and skirts.

Nelly didn't raise so much as a querying eyebrow on any of her Wednesday visits. But she was taking in the small signs and reporting to Guite, who months later laughingly told me of these regular updates. "All she eats is yogurt." "You should have seen her getting out of the lagoon this morning—heavens, she's put on weight!" "She's eating *cochonneries.*" I could imagine their expressions, a mixture of delight and fond disapproval: *cochonneries*, from the French word for pig, *cochon*, meant "rubbish" or "junk" and might have been a reference to an empty chip packet by my bed one morning. Little wonder our friends appeared unsurprised when finally, at the end of week 12, we told them. "We prayed for you while you were away," Guite told us simply. "All of us." She jabbed a thumb in the direction of her son, who towered over her: "Even him." At this little dig at his nonattendance at church, Alain shifted his weight to the other foot and pulled at the small white towel that hung perpetually around his neck. "Maybe He listened to me," he quipped, "seeing as He doesn't hear from me that often."

The phases of pregnancy had been described to me by friends but even so the force of the first trimester fatigue came as a surprise. It was like jet lag: you couldn't fight it. Then one day, just as I'd been told, the tiredness and nausea mysteriously vanished. The second trimester is aptly known as the blooming phase, and bloom I did in all sorts of ways. While Frédéric fretted throughout the pregnancy that something might happen, from this point on I totally relaxed. When a local nurse suggested at one point that my weight gain had rather surpassed the recommended limits, I was not concerned but indignant. My diet was healthy. I didn't feel overweight, I felt mighty. My energy was boundless.

The lagoon, which had long been vital to my sanity, became important to me in new ways. There was the physical relief of weightlessness as I grew heavier. And each stretching arm stroke seemed to create more space inside for my growing baby. More than ever I felt transported into an ethereal realm. Pregnant women often dream of swimming, apparently, especially in the early stages when their own bodies are filling up with fluid. I didn't have such dreams—or none that I could recall. What happened to me was that reality became even more dreamlike.

I began to play in the shoals after my swims. What was the rush? No lingering in the lagoon—was it really me who came up with that rule? My daily work schedules seemed silly now—as if something as fluid and tricksy as time could be broken into columns and straight lines. Somersaulting underwater gave me delicious tremors of dizziness. Sometimes I felt a flutter inside, an answering bump or kick as if to say, Hey, I can do that, look at me! Freud, with his theories on embryonic fantasies, would have had a field day with the symbolism. Was there any body of water more womblike than a reef-fringed lagoon? Could any human being be closer to sea water than a pregnant woman filled with amniotic fluid? We were practically one, the lagoon and I, made up as we were of the very same thing.

Perhaps my body's new life-giving generosity made me more generous spirited. The turd-like sea cucumbers no longer seemed so repulsive and for the first time I was moved to stroke one. And guess what? It didn't feel soft and squishy but quite firm; the texture was not slimy as I'd imagined but rather like very fine sandpaper. Perhaps the lagoon creatures had grown used to my presence, for I often swam alongside the pink whiprays now, as they shuffled along the bottom. The eagle rays were shyer. Elegant in their dotted black and white coats, they often took off as I approached, as if suddenly realizing they were late for a ball.

Seeing them like this made me reflect on the unseemly

spectacle I'd witnessed once on the other side of the island. Within the reef, near Taotoi Pass, is an attraction called Stingray World where tour groups can cavort with large pink whiprays. The day we went, there was much shrieking as the sea creatures—some of which had wingspans of more than a meter—pressed and wrapped themselves around the humans, sucking at them in search of fish handouts. "Aren't you coming in?" Frédéric had called, laughing as three slithering rays fought over him. I shuddered; there was no way I was stepping into the fray. That day decided it for me: I wasn't a fan of the practice of feeding sharks or any other sea life. There is a lot to be said for keeping a respectful distance. After that experience, the calm encounters during my morning swims seemed even more precious.

Thoughts of Henri Matisse on Fakarava came to me often in the lagoon during my pregnancy. The delirious perspectives and strange magnifications underwater had fascinated him. I found myself doing as the artist had done, looking up at the sky from the sandy floor at the clouds spilled like milk on the surface, or staring at my own hand underwater, which through the magical membrane had an otherworldly clarity. When I no longer knew which way was up, I'd lie back on the warm pillowy surface, legs dangling, head rolled back with my stomach sticking right out.

"You looked like a *motu*," teased Nelly one day. It's true, my bare dome must have resembled an islet. Once as I was swimming home I made out a stick figure standing on our beach. Whoever it was had their hands on their hips because the arms were bent at sharp angles. By the time I swam ashore the person had gone but later the same day my suspicions were confirmed when Guite's walking stick banged crossly up the front steps. She stood backlit in the doorway, slight but none-theless formidable, and shook a finger at me. She'd never been thrilled about me swimming so far and my pregnancy made her more protective. "*Aïe, aïe, aïe,*" she scolded. "You could be run over by a fishing boat. I saw you this morning, halfway to Tahiti, bobbing in the water like a little coconut."

⌒⌒

"Life begets life. Energy creates energy." The famous words of the French actress Sarah Bernhardt ring true for my preg-nancy, for these were not idle months. Once a week I drove around the island in an anticlockwise direction to Opunohu Bay, spectacularly flanked by the awe-inspiring peaks of mounts Tautuapae, Mouaroa and Rotui. On my return from Sydney I'd resolved to resume the private Tahitian lessons I started not long before leaving. They took place in a house next to the lagoon under the guidance of Lee, a former schoolteacher. I always felt slightly nervous. A kindly but no-nonsense Polynesian, it wasn't hard to picture an entire class squirming under her stern stare. The fact that British mis-sionaries carried out the formidable task of alphabetizing Tahitian supposedly led to linguistic affinities that make it simpler for English speakers than for the French. But as there are only thirteen letters in the language, mispronouncing one vowel can alter the meaning of a whole sentence. You can easily get by in the territory just speaking French, but many islanders converse in Tahitian. Hopeful of one day surprising Alain or Aima with some phrases, for a while I was diligent with my homework. *'A rave i t-e penitara! 'A horoi i tena tomati! T-e tamahino -o Tara*, I wrote in my exercise book. Take the pencil; wash these tomatoes; Sarah's daughter.

Languages are a way of understanding what matters to people and how they see the world, and it was the cultural insights I relished most. What might have been a tedious lesson on grammar was enlivened by an example of the two types of possessives. "My outrigger canoe" implies an intimate, absolute relationship, whereas "my wife" is nonexclusive. "In other words," pointed out Lee with a throaty chuckle, "in Tahitian your canoe is too precious to lend, but a wife or husband can be borrowed."

By sheer coincidence, around this time a few work opportunities dropped into my lap. One of the big cultural events on the territory's calendar was an annual film festival held in Pape'ete for documentary filmmakers from throughout the Oceanic region. The chance to help out came through a much-loved local radio journalist, Michèle de Chazeaux, whom I had interviewed for a story. In its third year, the festival was beginning to receive more entries from countries like Australia and New Zealand, and when the selection committee decided it needed an English speaker Michèle remembered me. It was upaid work but it was nice to feel useful and I gladly gave over evenings to viewing and note taking. Every so often there was a meeting to attend in Pape'ete with the other committee members. Held at the Maison de la Culture, these were relaxed, friendly occasions during which discussions about the eligibility of individual films frequently evolved into grand debates about the exact geographical parameters of Oceania.

As for the other opportunity, the travel editor had contacted me many months before about writing a feature. Finally, after a long delay then a spate of e-mails, a phone call had settled the question of which islands to include. Out-of-the-way atolls and drop-in-the-ocean islets were well and good, he said, but the magazine couldn't possibly run a long piece on French Polynesia that didn't feature Bora Bora. To my suggestion that the island had been photographed and written about endlessly, he pointed out that two recently opened five-star resorts should provide a fresh angle.

Tahiti might be evocative by name but in reality it's not a destination so much as a stopover—a place for visitors to catch their breath after a long flight from Paris or New York. To *experience* paradise for a week or two, the honeymooners and holidaymakers take one of many short daily flights to Bora. Paul Gauguin may have put Hiva Oa on the map and reignited the Tahiti legend but Bora won out with Hollywood romance and glamour. It was while filming *Mutiny on the Bounty* on the island that the (then) dashing Marlon Brando fell in love with his beautiful co-star, Tarita Teriipaia.

Despite its reputation or perhaps because of it, Frédéric and I had felt little attraction for the place—Bora Boring was the name given by American friends whose honeymoon there had been an unmitigated disaster. Granted, those overwater bungalows with aquarium-paneled floors were alluring but at roughly US$1000 a night, they weren't affordable. Yet this was *work* and someone else was paying, and Frédéric's enthusiasm soared accordingly. "I'll come and carry your bags," he chirped straightaway. We got on the plane like two kids off to Disneyland. Almost seven months' pregnant, I was beginning to feel very heavy. With another wet season under way, at night in our rather airless bedroom I perspired profusely. A luxurious, air-conditioned bungalow with a king-sized bed didn't sound boring, it sounded glorious. Bring on massages and facials and room service!

In a secret chamber of our minds, or rather our hearts, we all hold an image of an idyllic island, so it's said. An experience I had years ago with a hypnotherapist whom I saw for insomnia proved the point to me. "Picture a dream landscape," he had said, in a deep calming voice. "Somewhere safe and peaceful—a beautiful garden or a mountain lake. Or maybe a field full of wildflowers, bobbing in the breeze." When the image was fixed in my mind, he explained, my little finger would rise into the air, as if pulled up by a string. My eyes had almost snapped back open in disbelief; it crossed my mind I could fake it. But then an image began to form in my mind. "Ah yes," the hypnotherapist nodded after, "that's the most common dream landscape." Golden curving shores, waving coconut palms, sparkling aqua water. At some point I was amazed to realize my little finger had indeed floated up into the air.

My dream islet may have been a little flatter and smaller, but from the plane Bora Bora was as beautiful as people had said. Older than Mo'orea and Tahiti by a few million years, the island was further on in its evolution toward becoming an atoll. Its volcanic mountains stuck up like a pair of thumbs amid a wide lagoon in shades of blue from azure to beryl to sapphire and turquoise, rimmed with *motu*. It was on these islets that most of Bora's resorts were built. Sixteen hadn't sounded that many until we were speeding past them on the boat from the airport to the hotel. Overwater bungalows sprouted like spring leaves from branches connected to long trunks that crossed the lagoon. Mo'orea may have had the world's first overwater rooms but Bora had staked its future on them. Handsome timbers, no high-rise—you couldn't say the resorts were unattractive. But it was the same feeling I got seeing rare butterflies mounted and framed: the many man-made avenues over the water just looked wrong. Stranger still was the urge to build more resorts when many of the existing ones remained half-empty. Tax breaks provided by French law to encourage investment in the territory meant hotels were built whether or not they were needed and regardless of infrastructure considerations such as adequate water supply. "We like the jobs," the boat driver told me, when I asked what locals thought. Then he quietly added: "But a lot of people are saying these two new resorts must be the last."

"It was a supply base during the Second World War, did you know?" I asked Frédéric as we sat one evening, watching the sun set. Around us, honeymooners posed for photos, with the striking claw-like form of Mount Otemanu, the island's highest peak, rising in the background. It seemed incongruous even mentioning war, given the postcard setting. But were it not for Pearl Harbor and fears of another Japanese attack, Bora Bora might still be a quiet, preserved island, dependent on copra and vanilla. Anxious for the Allies to have a presence in the Pacific, the US Navy sent an armada of troop carriers, cruisers, destroyers and cargo boats to the then tranquil backwater. Among the 5000 Americans was James A. Michener, who later turned his wartime experiences into a bestselling novel which became the basis for the hit Broadway and film musical *South Pacific*. With the troops outnumbering islanders five to one, some critics called it an invasion but as far as occupations go it was jovial. Far away from the fighting the Americans spent a few idyllic—though not idle—years, building the territory's first airfield, organizing outdoor cinema soirées and fathering a great number of local babies. After the war ended, word of this Pacific gem spread. When Tahiti got an international airport in the 1960s, Bora Bora, with its capable runway, was the only outer island visitors could reach by air.

⌒⌒

A photo of me and Frédéric taken by Saki, our Japanese butler, probably best sums up our stay. It shows us sitting on the private deck of our overwater bungalow ("villa" would be more accurate, since there was nothing Robinson Crusoe-like about it), with a rainbow of tropical fruit spread on the teak table and Bora's lagoon sparkling behind us. More Tongan queen than slender *vahine*, I look glowing and grand in my five-star fluffy bathrobe. Frédéric, too, wears a bathrobe, along with a satisfied grin. With his deeply tanned face and wet hair swept off his forehead, he bears a tiny resemblance to Silvio Berlusconi. Near the fruit platter, almost right out of the picture, my notepad and pen lie forgotten—discarded—as though I'd all but given up on pretending this was work.

It was in many ways a baffling place, though. "Why do we

need *three* flat screen televisions?" Frédéric had wondered once we'd had a look around our luxurious abode. The clock radio had to be smothered with a pillow then finally unplugged and put away—three bricks high, it was bright enough to broadcast the time to a public square. If you were inclined to be picky—and I wasn't in these pampered circumstances—you might say the glass floor panel was more of a gimmick. There weren't a lot of fish. Tasteful imitation was the design code. Swimming pools were made to look like the nearby lagoon, with palm-shaded beaches and sandy shores; tropical gardens were manicured to look like outcrops of lush jungle. It was like stumbling onto a film set.

Yet these curiously seductive idyll-constructs tapped right into that powerful dream that under hypnosis had emerged from the seaweed of my subconscious. Throughout the ages, earthly paradise has nearly always been a walled garden or an island—a separate little world. And what could be more cut off and contained than an exclusive resort on an islet? During our four-day stay we left our luxury confines only once, to change hotels. Every island I'd visited so far had made me think deeply about something: on the Marquesas it was about being far away; on Fakarava it was about feeling small. Profound thoughts didn't come easily on Bora Bora, to be honest. But not long after we got home, in one of those memorable pregnancy moments, I found myself questioning our human longings. Why must we set our sights on paradise—or increasingly these days the dream of perfect happiness?

We were sitting out in front for once, perched on the steps, not looking at the lagoon but facing the mountains. It was impossible to name their color, which in this granular light appeared the result of careful scumbling: saffron upon musk-pink, mauve upon mint. Night would soon drop and the sky shone a blue at once rich and faded. "Denim," I said, searching for an apt description.

"It reminds me of Italian chapel ceilings," offered Frédéric thoughtfully. He was good with his blues.

If the colors were difficult to label I was in no doubt as to the name of the warm feeling inside. As I leaned back to allow room for my stomach and the little one growing inside, the feeling expanded into the new space. No one ever says, "When I grow up I want to be *content*." And yet this unassuming state confers a beautiful sense of fullness that felt to me like floating. It was a powerful realization, too enormous to voice. I kept to myself my private name for that special glowing blue of the sky. Spoken aloud, written on the page, it might sound soppy: the color of contentment.

SIXTEEN

At first sight Clinique Paofai had not appeared an ideal nest. One of several hospitals in Pape'ete, its exterior resembled any other peeling high-rise along the traffic-choked boulevard that sliced between town and the waterfront. Like every mother-to-be, I sought a safe, secure place to have my baby. Inside I had hoped for gleaming surfaces, an atmosphere of matronly efficiency with perhaps an eye-catching floral arrangement at reception or in the foyer. Instead, on my first visit to fill in some forms, it had reminded me of an underfunded state high school: the downstairs toilet was blocked and the walls of the main stairwell were smudged with handprints. My head flooded with stories remembered over the years about medical bungles and stillbirths and babies strangled by umbilical cords. Maybe we should go back to our original plan and return to Sydney for the birth, I worried.

But while the thought of being in Dr. L's care again was greatly reassuring, returning to Australia wasn't a simple solution. I couldn't just fly back, pop out a baby and then bundle it straight on a ten-hour flight to Tahiti: giving birth there meant arriving well ahead of my due date and staying for a minimum of six weeks after. With my parents having embarked on their merry perambulations around France, we no longer had a Sydney base. We'd need to rent an apartment, which would add to the considerable expense. Frédéric was able to take two weeks' paternity leave but after that it would just be me and the baby.

We thought of all the women in the past who had given birth in fields or alone—not to mention the Polynesians who continued to have babies on outer islands with barely a dispensary on hand. ("They're much more stoic than *popa'ā*," a French midwife on Mo'orea told me. "There's no screaming.") Clinique Paofai might not look much but it was a hospital with highly trained staff—a decent medical system was one of the gifts of French colonization. After asking around and being warned off Dr. So-and-So, who apparently found scheduled C-sections suited his social life, and another obstetrician who rated low on bedside manner, we found the gently spoken Dr. F.

"*Grossesse précieuse*," he had marked on my medical file at our first appointment. "Every pregnancy is precious, of course," Dr. F hurried on, with a slight smile. "But we use the term when there were many difficulties involved." Compared to "*stérile*" or "infertile" or "IVF patient," this was one label I didn't mind. History does matter, the words seemed to say. To my ears, "precious pregnancy" was a sweet acknowledgment of years of effort.

The French are fond of scans during pregnancy and compared to friends in Australia or England it seemed I had many, although it may also be that a *grossesse précieuse* is subject to closer monitoring. The one that stands out in my memory occurred at 26 weeks—a milestone in fetal life because from this point the very premature baby is deemed capable of surviving outside the womb. As usual, Frédéric and I had caught the early ferry from Mo'orea over to Tahiti. Through Vai'are Pass the swell seemed to hit at an odd angle and several times the boat pitched into nothing, prompting me to move to a window seat to stare fixedly at the lumpy horizon. Even in the new *Aremiti V*—sleeker and smarter than its predecessor—the ocean crossing from island to island could still feel like an adventure. In Pape'ete, there was the usual cheerful mayhem at the wharf with the tetchy fellow blowing his whistle at anything and everything. A rattly local bus pulled up and we piled on, hoping it went in the direction of the doctor's rooms on the outskirts of town. I liked riding in these traditional "trucks" as they were called. With their open windows and square ends, they had the endearing simplicity of a child's toy. There were spare places at the back but before we could edge up the aisle there was a shuffling along the front bench seat. With a hand buffed smooth by age, like the driftwood we collected, a *papi* wordlessly patted the space created for me. "*Mauruuru,*" I thanked him, squeezing in.

In the doctor's room, Frédéric fidgeted. Only when Dr. F reiterated that the baby was doing just fine did he relax and turn his full attention to the ultrasound image on the screen. Curled inside me, our child was perfectly profiled, offering us the clearest view to date of an upturned nose and prominent upper lip. "Look," I pointed excitedly. "Your mouth."

At that moment on the screen a hand bobbed up, displaying a delicate fan of fingers. *"Regarde, il nous fait signe!"* Frédéric exclaimed. In French *bébé* is a masculine noun, and in conversation our child was not "peanut" or "twinkle" or any of the other cute diminutives we'd heard parents use, but simply the pronoun *il*. When I was on my own, though, with a palm pressed to my tight dome to feel the movements inside, I spoke in English to "my little one."

"You don't want to know whether it's a boy or a girl, do you?" checked Dr. F, who had been busy measuring the size of the head, which although disproportionately large to our eyes was apparently normal. It was common for French couples to know the sex from the outset; it was me who'd insisted on keeping the surprise. But faced with this little waving person my resolve crumbled. "What do you think?" I turned to Frédéric, whose eyes instantly brightened.

Pressed to tell, Dr. F chuckled. "You can probably see for yourselves. There's no doubt, *c'est un garçon.*"

People had been telling me as much for months, especially Polynesians. Boys sit low, the fruit vendor at Mo'orea's port had advised, nodding at the bell hang of my stomach when I went to buy yet more *solo* papaya, the small sweet variety. A girl makes a higher, more spread-out bump, Nelly confirmed sagely. Yet privately I was convinced they were wrong. The child who for years had lived in my imagination was a daughter—for some reason this is most often the case for women who undergo infertility treatment. And so hearing the news in Dr. F's rooms, I was stunned.

I was hardly an expert on little girls but young boys were completely foreign territory. On many occasions with friends,

I'd been amazed—all right, appalled—at the surging hormonal energy of their sons. This rowdiness was much more evident in Australia than in France, where children were not permitted to charge through houses or burst noisily into adults' space or interrupt their conversations. Cultural and social factors must count for something, too.

Even very small boys made me feel out of my depth. I still recalled watching a friend change the diaper of her eight-month-old son, who had lain on the change table frog-kicking delightedly, his small penis—which proportionally speaking was huge—stuck up like a Dutch baby carrot between two rolling plums. An arc of pee shot Jane below the eye and kept on hosing. "Quick, the diaper," she called. Forgetting it was in my hands, I just stood there, dumbfounded.

A little boy with boy bits that would stage impertinent erections and get up to all sorts of mischief? It was time to delete for good the scenes of my imaginary daughter, skipping gaily in the red Bonpoint coat. It was time to come up with some new baby names, something other than Polynesian Poema and French Fannie (which had caused consternation among English-speaking friends—think of the teasing she'll get, they protested). Frédéric was elated. *"Un garçon? Mais c'est superbe!"* I was delighted, too. It just took a day or two to get my head around it.

⌒

A few cloth diapers for vomits
A million disposable diapers
Cotton-wool balls

Change mat

Baby wipes

Lots of face washers

And so on went the list for one and a half pages. One of my oldest friends, Sue had understood that no item was too obvious to mention. If the second trimester was marked by a dreamy playfulness, the final phase of pregnancy was driven by practical preparations. Other helpful lists were e-mailed from France, Sydney and the UK. Sometimes brands were singled out: BabyBjörn carrier got a tick; Peg Perego, whoever she was, had wheels that were too small. There was mention of a bouncy chair that vibrated and played music. But Tahiti, let alone Mo'orea, felt a world away from the designer strollers we'd seen powering along the esplanade at Bondi Beach the day of the pregnancy test. At the scruffy, Chinese-run general stores baby gear was roughly thirty years out of date. Strollers snapped open and shut like cheap umbrellas; they didn't have tires that needed pumping up or fancy carriages that clicked onto shapely frames. Living on the island we had discovered a simple truth: take away the plethora of choice in material goods and you don't miss it. Once in a while, remembering the flair and whimsy that went into Paris boutique displays, I missed the pleasure of window shopping. But there was beauty, too, in keepings things simple.

At the Carrefour hypermarket on Tahiti, we found cot sheets, cloths and tiny outfits in size 000. Soon enough we'd have to sort out how they fitted and fastened. In a matter of days we'd discover all sorts of uses for simple squares of fabric—sunshades, wraps, burp cloths, vomit mops, mosquito barriers for tender flesh. In preparation for the baby's arrival

I washed everything in gentle soap. Pegged on the line, blousing in the sunlight, the cotton singlets and bodysuits looked so sweet and innocent. All-in-ones with feet took merry steps, stirred by the breeze. Frédéric went back inside for the camera and then we stood staring in wonder. How exactly did one swaddle? Would our little one really be that little?

For all the romantic ideas I may have had about motherhood, childbirth itself inspired far less fantasy. Terror might have first been stirred by a childbirth video we had been shown as part of Year 10 human biology at school. It was probably tamer than I remember and certainly it ended happily, but to impressionable sixteen-year-olds, watching the baby's head crown between a pair of legs was like a horror movie. We did not marvel at the creative potential of our own bodies. There were shrieks of "Oh my God" when it was revealed that sensitive parts might tear or have to be cut. When one girl asked in disbelief "Why would you?" her remark didn't seem facetious. "Well, if your own mothers hadn't been willing to go through it you wouldn't be here," the teacher had pointed out mildly.

Years later, when friends began having children, few painted the actual birth process in terms of the elation and empowerment so often described in books. One dear friend, a fabulous mother to two teenage children, spoke of a lingering sense of failure. "I completely fell for the whole natural-birth fantasy," she sighed. "I wanted to be one of those women who pushes through without pain relief. Instead I screamed the place down for someone to just come and kill me." There was no postpartum hormonal high, either. Instead she described a "perfect stillness" cradling her daughter for the first time.

Once, when a friend rang from a Sydney hospital to announce the arrival of his son—born healthy but following a full-blown, drawn-out emergency—unthinkingly I rushed into congratulations. "Amazing news," I gushed, "just amazing." In a voice cracked by fatigue and the emotional trauma of his wife's suffering, he repeated my word as though it were in a foreign language. "*Amazing?* I suppose that's one way of putting it," he answered at last, then started to cry.

For those lucky enough to experience it, perhaps the supreme joy of giving birth is simply too momentous to describe. When an Australian friend in Paris decided to have her third child at home, complaining that the French system was too interventionist and conventional, she seemed to me insanely brave. The baby came so fast there was no time to light the scented candle or play Bach: her daughter was born on the bathroom floor while the midwife was stuck in traffic. In photos taken minutes after by the shell-shocked husband, my friend sat atop a pile of blood-soiled towels. Babe in arms, lipstick freshly applied, she looked not only euphoric but radiantly confident, as if after this ultimate accomplishment her body could do anything.

Still, when Dr. F had said a caesarean was strictly necessary, I felt not disappointment at missing a transcendental life experience but relief. Abdominal surgery was something I knew: it was an operation some years before involving a deep, vertical incision that now made natural birth too risky. After all the medical intervention with IVF treatment it seemed pointless to worry about more. The caesarean was scheduled two weeks ahead of my due date, a standard precaution aimed at reducing the risk of going into labor before. It would take place in the morning. I was given instructions to arrive at the clinic the previous afternoon with my hospital bag plus my own pillow and bed linen.

⌒

At Tahiti's Beachcomber hotel, the *tiare* behind Frédéric's ear pointed up jauntily, as if at any moment the bud might launch into the stars. My scarlet hibiscus bloom kept falling out and I wondered again how Polynesian women got theirs to stay put. "Wrong ear," Frédéric pointed out helpfully. "It should be your left." I could never remember which side meant "happily taken" and which side signaled availability. Some fifteen kilometers away, Mo'orea rose black against a gold-leaf sky that was fast acquiring an antique patina. Nearby, the swimming pool glowed like a green candle. On our table, champagne fizzed festively in our flutes. Next to my camera lay a packet of Frédéric's favorite slim cigars. While I might not be having much of a last hurrah, he was up for a night of celebration.

"*Manuia*," he said, raising his flute. "To us. To our baby. To a new life."

Actually I don't recall what we toasted. Only the hot pain that was still wringing my insides as our glasses chinked.

For a few months now I'd been getting the mild Braxton Hicks contractions that are the body's way of preparing for the real thing. That morning in the lagoon, they'd come on a bit more intensely. By now my stomach made quite a drag in the water and I swam slowly, letting the lagoon take my weight. Uncomfortable though the spasms were, they didn't really hurt. After a few minutes of me treading water the cramps stopped. To be on the safe side, I headed back to shore.

"*S'il vous plaît*," may we see the wine list? Frédéric addressed a slim-hipped *rae rae* waiter, then turned back to the menu. "I can't decide between the New Zealand lamb and the tuna," he murmured.

By the third wringing pain I was wishing I'd paid more attention in my prenatal class. Going into labor was not meant to be part of my birth experience. All the talk about waters breaking, contractions, breathing and pushing had seemed irrelevant. Was this *it*? These contractions felt very different from the benign Braxton Hicks variety. Each one rolled and squeezed, more powerful than the last, as if my body was building up to something.

I cleared my throat. "Er, I think we'd better go to the hospital." I had no desire to cut short the evening but I confess it was a bit of a thrill to deliver that line. Briefly I explained the pains.

Frédéric looked disbelieving. "But your due date's not for another two weeks." Walking to the car park he assured me, "They'll tell us it's a false alarm."

There was an acceleration of activity once the midwife examined me. A phone call to my obstetrician, who gave instructions for medication to be administered to try to calm the contractions. Then more phone calls to other parts of Clinique Paofai. "The caesarean will be first thing tomorrow, a day early," the midwife explained. "Assuming the medication works, otherwise it will take place during the night." She said something about centimeters and my cervix but the stages of dilation were another aspect of natural birth I hadn't taken in. Frédéric had the crestfallen look of a man who knew he would never get his rosemary-basted lamb, red wine and cigars. I felt a little shocked, too. Everything had seemed so neat and planned, down to our booking at the hotel for a last night together and the definite delivery date. Now Mother Nature had pipped us all—our son was ready to come into the world. The midwife looked at us in an amused way, as if she'd just noticed something. "This is your first," she stated. "There's nothing to worry about. Babies come when they're ready." And so the birth day was moved from Thursday to Wednesday—an insignificant detail in the scheme of things but with one important consequence. The hospital roster was not the same.

Early on in the pregnancy we had raised with Dr. F the issue of Frédéric attending the birth. It wasn't usual in the territory for husbands to be present during caesareans but Dr. F had willingly agreed, as had the anesthetist. But ultimate power rested with whoever was responsible for the *bloc opératoire* on the day. Now that I was to have the caesarean early, the senior nurse who had given her consent would not be on duty. After greeting us the next morning Dr. F lowered his voice. "*Bonne chance,*" he said sympathetically. "I'm afraid this one never says yes."

As I lay ready in a cotton hospital smock, showered and shaved, a thin, frowning woman blew into the room, as briskly efficient as the hospital air-conditioning. "*Bonjour madame,*"

Frédéric began politely. "My wife and I—we talked this over months ago with Dr. F who is quite okay with it—we are very much hoping I can attend the birth. Sarah, you see, is Australian and most hospitals there let partners attend so this really means a great deal to her."

I thought this might be too much information and apparently so did the nurse, because she glanced up sharply from her clipboard.

"It may be the *fashion* elsewhere," she said frostily, "but it is not the practice at this hospital. This is a surgical procedure, monsieur." She gazed unblinkingly at him over no-nonsense reading spectacles. "I'm afraid it's out of the question." Tutting in the French manner, which always sounded to me like Skippy in a poor humor, she strode out of the room, muttering to a junior nurse about how the last husband had fainted on her.

Given the chance, I would have made a scene—begged, shouted, wept. But all I could do was shoot Frédéric a distressed look as my trolley bed was wheeled out of the room and down the corridor toward the operating room, while he tore in the opposite direction after the nurse who never said yes. But by the time the anesthetist inserted the long needle into my back Frédéric was there, kitted up in gown and hairnet, looking extremely pleased with himself. "How did you change her mind?" I asked later. I thought perhaps he had got furious and demanding. Or poured out a sob story about having waited not nine months to witness this event but many years. "*Mais non,*" Frédéric shook his head emphatically. "That would never have worked. I told her how much I esteemed her professional judgment and that of course she was right to have the interests of mother and child at heart." He held up a tutorial finger. "You have to start with flattery. The aim is to seduce the person with your respect."

"Like a courtier trying to win a favor from the king," I'd joked.

He nodded. *"Exactement."*

⌣⌣

My upper body had been cut off from my lower body: that was how it felt once the epidural kicked in. A white screen stretched across my rib cage, blocking any view of my lower half. Lying on my back, I could just see the masked faces of my obstetrician and five or six others down by my feet. There was a whirring sound followed by a faint but unmistakable odor of burned flesh—mine, presumably. The first incision goes through the abdomen, I'd read in a birth book. The "bikini cut" it was called, as though it were something you might get done for fun on holiday, in the same manner as tattoos or dreadlocks. A second, smaller one opens up the uterus, though it may be made bigger by tearing, which apparently causes less bleeding than cutting. It was surreal knowing this was happening, but the idea was not troubling— the pethidine had worked its charms. The room was very quiet. Frédéric sat beside my head as instructed: under no circumstances was he allowed to glimpse the procedure, the strict nurse had lectured. We exchanged a few whispered words but mainly we just squeezed hands excitedly.

It was when they started rummaging inside me that things started to feel odd. It seems an omission now but no one, not my doctor nor the birth book I'd read, nor friends who'd had C-sections, had mentioned that the business of extracting the baby might be very physical. While natural birth required pushing, I wasn't aware that caesarean births involved so much pulling. No one had described being able to feel the pressure of being pinned down by nurses while the doctor tugged. Or the squelching: it sounded as if they were ankle deep in mud on the other side of the white curtain. With only a little encouragement I thought the baby would slip out, seal-like. It would be very clean and clinical.

"Excuse me," I said faintly. "Is something wrong? Is the baby stuck? I feel a bit funny."

Behind the surgical masks, there was murmuring. A male voice spoke reassuringly: "Everything's fine, not long now." More anesthetic or gas must have been administered, because the squeamish feeling faded. I had lost track of time—later it would be astonishing to learn that only ten minutes had passed since the first incision. All of a sudden there was more pressure and then a new energy in the room: quick footsteps, louder talking, movement. There was not the bleating *weeh weeh* cry that I'd thought all newborns made. No *happy birthday, baby* cheers from the medical staff, as I'd seen once in an American documentary. But my son was here now, I just knew.

What he made of his entry will remain a mystery—unless of course one day he embarks on one of those rebirthing experiences. The journey from the secure, watery womb into the wide world of air and breath must surely be the most extraordinary any human being undertakes—apart, perhaps, from the journey that awaits us at the other end. Occasionally, lingering in the shoals, I had squeezed my eyes shut to try to imagine how my baby must feel, floating in darkness. By the end, pushed against my curved walls, it must have been claustrophobic. Was it liberating to break out? Perhaps after the confining security, the new space felt like a disorienting void—like my first glimpse of bottomless ocean as a scuba diver. Was the air-conditioned room cold and dry after the warm amniotic waters? The operating room with its harsh lighting and shrill sounds must have seemed unfriendly. But then amid the noise and flashes he might have discerned one voice he knew from the inside.

Frédéric had crossed the room and was standing by a nurse and they were both leaning over an unseen table. It seemed aeons but it was only a few minutes before he returned, aglow with tender pride, carrying his son in his arms. *"Tout va bien, tout va bien, tout va bien, il est superbe,"* Frédéric reassured me. The neonatal nurse then gently lifted our baby from his father's arms and carefully laid him across my chest. She spoke softly. "Have a cuddle with *Maman, bébé.* Don't move, *Maman,* that's the way, you need to keep very still for the doctor."

There remained six other people in the room to sew and staple me together, layer by layer, in what is the most drawn-out part of the operation. But from then on I was only aware of the three of us. Cocooned together in this windowless room of stark whites and easy-to-wipe metal surfaces, we were our own little island. "Hello my little one," I whispered to the darling face with the high forehead, the head smooth as a bubble, the mouth with the defined top lip, the soft fan of eyelashes, the purple filigree of blood vessels across the closed lids, the shell ears, the satiny suggestion of eyebrows, the sweet nose, the starfish hands. Given the size of my stomach by the end, I'd expected something more robust than this detailed, delicate creation. I couldn't believe how smooth his skin was, how long his bandy legs were. "Hello Oliver." We'd wanted something easily pronounceable for French and English speakers, and that was the one name Frédéric and I agreed on, once we knew we were having a boy. "It's you, you're here." After all the prayer candles, after the hoping and trying, they were my words.

It was an agreeably uneventful day in the maternity ward at Clinique Paofai: three healthy babies and straightforward deliveries; mine was the only caesarean. Around the world, approximately 250 children shared the same birth minute as our son. By the end of the day there would be half a million new lives on Earth. The numbers were insane. Yet every one of them was surely a little miracle—each one merited a message inscribed in stone, like the plaques I used to read in Paris nailed to the church wall. Only a single tile would not be big enough to contain my gratitude.

I stared in awe at my baby boy, whose pink fingers wrapped like teeny tentacles around one of mine. Words, wonderful words, sounded a joyous carillon inside my head.

It's not a crime to hope, you know.

A lovely embryo.

Une grossesse précieuse.

Maman, the nurse had said.

SEVENTEEN

They were a blur those first weeks and months. One day ran into another, day into night, and no doubt fatigue smudged everything more. A newborn baby has no concept or care for conventions of time and we lived by what seemed at first a most erratic cycle of feeds and sleeps. With me still shuffling around after the surgery, Frédéric had taken some time off work. Yet even with the two of us there, the task of giving a tiny person a bath, say, could swallow up most of a morning.

At about three weeks of age, just as we were getting into the swing of things, our placid son discovered his lungs. When darkness fell in the sudden way it did on the island, Oliver became inconsolable. According to the literature this new phase of wakefulness was part of a growing awareness of the world. Yet knowing it was normal did not make it less bewildering. The bellowing, which could last several hours, set off one dopey dog after another until a daisy chain of barking extended around the coast from our house. Against the moonlit lagoon, father and son would be one shadow, pacing up and down the beach until eventually the crying subsided.

Toward the end of the first month Mom flew in. Dad stayed back in France to finalize their purchase: after scouring the country's southwest they had found their dream home. Placing the small bundle in her arms was a moment of sweet symbolism for me, underpinned by a strong sense of being part of a cycle. There I was, a mother in front of my own mother, and there was Mom, a grandmother for the first time, holding her grandson. Like saying the words "I'm pregnant," this was a scene I had imagined many times. My parents had followed each attempt, remembered the dates of my final blood tests, and then after debating whether to call had to search for the right words of encouragement and sympathy. They'd worried for me, though they'd tried not to show it. My heart swelled with pride as she sat on the cane couch outside, no-nonsense Mom not noticing the lagoon or the view, tenderness all over her face as she nodded at Oliver. "Look at you. Aren't you a clever boy? Yes, you *are* beautiful."

⌒

"He made this really odd sound today," I reported one evening to Frédéric, who by now was back at work. We were sitting on the back porch eating the fish pie Mom had made. Oliver was soundly sleeping. "It was a totally different cry," I went on. "Not upset but feisty, like he just didn't want me changing his diaper."

Mom nodded. She'd spent most of the day in the kitchen

baking but she had witnessed the little turn, too. We'd both been so struck that we'd just stared at Oliver, lying red-faced on the change table, barking furiously at us. "It was like he was yelling NO," I added.

"Maybe he's going to be like me," Frédéric grinned. "I used to throw awful tantrums."

I turned to look at him. "Really?" It was hard to picture; he was such a gentle man.

"Oh yes, I was terrible," he chuckled. "Once, in a golf competition, I got so furious with myself I hurled my club into a tree." Frédéric beamed proudly. "I got suspended from the club for that."

"I'm sure the little boy was just hungry," Mom offered, seeing my face.

"And I was *always* talking, I never shut up," continued Frédéric, the childhood memories unspooling now. "*Arrête, mais arrête, tu es un moulin à paroles!* My mother was always saying that."

"A windmill of words," I translated for Mom. Inexplicably I felt put out by these revelations. Who knew what Oliver's cry meant? But staring at the small person in my arms, I sometimes pondered his pot-luck inheritance. With all the possible genetic combinations, one set of parents can produce literally trillions of different children. Which resemblances or personality traits would bubble to the surface? Would our son have my father's unfailing patience or my father-in-law's legendary impatience? What flaws and strengths were part of Oliver's makeup already and which other ones would he learn from our behavior? It was way too soon to know. But I learned something about my husband that night. Up until then all the family stories had been about how engaging Frédéric was as a boy, how enthusiastic and interested he was in everything. There'd been no mention of tantrums or verbal diarrhea.

Now you tell me, I felt like saying.

There'd been one last ten-day deluge to mark the end of the wet season just before Mom arrived. Before putting Oliver to bed I shook every fold of his mosquito net, checking and double-checking there was none lurking in the veil. I went around the garden overturning all the potted bromeliads, whose stiff, fanning leaves collected rainwater, creating tiny pails that were perfect for egg-laying. There was good cause for extra vigilance: this wet season so many cases of dengue fever had been reported that anyone flying from Tahiti to New Caledonia automatically had their temperature taken on arrival. A high fever—a symptom of the mosquito-transmitted virus—meant being immediately quarantined. In French Polynesia seven or eight children, mostly very young babies, die of the disease every year. At night Frédéric would swipe the air dementedly with an electrified insect racket he had found at a Chinese corner store in Pape'ete. "What an invention," he'd enthuse. Like a chef proudly show-ing off a dish, he would hold up the racket while a mosquito sizzled on the wires: "*Moustique grillé, merveilleux!*" I'd have to prize the treasured toy from his grip to get a go. The burst of crackling was a most satisfying sound. We only regretted there was no counter on the racket to keep tally.

Still, when Mom started feeling tired and nauseous toward

the end of her second week we didn't think to blame mosquitoes but a stomach bug. One morning she got up looking pale and drawn. "I'm fine, I'm fine really," Mom assured me feebly. "Perhaps I'll just go back for a little rest." A moment later there was a sickening thwack from the spare bedroom. Racing around the patio I found my mother slumped crookedly on the hard tiled floor.

At the small but brand-new emergency wing of the island's clinic, the doctor examined the red, itchy patches across her chest and hands. Temperature, headache, vomiting, rash— even before he made the pronouncement I recognized the symptoms of dengue fever. They let her come home the next day but for the remainder of her month on the island Mom needed a lot of rest. "Fat lot of good I am," she said ruefully. "I came here to help and now look at me." Guite, bless her, popped by with a wholesome lamb-and-lentil stew; Alain called in with freshly made *poisson cru.*

It would be a full year before Mom got her old energy back. "She's seventy," the doctor on Mo'orea had told me. "It's going to hit harder." I suppose seeing Mom look frail was a poignant reminder of the life cycle, too. A new generation comes along and suddenly we're parents and grandparents, and like it or not, we're all one link further along the chain.

It was at night, when Oliver and I were the only two awake in the house, that I became aware of the complex chemistry of motherly love. Perhaps it had something to do with feeling safe inside by the soft glow of the bedside lamp, draped in one of my sarongs, while outside the darkness hinted at unknown dangers. "Love" seemed far too simple a word for the waves of emotion I got staring at his small, frowning face as my milk filled his tummy. Fear, it is said, lies at the heart of the mothering experience.

As Oliver's eyelids flickered and grew heavy I'd silently pray and lecture. Please God let him have a long life. Help him grow up to be healthy and strong and sensible. Motorbikes are out of the question, little one. I did not feel hypocritical in the slightest laying down this rule, despite having ridden for years on the back of a Kawasaki 1100. I thought a lot of my own mother and her ceaseless, shifting anxieties for her children. "I'm moving on from you," she used to announce occasionally. "My new worry's Mark/Anna/Sarah." She still says that actually.

Hats and sunscreen were incidental in our house, but for much of her working life Mom, a physiotherapist, treated young quadriplegics and paraplegics, and understandably she had an obsession about spines. Instructions were issued threateningly as we tore out of the house: Don't you go diving into the shallow end, don't you go breaking your neck. Mo–om, we'd groan sometimes. We kno–ow. Usually we grinned and rolled our eyes because, of course, we were immortal.

Well, my friend, I nodded sternly at Oliver, captive in my arms. You can grin and roll your eyes at me all you like.

By then his eyelids would have fluttered shut. Sleep comes over babies like a spell. A hand might be caught hovering like a star in the air. When this happened I'd gently close the splayed fingers, lower the small arm and then kiss his brow, happy to note the little crease had gone.

After Mom left I found myself alone for twelve hours a day with a baby who grew not more settled but increasingly discontent. Distress was triggered by the most minor events: burping, farting, pooing and feeding. His body would go rigid as he wailed, his legs stuck out like rods, his fingers splayed, though he was unable yet to produce tears. A lot of the milk that went down came back up, though it took me a while to realize this meant his tummy was empty and he might be hungry. At Clinique Paofai, seeing Oliver for the first time, Guite had affectionately likened him to a prawn. And compared to the solid Polynesians with their thick thatches of black hair, he had looked small, pink and peeled. Now her description acquired new meaning. My baby wasn't thriving. "He really is a shrimp," I told Frédéric tearfully one night.

"Colic." The pediatricians's unperturbed tone after I'd described Oliver's symptoms was an immense relief and for this alone I could have hugged her. "He might have a bit of reflux, too." Formerly the head of pediatrics at Tahiti's main hospital, now semi-retired, Yvette was neat, direct, sensible, a bit old school—which suited me just fine. Thirty-five years of experience provided a long perspective on trends and about-turns in medical thinking. "It's not the recommended position," she told me, "but you might find sleeping him on his tummy helps." After checking Oliver's weight she advised supplementing breast milk with formula. Holding him more upright while he fed was another tip.

It was Yvette who gave us the first clues to our son's personality, when he had reached the grand age of just three months. "*Très éveillé*," very alert, she declared after checking his reflexes, eyes and ears. His young fingers gripped hers forcefully as she pulled him up to a sitting position. She bent down so they were at eye level and he studied her glasses with interest. "*Benh oui*, you're going to be a busy boy. You'll keep Mom on her toes, I can see that." Her eyes slid over my fatigued face as we sat down again, either side of her big desk. "*Eveillé* babies tend to be *exigeants*," she told me. "They're full-on but wonderfully rewarding. He'll have a zest for life this one, you'll see!"

That evening as I recounted our visit to the pediatrician to Frédéric, I was reminded of a consultation in Paris years ago when the word "*exigeant*" also came up. "That's exactly how the vet described Maddie when he examined her the first time," I said a bit flatly. In fact, Yvette might have been describing a West Highland terrier—zest for life, rewarding, demanding.

We both stared at our dog, asleep on the terrace some meters away. In her youth she had been crazy about children but so far she'd paid Oliver scant attention. At eight, she was getting on and a few licks of his ears had sated her curiosity. "Maddie Mads," I called sweetly. "Maddie." I patted my thigh. Needless to say, back in Sydney far less encouragement would have brought my brother's two boxers bounding over, spraying slobber everywhere. But West Highland terriers don't stoop to devotion. One brown eye cracked open, considering. Then closed again. Stubborn, plucky, joyful, companionable, our Mads also had a healthy sense of her own importance. It was startling—scary—how little our careful parenting had done to mold her Scottish character.

"She said we'll need to be firm with him later on," I said, getting back to the visit to the pediatrician.

Frédéric and I had already had the discipline discussion countless times—well before Oliver had been conceived. Years of observing other families had provided a parenting school of sorts. Many times we had hypothesized as to what *we* would have done had a certain misbehaving child been ours. Neither of us saw any harm in the occasional little smack on the rump. Having lived so long in France, we were both suspicious of the child-rearing fads that swept through English-speaking countries, the many books espousing the latest theories. While cultural differences might conceivably have divided us, a common view had evolved over the years by means of a cherry-picking process. At mealtimes and at restaurants our son would behave like *French* children. Evenings were to be our time, adult time—at least just as soon as Oliver had settled into a routine. I entertained another fantasy, too, gleaned from Paris dinner parties where children filed out to peck the guests politely on both cheeks and then quickly disappeared. There was a lot to be said, I thought, for the way the French raised their children.

Australian youngsters, on the other hand, seemed to have little concept of being seen and not heard. At barbecues and dinners they often buzzed boisterously around the table and the adults. I wanted to shoo them away, though this is a privilege reserved for parents with children. Yet these same kids also exuded a charming spontaneity and lack of inhibitions. There was a frankness to the way they looked you in the eye. "I hope Oliver is like that," Frédéric said a few times.

Needless to say our expertise on the subject of raising children was entirely academic. Hypothesizing and cherry-picking were all very well but what we didn't have was hands-on experience. There was nothing by which to measure our potential as parents—unless you counted Maddie.

"You've been firm with her and look how she's turned out," teased Frédéric. I shot him a look. When it came to discussing her failures she was invariably *my* dog.

Maddie, bless her, chose that moment to belatedly obey. A slow stretch rippled her hull, which had been lying beached on the porch like an unseaworthy sailing boat. With a sigh she drew herself up on her stout legs and ambled over. Island time suited Mads. "Good girl, good girl," I cheered, vindicated. Reaching my chair she sat and sniffed the air a few times, detecting the remains of chicken on my plate. Her laser gaze bore into me. The insistent heat of it was unmistakable: not obedience nor anything as demeaning as devotion but blatant self-interest.

"Aïe, aïe, aïe." Above my son's wailing I could hear Guite tutting as she walked up our drive. At seventy-nine she was as alert and energetic as ever but a bad hip made her hobble. At some point during her visit she might ask if I'd seen the walking stick she was now supposed to use and express irritation at having misplaced it yet again. But it seemed to me she was happier without it. "It makes me feel old," she grumbled. "How am I supposed to garden with a walking stick?" It was pointless reminding her she wasn't meant to be gardening, not for the moment. Her doctor had warned pruning with heavy secateurs was not helping.

She took Oliver from me, her eyes soft. "What's all this

misery, eh? Why all the noise? Tell *Mamie*." She flipped him onto his stomach and lay him across her knee as easily as if he were one of her *beignets de bananes* in a pan. *"Raconte, raconte,"* she encouraged, stroking his back. Oliver stopped crying and cocked his head, showing off his new neck control. When it came to handling him, she and Nelly had none of my initial tentativeness and often they managed to calm him when nothing I'd done had made the slightest difference.

The *miri* bath was their idea. It'll soothe him, help him settle, was all they said. Only later did I discover the true purpose of the wild basil bath: it was the old Polynesian remedy for chasing away evil spirits. Whether or not either Guite or Nelly believed in traditional healing methods I couldn't say—certainly both of them relied on conventional medicine. But then faith in one did not preclude belief in the other. When a traditional healer from one of the outer islands arrived for a short stay on Mo'orea, so many people flocked to see him that the vehicles on the roadside were declared a traffic hazard by the gendarmerie. Perhaps when it came to the *miri* bath, they simply thought anything was worth a try.

Like a couple of witches, I joked when they told me about picking the wild basil the day before, then boiling the leaves for many hours in a cauldron of water. This cracked them up—Guite laughed so heartily she had to wipe her eyes—though it didn't occur to me I'd hit the nail on the head. I scooped up some water in my hand. It was tea colored and warmed to just the right temperature. The aroma was mild and earthy, only faintly reminiscent of basil.

Oliver lay in the warm, dark water, pale and pleased, waving a little hard-on as the two women gently sponged and splashed him. Nelly wore the solemn expression she reserved for important occasions; Guite clapped and showered Oliver with compliments, calling him *petit prince* and *beau* and well-endowed. Afterward he was laid out on the couch on his stomach, beneath the photo of Guite as a young woman, looking like a Tahitian princess with cascading hair, flower and smile. Four hands massaged his back and buttocks with *tiare*-scented *monoi*.

"*Il va mieux*," Nelly smiled one month later.

She was right. Oliver no longer looked like a shrimp. He had put on weight and was crying less. Yet he was an *éveillé* little fellow, there was no doubt, and my own fatigue had not abated. Some days I thought of going to collect leaves to make my own witches' brew. How lovely it would be to loll in a tub of curative warm tea. Oh yes, a *miri* bath might be just what every new mother needs.

EIGHTEEN

"I'm going stir-crazy," I confided over the phone to Sue, my old friend. I felt guilty saying it, like she might think I wasn't happy being a mother. Maybe an increased capacity for guilt is one of the unspoken legacies of success through IVF. Having had my longing fulfilled, it was hard to admit to ordinary frustrations and difficulties. Though with two children of her own, Sue was already familiar with the way your world suddenly shrinks when you have a baby.

"You've got to get out more," she advised sensibly. "Why don't you go to the local park? You might meet some other mothers. Take him for a walk, babies love being in strollers. It'll do you good, too."

It was moments like this that I felt I inhabited another planet—one very different from the world I had glimpsed in Australia, where mothers with young children met at cafés that offered crayons and babyccinos, or at outdoor playgrounds with childproof gates and spongy surfaces. Friends spoke of story readings at local libraries, special cinema screenings for mums and bubs, art talks for adults tailored to the time constraints of small children. I would have jumped at the chance to join in any of these activities—a mothers' group would have been good. Yet the concept of strangers getting together for social purposes is quite foreign to the French. In Paris, women often returned to work when the baby was three months old, which was pretty much how it went in this territory, too. As for Polynesians, surrounded by relatives, they had no need to create support networks.

To friends cooped up in tiny apartments with children, snapshots of our daily life would have appeared idyllic. Meandering about our large garden, Oliver in my arms, picking delicately fragrant *tiare* buds and the more potent *taina* blooms. Or the two of us sitting on the beach, watching the afternoon ferries from Pape'ete grow rapidly into bigger dots as they drew closer. Some mornings I even managed to get a swim in before Frédéric left for work. Yet Sue had underscored a truth known to every stay-at-home parent. For sanity's sake, you need to get out of the house. Possibly Oliver needed to, too, now that he had passed his first half-year milestone. While his colicky symptoms had improved, late afternoons—the witching hour—remained challenging. Sometimes I wondered if his grumps weren't just frustration at being in the same place, day after day.

"There aren't any parks," I told Sue. "Or footpaths." Saying this aloud brought home the truth. There was *nowhere* to push a stroller. Even Pape'ete, which involved a half-day excursion, offered no possibilities for a pleasant walk in the shade. Yet our conversation got me thinking. It was no good sitting at home feeling stuck. We had to go somewhere; we had to do something.

A few test drives on one of the short dirt tracks near home put paid to the idea of afternoon promenades in the stroller. It was a fancy one, too: smart green with large capable wheels that were supposed to roll smoothly over most terrain. Frédéric had protested indignantly upon discovering that I'd asked Mom to bring it over with her. It was precisely the sort of expensive baby item we'd vowed not to buy. In the event, the large wheels had not been up to the potholed surface. On we jounced for a few hundred meters in what must have been a jarring ride for the small passenger.

By now Oliver was old enough to sit in a front-facing, strap-on baby carrier—a confusing arrangement of flaps, straps and clips. Before his birth, hiking had been one of our regular weekend activities. With a bottle of rosé, some cheese and a baguette in our packs, we'd scramble up one of the steep trails that led to a pass or ridge with spectacular views. With Oliver I opted for something less ambitious. Ma'atea was only a ten-minute drive from home. There, a dirt track wound past the houses on the flat and climbed gently inland and up. It wasn't a strenuous hike nor was it a tranquil promenade. In a pack on my back I carried a large bottle of water and we wore sunscreen and hats. If we didn't dally we could get to the old mango tree, which served as a turnaround point, and then back to the car within just over an hour.

"Look at the bright curtains," I chattered as we passed the

last of the painted weatherboard houses and trees practically ringing with bells of fruit. Although the sun was easing itself down the sky, the bowl-shaped valleys trapped the afternoon heat and Oliver quickly grew clammy in the fabric carrier. But he would chirrup sweetly, grabbing fistfuls of the thick air which he tried to stuff in his mouth. Sometimes a stray dog would follow us, attracted by Maddie or the possibility of friendly human company, but if there was more than one I'd raise my stick and send them scrambling. I'd become wary of the hostile possibilities of the pack since being surrounded by snarling dogs once on the wild end of Temae beach.

After about twenty minutes the trail emerged from beneath the forest canopy, giving us a first glimpse of the island's green heart. It was the abrupt verticality that made the vista so breathtaking: the peaks may have been less than 1000 meters but their height was exaggerated by their spire-like forms. My skin always prickled at the sight. Here the sun did not fall in a soft, dappled way but vaulted from pyramid to pyramid, creating a resplendent pattern of light and shade. The colors were so densely textured you could almost taste them—lime, banana, pomelo, papaya, passionfruit!

Intimidating though they had seemed at first sight from the ferry, I now saw the mountains as friends. It comforted me to look up and see Mouaputa, keeping an eye on things with the hole through its peak. The remarkable formations called for a powerful, feminine voice on the car stereo during our many tours of the island—something that could dip and soar. Not Jane Birkin or Carla Bruni but k.d. lang belting out "Hallelujah," Sinead O'Connor hollering her heart out. On our painting expeditions what I so wanted to capture, but couldn't, was this surging earthly power—so different from the evanescent, lyrical, horizontal beauty of the lagoon. While I'd yet to think of a painter who might capture the dancing light in the water, the mighty volcanic mountains sang out for Cézanne. With his masterful sense of architecture in nature, the French artist would have done justice to the structure and sculpting.

The rattle of a ute coming down the hill in our direction interrupted these thoughts one day. On weekends, we occasionally passed a family tending their fruit trees, and we could never walk by without having a bag of grapefruit, papaya or limes pressed into our hands. The generosity of Polynesians might be legendary but it's no myth. Weekdays were quiet however. Never before had I encountered anyone this far up the road.

The ute stopped level with me and the driver rested an arm on the open window. The unexpected appearance of an unsmiling stranger made me wary. It is not being alone in nature that we fear but the possibility of meeting other human life.

" *'Ia ora na*," I said, stopping. He didn't say hello back.

"What are you doing here?" he asked curtly. "Where are you going?"

"We're just going for a walk." I smiled ingratiatingly, suddenly wondering if I was trespassing. Was this a private access way? Had I missed a sign saying *tapu*?

"Avec bébé?" He stared hard at me, without glancing away as the younger men often did, as if trying to decide whether the truth was really that simple. It would take a dippy *popa'ā* to hike up a mountain with a young baby in this febrile heat;

252

Polynesians knew to stay indoors in the afternoon. He glanced at Maddie, herself a curiosity compared to the short-haired island dogs with their lumpen heads full of survival skills. Sprawled and panting on the track, her white fur smeared with whatever manure or carcass she had rolled in, she did her pedigree proud.

Although I was standing up and the man in the car was sitting down, somehow he had the advantage. With a woven, worn brim shielding his face, it was difficult to pick his age. But from his patriarchal posture it was obvious he belonged to the generation of elders whose sense of identity was rein-forced by the memory of how things once were. The sort of Polynesian who dressed up for church and never exceeded 50 kilometers on the road and was more comfortable speaking in Tahitian—even if in his day schoolchildren were punished for using a language other than French. The type of *papi* who could show his grandsons exactly how to tie a knot so their precious pirogues would never float away, if only they'd listen.

Beneath his sun hat his eyes scrutinized me. I refrained from telling him the truth. "We were going stir-crazy" was unlikely to win much sympathy. Instead, in a tone that was slightly defensive, I said: "I've got plenty of water."

He nodded, unimpressed. "Where's your car?"

I pointed. "By the river."

He looked straight ahead, as if addressing the houses a kilometer down the road, hidden by lush vegetation. "You shouldn't come here. It isn't safe. You and *bébé* should go home."

I declined his offer of a lift, partly because I didn't fancy hopping into a stranger's car but also because something in me bristled at being ordered to leave. Was it because I was *popa'ā*? Nelly, too, had warned me about my walks—there's too much drinking, too much smoking *paka*, too much fighting in the valleys, she'd said. Though if I listened to Nelly I'd never do anything. This explicit message from a frowning stranger was more difficult to dismiss. As the dust cloud kicked up by the ute melted into the mango sunbeams, I meekly turned and trudged back down the hill.

The truth sank in a few days later when I learned the reason for his insistence. In his prickly way the fellow had been caring. At the time of our encounter, police were still searching for a man who a few days earlier had assaulted a longtime French resident, a woman, off that very track.

⌒

Increasing violence is not an aspect of life limited to island communities. In Australia, I would not dream of heading into the bush alone. But this incident fitted into a broader context of change which, like so much else, seemed curiously amplified on our small island. Elderly Mo'oreans who could recall when the ring road was a rough dirt track and no house was ever locked described the impact of modern life in catastrophic terms. "Life changed too fast here," said Lee, my Tahitian teacher, once when I managed to divert her attention from grammar. She stared out the window with a faraway look in her eyes. "One day people were living off what they could fish and grow. The next, *boum!*" She smacked her hand on the desk. "We were in the atomic age, in the very center of it, literally."

It was in 1995, my first year in France, that Jacques Chirac, who was then president, decided to resume the nuclear tests, sparking international outcry and the worst riots Pape'ete has ever seen. But it wasn't until we moved to the territory and I went to places like Fakarava that the terrible paradox really struck home. France—all the while energetically promoting the territory as paradise to attract French settlers and tourists—violated it an estimated 200-odd times over almost four decades. One can only imagine how the underwater detonations beneath Moruroa and Fangataufa, at the extreme end of the Tuamotu chain, have ravaged the atolls' structures and coral reefs. How much radioactivity was absorbed by the fish and the islanders who continued to eat them because there was no alternative? It's hard to say given the intractable secrecy the French authorities have maintained over the details and data.

But the impact explained by my Tahitian teacher was one I hadn't considered. Beginning in 1963, the nuclear testing period in French Polynesia brought jobs and big salaries. People were needed to build infrastructure. Islanders abandoned villages and plantations, lured by the generous state-paid salaries. With no one growing or producing, the territory's modest but steady exports diminished, while imports skyrocketed as Polynesians developed a taste for Western foods, clothes and new cars. The closure of the testing facilities in 1996 put an end to the nuclear era and the high wages. The French authorities would argue the territory has been amply compensated by a most generous funding package, adroitly negotiated by Gaston Flosse. But many say this era was the final blow to the Tahitian way of life. After that there was no going back, no reversing the rampant consumerism.

"Keeping up with the changes was not a struggle for *popa'ā* and *demis*," Lee said. "They took advantage of them and got good jobs. But not *le petit Polynésien*."

"Is that why you set up this center?" I prompted. The house where I had my lessons was a meeting place for neighborhood youth, who came after school to learn their language and culture and get help with their homework. Lee nodded.

"Ordinary people are just falling further and further behind," she said with a heavy sigh. "It's like another bomb waiting to go off."

⌒⌒

One morning about a month after the news of the valley attack put an end to our afternoon walks, a slight sound at the door made me swivel around fast in my chair. In the rather dim, air-conditioned spare bedroom I was arranging papers and files, having relocated my office when it had begun to stretch across four corners of the living room. After our early spate of *visites*, eighteen months had passed since the last intruder had left wet footprints across the veranda to the back sliding door, which fortunately had been locked. Now, though, the door handle was turning; slowly, quietly. Whoever was about to enter the room didn't want to be heard. I recall an instant of disbelief, as if this suspenseful moment had been cut from a film. But while my heart raced, my thoughts were quite lucid. There was no other exit, nowhere for me to run. Quite possibly he didn't know I was here, which gave me an advantage. *I* must scare *him.*

At the ready, I roared and charged the instant he stepped into the room. Once again only scant details registered, though this time I would not bother the police with them: twenty-something, medium build, shoulder-length black hair, shorts, well built, bare chest. Was it the same guy who had broken in as Isabelle slept in this room? I would wonder later. Fortunately the "visitor" instantly took flight, saving me from having to decide on what to do upon reaching him. The tendency of local men to run from confrontations often leads *popa'a* to label them, disparagingly, as *trouillards*—scaredy cats. Though an intruder who flees seems to me infinitely more decent than one who hangs around.

I tore around the veranda to our bedroom to check on Oliver. The sight of him through the soft folds of mosquito netting, sleeping innocently, must have hit my maternal button. I raced into the living room. Our Polynesian friend Claude kept a baseball bat for such occasions and I grabbed the closest thing we had to one, then ran in the direction the young man had gone, descending the front steps in one leap and running out onto the road. It was empty, suspiciously quiet. There was no sign of anyone. No witnesses. Daniel and Catherine, our dive buddies, were away. Guite was over on Tahiti. Up high, the coconut palms whispered among themselves. He was out there, I knew it, hiding behind a fence, waiting for me to go back inside to make a clear getaway. I stood rigid, hardly breathing, straining to hear a telltale rustle or movement. But the only sound was a whooshing in my eardrums of my own coursing blood. Something primal erupted in me. "You ever come back here I'll kill you, you hear me?" I raised my voice and let rip. "I KNOW YOU CAN HEAR ME. NEXT TIME, YOU'RE DEAD!"

After a minute or so my fury was spent. Delayed shock and fright made my legs feel wobbly. Standing in the middle of the road waving a didgeridoo, handsomely painted with cross-hatching patterns, I must have appeared more nutty than scary. The Indian myna birds didn't swoop as I went through the gate but jiggled and twittered among themselves, excited to see me in such a state. They, too, had seen but would not tell. Perhaps I would ask Clet to pop them off after all.

⌒

When it comes to Tahiti, foreigners either uphold the myth or debunk it. It's a tradition Polynesians are heartily sick of, and in writing about these incidents there is a risk I am simply perpetuating it. If these events gave impetus to our departure, they did not on their own trigger it. Coming face-to-face with an intruder had certainly been unpleasant and there was no doubt that having a baby had increased my sense of feeling stuck and cut off on the island. But equally, it had always been our intention to leave. We had stayed over three years, longer than intended. True to his word, ever since our first Saturday night out on Mo'orea, Frédéric had kept count of our tours of the island. When he announced we'd completed one hundred circumambulations, this milestone seemed another sign. It was time. Creatively speaking, that space inside me no longer felt so empty. The lid may not have blown off the wasabi paste, to use Frédéric's metaphor, but the possibility of squeezing something out one day didn't seem so far-fetched. I grew impatient to get back to the world of public libraries and art exhibitions, of old friends and cinemas, footpaths, parks and cafés.

For some time our departure had been a mirage: every time we got close it shifted into the distance again. As long as Frédéric kept doing his job, head office was in no hurry to relocate him. But then an idea that had been raised some time before was unexpectedly brought back to life. Would he be interested in setting up an office in Sydney? At first we were thrown: Australia? Returning to Paris and our renovated apartment with its not-quite-new elevator had always been our assumption. France was where Frédéric's father lived, his sister, and also my parents now. My sister still lived in London.

Yet the more we thought about it, the more the job seemed like a rare opportunity. Hadn't we in the past talked about living in Australia one day? It would be a fresh challenge for Frédéric—his first experience of living in an English-speaking country. After more than thirteen years away I was no longer sure where I belonged but this was a chance for me to reconnect with my homeland and for Oliver to get to know it as well. In my mind, I drew a line on the world map, tracing our journey from Paris to Tahiti several years before. One option was to backtrack to France; the other was to continue south in a fresh, forward direction. Moving to Australia started to make sense. Perhaps our voyage was always meant to be a longer arc?

There were many details still to be worked out but when a replacement was found for Frédéric in Tahiti our departure was fixed. It was still five months away but the existence of a plan was energizing. I sat down and wrote yet another list: things we had to do before we left.

NINETEEN

In satellite photos taken from space, the oblong scribble of Fakarava reveals many pale, shallow channels across its thread-like width but only two deep, dark openings. Garuae Pass, the gaping gateway we'd hurtled through on our first alarming "drift" dive, stands out clearly, however the slit at the opposite end of the atoll is easy to miss. Indeed, most people have never heard of Tumakohua Pass. Yet to scuba divers it is one of the world's wonders. It was in this channel's gentle currents that the ardent Italian tourist claimed to have flown like a bird; it was there he met God. And so as our departure for Australia grew surer, I planned our fourth and last trip to Fakarava. Only this time, instead of remaining near the main village, we'd take a boat across the immense lagoon to stay in one of several small pensions that house the only human life on the far southern shore.

Low-lying atolls have always mesmerized me and at the sight of the first Tuamotu island any lingering anxieties about our trip dissolved. The night before I'd flown into such a panic about leaving Oliver that I'd insisted on writing a will. Just in case both his parents were taken by tiger sharks or vanished into the deep—as had occurred only recently on Tahiti in a mysterious triple tragedy involving experienced scuba divers whose bodies had never been found. It wasn't simply leaving Oliver for four nights that made me fret but our remote destination, sixty kilometers by boat from Fakarava's airport. While we would be in phone contact there was no fast, direct way for us to get home should anything happen in our absence.

Daylight helped restore perspective, as did Oliver himself, who appeared almost indecently cheerful when we departed. *Na-na, na-na*, he called in Tahitian from Nelly's arms on the front porch, flopping his wrist encouragingly. Now in the air it was as if my own wings were stretching. It felt fantastic to be out of the house. Our reasons for leaving him behind began to sound rational again. A remote islet a sea journey from the nearest pharmacy was not a safe place for a twelve-month-old toddler, unsteady on his feet but a lightning-fast crawler. We'd have spent the whole time worrying about him choking on a piece of broken coral or bolting into the water. My attention shifted back to the circular scribbles below. They had the poignant beauty of garlands laid on the ocean in memory of a surfer and I felt a pang of regret that they might one day be gone.

Depending on the sea, the boat trip to the far side of Fakarava could take two hours and the idea was to set out as soon as we'd landed. But atoll time is even more relaxed and elastic than island time. The owner of the pension where we were booked to stay had apparently partied hard the night before, having arrived at the main village the previous day. After he met us at the airport, there was still the dive gear to collect along with our instructor, and food supplies had to be bought at Rotoava's one-stop store. It was nearly four in the afternoon when we started speeding across the water and I thought how easy it would be to lose your bearings in daylight, let alone in darkness. Fakarava's lagoon felt like open ocean, only without the swell. There was no sign of land ahead, nothing but an unruly hedge of cloud on the horizon. Pretty soon the shore behind us had disappeared from sight, too. Even the chalk mark of our wake was quickly rubbed out. There was no up or down, no sky and earth, just our boat buzzing along like a tiny insect that might easily be crushed between the hemispheres of blue.

Our dive instructor turned and flashed us a relaxed grin. In over two years on the atoll Guillaume must have done this trip countless times yet he sat like a sea dog on the front of the boat, nose to the wind, sun-bleached hair streaming. We grinned back. My hair whipped across my face and Frédéric's stood up on end as though the emptiness had made it electric. Steering the boat lightly with a couple of fingers was our host, Manihi, who owned the *motu* and ran the guest bungalows where we'd booked to stay. A Polynesian of mixed European and island heritage, he was a tall, powerful man whose loose sarong attire didn't seem to fit with the harsh angles of his flat-top crew cut. His appearance, combined with the ease at which the Hinano beer cans were opened and emptied, gave him the dangerous air of a rogue colonel in *Apocalypse Now*, and possibly this heightened the sense of adventure.

Land, when at last it came into view, had an eked-out appearance, as if the long string of atoll we'd left behind had been laid too rashly, leaving only the odd droplet for the southern side. Manihi's *motu* sat fetchingly on the twilit lagoon—all the more fetching for the wind-whipped *aito* trees that stood about 10 meters tall. It must be an ancient survival instinct that makes you scan flat atolls and islets for something to climb.

The next morning Faro, who drove the dive boat, took us to the ocean entrance to the channel, which ran between two *motu*—two little blinis, covered in the typical atoll scrub that looked like mashed peas. Barely 200 meters across, the southern pass was nowhere near as intimidating as Garuae, which was four times as wide. The current would be less frantic, too, Guillaume assured us. We adjusted our masks and I blasted air out of my regulator a couple of times, just to be on the safe side. The sea shone as if it had been polished overnight. "Visibility's going to be amazing," Guillaume enthused. Yet looking overboard I could make out nothing. Deep navigable passes are considered the crown jewels of atolls—literally lifelines for both ocean and humans—but Tumakohua was keeping a lid on its treasure.

As my head slipped beneath the pane and I stared down into *le grand bleu*, fear fluttered in my stomach. Emptiness, exterior or interior, in water or on land, isn't my thing. But before there was time to reach for anyone's hand, the current had carried us firmly but not forcefully to the mouth of the channel, where the floor rose. Then we were skimming through a canyon that widened to a gentle valley, over coral hills and smooth sandy plains rippling with refracted light.

To say the pass was *teeming* with sea life would not adequately convey the surging congestion, the columns of color, the shimmering shoals so dense they caused eclipses, the glittering disco lights that occasionally morphed into ribbons of tiny fish then back into balls again. Several times I braced myself for impact only to find at the last second the "wall" miraculously swerved or parted, after which it would coalesce, not minding me at all. Here were the fish "stained and striped, and even beaked like parrots" that had enraptured Robert Louis Stevenson; the "stupendous fish" that had astonished Matisse—in their hundreds of thousands. Barracudas tracked us like silver arrows and to my delight a jolly Napoléon wrasse bustled over, its plush pattern jiggling a fantastic color inversion. It was terrible to think that across the tropics the numbers of this curious, trusting fish were threatened by the demand for live seafood. In parts of Asia its lubber lips are considered a delicacy, while a whole Napoléon wrasse served straight from a tank can fetch thousands of dollars. By contrast, a surly titan triggerfish took no notice of us and we knew better than to approach as it kicked up a dust storm, building a crater in which to lay eggs. The pass was not a quiet place. Even above the sound of my own gurgling breath I could hear the clicking, chipping, pinging and crunching.

Once I had witnessed another remarkable flux in the natural world, the wildebeest migration in the Serengeti. Yet on the savannah, surrounded by other safari vehicles filled with tourists obsessively snapping pictures, I had felt oddly dispirited—so much a spectator that the wilderness might as well have been a zoo. Whereas now I was simply one fragment of color in an ever shifting kaleidoscopic pattern. For the first time underwater I didn't feel like an intruder. In this vital artery I was just another living creature swept along by the inflow of sea water on its way to flush and refresh the lagoon, carrying with it nutrients for the feeding fish.

This was diving as I'd dreamed it—light, free, effortless. Keeping balance and staying horizontal came naturally in a steady current that didn't threaten to rip off my mask or snatch my air source. Swooping down into bedrock basins, soaring over ridgelines, I wanted to whoop.

I'm flying.

As we entered the lagoon the current eased and a very different wonderland opened up in front of us. My depth gauge read ten meters, eight, then six. Water turned into glass. Gliding over an endless meadow of massive, sculptural blossoms I fell into a blissed-out trance. Until now I'd never paid much attention to coral. Scuba diving off Mo'orea, where much of it was bleached or damaged, it took a leap of imagination to think of it as anything other than some kind of dead plant life. Whereas the fanning, branching, mushrooming formations below were moving testimony to the time and effort put into their creation by millions of tiny creatures whose skeletal remains built up layer upon layer.

Fantastique, incroyable, magnifique, sublime, superbe. Fountains of superlatives spurted from our mouths as soon as our heads were above water. Frédéric and I couldn't stop laughing. Guillaume flicked his shoulder-length hair off his face and grinned at his charges, happy to see how Tumakohua Pass had affected us. Still three dives to do, he promised.

After dinner that night Frédéric and I lay on the jetty staring at the lavishly starlit night, each of us meditating on the unforgettable day. The breeze was light and warm. Only the occasional loud splash nearby interrupted the stillness—a reef shark making a lunge perhaps. The night predators were on the prowl. I thought of the sharks we'd watched on our thrilling second dive that afternoon, grays and whitetips mostly. Two hundred or more hovering in the drop-off, getting on with their business, not minding us at all. These ones didn't get handouts and while our presence didn't worry them, they didn't come sniffing like dogs either.

All we'd done in the pass was go with the flow but lying on the jetty I felt a delicious muscle fatigue as well as a profound sense of peace, and the combination was like a drug. An image of Oliver contentedly sleeping drifted across my mind. Nelly would probably be in bed, too. Asleep on a mattress thrown on the floor by his cot, because no matter how many times I told her to use our bed, she insisted on sleeping right beside him.

Earlier over dinner Manihi told us that when he and his wife, Tila, had first bought the *motu* in 1985 it was nothing but a barren pile of broken coral inhabited by a few birds. A "*tahuna d'oiseaux*," he'd called it, mixing Tahitian and French in the usual way. It wasn't on any map. For many years the islet had disappeared and reappeared at the whim of the ocean and weather. Twenty tonnes of earth had to be ferried across the lagoon and at first only the hardy *aito*, or iron tree, took to the harsh environment. Gradually the gardenias and bougainvilleas were coaxed into survival, creating the pretty garden setting that made the *motu* surprisingly green and fragrant. The attractive guest bungalows were built over many years from local *kahia* wood, with woven coconut palm for the walls and pandanus for the roofs.

From the head of the dinner table Manihi had waved a hand. "When I die I want to be buried here. Right here, in my paradise."

As the lagoon tinkled softly beneath the jetty, I pondered his words. How many times in the last few years had I heard different islands described as paradise? And yet this tiny *motu* couldn't have been more different from, say, famously paradisal Bora Bora. Here there was no stagey romance, no fish-tank floors, no televisions, flat screen or otherwise, no cocktail bars built for sunsets; if you wanted wine with dinner you had to supply it. Everyone on the *motu* ate together under an impervious neon light. Still, of all the islands I'd been to, this windblown islet came closest to the dream landscape I'd imagined years ago under hypnosis. Far from thinking Manihi was mad, his obsession with the place made sense to me—even if I have difficulty putting into words the special charm of a low coral mound that you can walk around in a minute. Perhaps we all want a little kingdom, of which to be king or queen.

I couldn't help thinking that for a man like Manihi, who exuded a reckless energy, such a place might be a salvation. That, or else it would drive you to drink. Heaven or hell: the debate over islands has gone around in circles for centuries, from at least the time of Thomas More's *Utopia*. The essential separateness that makes them seem like havens also triggers fears of being trapped. I have never been attracted to sailing, for example, partly because I hate the idea of being stuck on a boat. Even on comparatively large Mo'orea notions of imprisonment were never far away. *La promenade des prisonniers*— that was how Frédéric jokingly dubbed our Sunday afternoon walks along the rugged beach at Temae, where the reef was so close to the shore there was no lagoon at all. When Maddie sat on our beach gazing out to sea we teasingly called her Napoléon: like the emperor immured on St. Helena, she seemed to be dreaming of escape. "Every remote island is a potential Alcatraz," wrote Thurston Clarke in *Searching for Paradise*.

With little in the way of nourishment and fresh water, survival on a coral atoll is not simple and it says a lot about the resilience of the ancient Polynesians that they so successfully colonized *motu*. Recently I'd read the true account of a white man who lived Crusoe-like for many years on a desert islet. The cover photo of *An Island to Oneself* shows the author, Tom Neale, in a loincloth, knocking a coconut from a palm tree with something spear-like. For a total of sixteen years beginning in 1952, the New Zealander lived alone on Suwarrow atoll, 320 kilometers from Pukapuka in the Cook Islands, the closest human life. Without so much as a sailboat, he was stuck there by choice.

The idea had obsessed Tom Neale for many years before he managed to convince an island schooner to make a detour and drop him on the atoll. Like so many supposedly carefree existences—those of artists come to mind—his was founded on rigor and routine. Neale was fastidious down to the last detail. The teapot was heated before making tea and drinking glasses were held up to the gaslight after washing and drying, to check for cleanliness. Sundays Neale boiled his sheets. Desert-island life was anything but idle: the vegetable garden needed constant tending; there was a chicken coop to build and, less imperatively perhaps, a pier worthy of his beloved island. The hard toil took its toll when Neale injured himself so badly he was bedridden. Only by an extraordinary stroke of good fortune was he rescued by a rare passing boat—far from shipping lanes and yachting routes, the atoll received no visitors. It took the New Zealander six years to find a way of returning to his Pacific paradise. This time he learned from his mistakes: "In a curiously ironic way, I had unwittingly imposed on the timeless quality of the island the speed and bustle of modern cities from which I had been so anxious to escape."

My own island life was, of course, nothing like Tom Neale's. Yet even on Mo'orea I could relate to the obsession with time, the impulse to control it. How many timetables had I carefully drawn up? It has been suggested by some that Neale was a difficult, complex person—certainly it does seem strange that *An Island to Oneself* mentions neither the woman he married nor the two children the couple had before he decided to return to the atoll, alone. Still, there's no doubt he was one of a rare breed. Noel Barber, who visited Suwarrow at one point during Neale's stay, half expected to find an unwashed, rambling hermit. Instead the British writer was surprised to be met by a lucid, precise man who appeared deeply content.

"No man is an island," wrote the English poet John Donne back in the seventeenth century, though history is dotted with famous hermits who have found enlightenment through their isolation. Had my comparatively mild experiences on Mo'orea taught me anything? Had my daily swims or observations of the clouds, for example, conferred any insights? Put to the solitude test, I knew I wouldn't make a wise hermit but the crazy kind who babbles to herself and laughs aloud at private jokes. Yet I had learned, too, that you don't always need other people to make you feel alive. Beauty, light and color in nature make you feel viscerally human, too.

We spent four days at Tumakohua Pass and it went in an eye blink. But what an eye blink. Henri Matisse spent the same length of time on Fakarava eight decades before. "The memories of my voyage to Tahiti have come to me only now, fifteen years later, in the form of haunting images," Matisse told the photographer Brassaï. According to Hilary Spurling, the artist would draw on what he saw during his atoll stay for the rest of his life. If the revelations he'd sought from the trip were slow to come, Matisse himself seemed to accept that creation was a mysterious process that required "storing away," "distillation" and "absorption." Those who witnessed him making his famous cutouts were mezmerized by the magical way the shapes fell from his swiveling scissors. So impressed was Pablo Picasso that he had a magician perform for the artist as a tribute. The immediacy of the technique apparently took the struggle out of the creative act for

Matisse, who described the method as "the graphic, linear equivalent of the sensation of flight."

In Paris I'd seen one of his famous Tahiti-inspired works, *Polynesia, the Sea,* but it wasn't until our dives in Tumakohua Pass that I appreciated Matisse's genius. Only by cutting directly into paper could he re-create the crystalline silhouettes he saw underwater. Only by paring back his palette to white and dazzling blues could he convey the purity.

As we rose for the last time into the radiant shoals, a school of needlefish flashed like crystal wands and a jellyfish floated up to the light, its frilly bell more beautiful than anything blown from glass. I felt exultant but already nostalgic. The water was so transparent it was almost air. The ancient Tahitians believed that God was not in the sky but in the lagoon. And right then, hovering in that spangled space watching baubles of my own breath race to the surface, I did too.

TWENTY

Water, quick. I knew I had to get him under water.

This realization hit almost as soon as I flew into the kitchen and saw my golden-haired boy in his sweet striped T-shirt and diaper, wild-eyed and roaring. Thoughts came fast and abbreviated after that; my eyes seized the obvious. The kitchen tap, quick. Dear God it's on his face, his precious little face. Get it off his chin. Quick. Then I saw the soup had run inside his T-shirt; Christ the sink isn't big enough. Water, more water. The shower. Quick quick quick. Only in the bathroom did I rip off his T-shirt and see the extent of it. Oliver would pay dearly for this delay. His top had cupped the boiling soup to his body. "The most crucial factor in reducing a skin burn is how quickly you get water to it," a doctor would tell me later. "Every second counts."

The sight of my son naked made me want to scream. It looked like he had been skinned alive, from his chin right down to below his belly button. His pale, perfect chest was a ghastly, livid pink. I couldn't say how long I kept him under the shower—six minutes? Eight? Twenty minutes under cool but not cold water is the recommended procedure I now know. By the time I carried him out we were both soaked and his small body was trembling violently from shock. His skin was beginning to bubble and blister.

Hospital, he needs to go to the hospital. The realization winded me, though in retrospect it was the obvious next step. Size is a crucial factor in determining the severity of a burn: if it covers an area bigger than your hand or more than 20 percent of the victim's body *go to the hospital.*

I raced outside carrying Oliver and put him in his car seat. Desperately I tugged at the straps until they gave just enough to stretch over the small towel filled with ice that I pressed to his chest. Another error. Water yes but not ice: never put ice on a burn. The pressure of the belt across his wound must have been horrendous and I can scarcely believe now that I did it. But in my panic I was weirdly attuned to other dangers. Strap him in, drive carefully, you never know on this island when an overtaking vehicle from the opposite direction might come hurtling toward you. Even in ordinary moments the buckle confounded me, and with my hands trembling it took numerous tries before the teeth fitted together, *snap.* Oliver shrieked like a trapped animal, his whole body bridged up. Please God please have mercy. Make him pass out.

I jabbered on in a tremulous voice driving to the clinic. "It's going to be okay, I promise, just hold on tight darling, breathe sweetie, breathe, Mommy loves you, the doctors will make it better." Anything to block out the unbearable shrieking. Raw and hysterical, the sound had not slowed or diminished since it ripped through the house. Though oddly my first reaction on reaching the kitchen was relief: no blood. There Oliver stood straight as a broomstick, not a limb bent out of place nor a single finger missing. But covered in something orange, oh Jesus the soup, not just hot but straight off the boil. Thick pumpkin soup: the ultimate comfort food. It sticks to the skin like paste.

With the front windows down we may as well have had a siren strapped to the roof for the noise coming out of the car. Children and adults on the roadside stopped to stare as we drove by. What's happened? What's wrong? Isn't that so-and-so's *popa'ā* tenant, the one who lives in the white house *côté mer*? Their faces registered concern and questions for which they would soon have answers. News travels fast on a small island.

It was a peaceful day at Mo'orea's clinic. There'd been no births on the island; no one had come off a scooter or a bike. Against the soft murmur of the distant reef, the doors swung open with a sound like a whip crack as I charged in without pausing to announce our arrival to the fellow at the entrance window. A nurse was already hurrying down the corridor in our direction, alerted by the heartbreaking screams of a suffering child and now the distraught cries of a heartbroken mother: *mon bébé, mon bébé.*

⌐⌐

"His life isn't in danger," the young French doctor said when finally Oliver lay calm, knocked out by the morphine. The words were meant to reassure me but this reference to death—even to rule out the possibility—only underscored the gravity of his injuries. On the way to the clinic I'd been hoping that Aima would be on duty; our friend and neighbor had by now graduated and become a nurse. I'd never met the solid Polynesian woman who patted my back as the medic continued. A second- or third-degree burn, it was hard to tell. "But it's extensive; he needs specialist treatment. He'll have lost a lot of fluid through the burned skin and the crucial thing now is to prevent infection." I don't know whether it was a delayed reaction to shock that brought on my tears or the natural way the nurse's aide wrapped an arm around me. Human touch is a magical thing and to me, the mother who had allowed this terrible accident to happen to her child, her warm, steadying hand felt like a form of absolution. "*Ça va aller, Maman,*" she said. "It's going to be all right."

One hour later the emergency helicopter rose in the dark with me and Oliver in it. I clamped the headphones firmly to his ears, intent on protecting what I could of his damaged body, though he was too drugged to be aware of what was going on. There'd been uncertainty as to whether there was room aboard for even one parent to make the flight to Tahiti. The doctor had pleaded and the emergency medics had allowed me to squeeze in, cradling Oliver. As the helicopter lifted up, Frédéric watched from the ground, shielding his eyes against the aircraft's powerful night beams. His pale, worried face grew smaller. Half an hour before, he'd cheerfully returned home expecting to see mother and son on the couch poring over a picture book, only to find the place unlit and empty. Tomorrow morning he'd be on the first ferry to

Pape'ete but for now there were no more boats or connecting flights. There was nothing to do but return to the house, where he kept glancing across the dark ocean at Tahiti, trying to discern which of the bright lights belonged to the main hospital.

⌒

The wound had to be cleaned and the damaged tissue scraped away every few days, a procedure so excruciating it must be performed under general anesthetic. Oliver had it four times during his ten days in the hospital. Although debridement, as the method is known, is widely practiced, later at one leading burn unit in Australia we were told that removing the newly formed layers of skin only worsens the scar. By the third anesthetic Oliver knew exactly what was in store when the masked nurse emerged from the operating room to collect him. He wrapped his arms and legs around Frédéric, clinging like a koala to a branch. "*Pa-pa, Pa-pa, Pa-pa.*" With forced cheer we tried to reassure him. "*Ça va aller mon petit père, ça va aller.*" "You're such a big brave boy, darling, you're just going to go dodo for a while; we'll be here when you wake up." But as the nurse reached for him, he clung even tighter and the handover turned into a struggle. Whisked finally into the operating room, Oliver shot his father a look of such anguish and betrayal that when the doors swung shut Frédéric's face folded in on itself.

Emotionally we were all over the place, as two realizations sank in.

His burn was far graver than we'd first thought.

His injuries could so easily have been much worse.

"We really worry if genitals are affected," the specialist burn nurse said, after examining him the first time. "It was lucky he didn't swallow any soup." The thought made me wince. Along with depth and surface area, location is another criterion for determining the severity of a burn.

Bound firmly from neck to hips, Oliver resembled a small mummy. I was enormously grateful for the bandaging, which he had to wear for weeks: the very last thing I wanted to see was his skin. It was months—years, in fact—before I could look at his scar without flinching. The hospital staff did their best to manage his pain yet inevitably victims of severe burns suffer long after the accident. The twilight zones between the doses of painkillers were the worst. Most nights both Frédéric and I stayed on Tahiti, sleeping on thin mattresses squeezed onto the floor space of Oliver's tiny room. Neither of us wanted to be at home, cut off from the hospital by sea and lack of transport, though once or twice one of us slept at a friend's place for a better sleep.

"Ouchie Mama, ouchie." It was a soft, plaintive cry but I was only half-asleep and I sprang up to find Oliver on his feet clenching the bars of the cot. If Frédéric's most vivid hospital memory was the look from his son as he thrust him into the arms of the masked stranger, this was mine. In the slash of uncaring light from the corridor, I could see his cheeks were awash with tears. This quiet despair was almost as terrible as his agony when the accident happened. There was little I could do except call the night nurse, who would only check the clipboard and say it wasn't time yet for his next dose of painkiller. I couldn't even give him a proper cuddle, his chest was too sore. "Come here, sweetie, let's go for a walk," I whispered. Up and down the empty corridor we went, Oliver sitting in his stroller murmuring "ouchie, ouchie." Each brave little sob stabbed at my heart.

"You did everything you could, it wasn't your fault": in Frédéric's eyes I was Oliver's rescuer. "At least you knew to get him straight under water," he told me. Later I would wonder how I would have reacted had the situation been reversed and he had been the responsible parent when the accident happened. Would my understanding have been as unwavering? Would I have *praised* him? Or under duress does the maternal instinct to protect override other loyalties?

In rational moments I didn't blame myself. Accidents happen and by definition they cannot be predicted. Hadn't our wise pediatrician said *éveillé* babies were a challenge? In many ways Oliver had become easier to manage. He slept soundly at night and didn't make a fuss whether he was put to bed in his own cot or on a mattress on the floor at friends' places. He enjoyed almost every food put in front of him—fish pie, chicken, rice, eggs, vegetables, potatoes, *fei* bananas, papaya, pineapple—and he had a special fondness for Guite's lentils and lamb. But he had two settings: on and off. When a friend once remarked how she loved waking in the morning to the contented, mellifluous babbling of her baby, I could only wonder how this might sound. From the moment Oliver's eyes snapped open he was calling urgently to get out of his cot. Every move he made was a lunge, grab or dash. When he fell, which happened often, it was not a cuddle he wanted so much as to get straight back on his feet.

"It'll be his Tahiti war wound," Frédéric reassured me, referring to the scar, which for the moment was still a raw wound that covered his entire chest. "Remember, he got to ride in a rescue helicopter."

But of the dramatic night flight, along with the accident and his hospital stay, we both knew a fifteen-month-old baby would remember nothing. The only memory of the experience that would linger was the pain. Young skin, like very old skin, is thin and it scorches easily. Over time I'd learn from specialists of the excruciating nature of second-degree burns: with the nerve endings intact, the victim feels the skin layers melt and sear. I'd read how medical thinking on infant pain has evolved from miscomprehension to understanding that babies as young as six months form a memory of it, which in turn can influence their response to pain in adulthood. Not that it took an expert to know the incident would leave an imprint on his mind as well as his body. I was there, I saw his eyes, panicked, pleading. I heard the screams. I'm his mother. I was responsible.

In my moments of self-reproach, the chair preyed on my mind. He'd been so thrilled to stand on it and throw vegetable peelings about while I chatted and made his dinner. If only I hadn't left it in the kitchen. To a boundlessly curious, on-the-go toddler the challenge of pushing the chair back to the bench and standing up on it to reach his dinner must have been irresistible. While of course everyone must go to the toilet, part of me wondered if I hadn't lingered too long, content for a precious moment alone. And if only I hadn't shown him where I put his soup. To Oliver's distress, after pouring some from the pot I had set his plastic frog bowl aside to cool. "I know you're hungry, sweetie," I told him, lifting him up so he could see the steam blossoming from the high counter. "But you have to wait, it's hot, see." Though it wasn't just hot; only seconds before it had been bubbling like lava. He wouldn't have known where to reach had I not shown him. At times I tried to picture the scene I had not witnessed: the lip jutting in determination as he climbed onto the chair, the sense of achievement as he stood to reach the bowl, which he could only just do with his fingertips. Perhaps a split second passed before the shock registered.

All that matters is he's safe, we kept saying. Like any grave accident or close call, Oliver's burn made us count our blessings. It might sound a cliché but it made us realize how precious life is—and how precarious. It taught me that events of great consequence can take place in the time it takes to snap your fingers. What we call the present is a pinprick. Life is but a series of instants and each one offers myriad possibilities. This arbitrariness had never bothered me before but when it came to my child's life it was intolerable.

There wasn't any time for dwelling on these thoughts when we left the hospital. The flashbacks came later, followed by stern lectures delivered by me to myself about not turning into an overprotective mother and not passing on fears to my child. With our move to Australia only five weeks away, back home on Mo'orea we threw ourselves into organizing and packing up. In the bathroom where I'd removed Oliver's top and then dried him after his long, cold shower, a scattering of pale peelings on the floor caught my eye. They were the finest, tiniest flakes, like the scales of a small fish, and as one crumbled between my fingers it dawned on me what they were.

I got the broom, swept up every last one and threw them out.

TWENTY-ONE

During his first two-year stay on Tahiti, Paul Gauguin settled happily for a time in the remote district of Mataiea, away from Pape'ete and its many distractions. But life on the far side of the island became lonely, and pretty soon he announced to his landlord, Anani, that he was leaving. According to the artist, the news prompted Anani's wife to puzzle sadly over the strange ways of Europeans. "You come, you promise to remain, and when we have come to love you, you leave," she said. "To return, you say, but you never return."

To me those words from *Noa Noa* capture a truth about Tahiti—even if on that particular occasion, the wife of Anani was proved wrong. Gauguin was not bound for the other side of the world but simply setting off around the island in search of a solution for his solitude. Within days he was back in Mataiea, disembarking the horse-drawn public coach with his new thirteen-year-old "bride"—Tehura he called her in *Noa*

Noa, though with typical ambiguity, elsewhere Gauguin records her name as Teha'amana.

Given the painter's propensity for embellishment and his huge ego—"monstrous" was the estimation of his loyal friend Georges-Daniel de Monfreid—you have to be a bit circumspect. Though it's possible Anani and his wife were sad to see him go, they may have been more disappointed when their impoverished tenant *came back*. Still, as Frédéric, Oliver and I prepared to leave the territory ourselves, those lines from *Noa Noa* came to mind. Ever since the arrival of the first European explorers, these islands have had to cope with a constant ebb and flow of outsiders. At Pape'ete's wharf, farewell scenes were once common: the abandoned *vahine*, eyes wide with sorrow, her figure not yet showing the baby who would be borne to the French or American sailor returning to life and sometimes a wife back home. Beginning in the early 1960s, the nuclear testing period brought what some have termed an "invasion" of French military personnel, who were stationed throughout the territory. When the experiments ended in 1996 and the facilities were closed, *les militaires* went home too, mostly. While some islanders may have mourned them—or at least the state salaries that went with the era— then as now, there were surely many who bade farewell to Europeans with a silent good riddance.

More recently this message was delivered clearly by the pro-independence president Oscar Temaru, who referred to French residents in the territory as "rubbish" or "waste." Unsurprisingly many *popa'ā* were outraged and some Polynesians also thought he'd gone too far. Later the criminal court of Pape'ete would find Temaru guilty of racial discrimination. The insult touched on deep-rooted sensitivities and in-securities: from the beginning, charges of mediocrity and small-mindedness have been leveled at the French settlers, by islanders and also by their own compatriots back in *la métro-pole.*

As our departure approached, I realized that I'd never felt completely comfortable being part of this transient commu-nity. It wasn't that I agreed with the "rubbish" statement. Cer-tainly there were some who fitted the negative stereotype, who swaggered about with a sense of entitlement or com-plained constantly about how expensive everything was. But there were also plenty of down-to-earth *popa'ā* who made a sincere contribution to the place. Maybe my unease was sown by my car accident and the furious words flung at me by the driver: Go back home; how dare you come here and take our jobs and land? Perhaps the problem was that there were *too many* comings and goings for a faraway island. Or too many expectations and projections of paradise for one small place. I couldn't quite put my finger on it.

⌁

Circumstances exacerbated the usual stresses of moving, and Frédéric and I bickered in a way we hadn't since packing up our Paris apartment. What have you done with the masking tape? Have you pinched my scissors? Oliver was still swathed in bandages, still on painkillers and antihistamines for the maddening itch, which typically occurs as burns heal. None of us was getting enough sleep. Every five days or so I would take Oliver on the ferry to Pape'ete to have his bandages changed. The procedure, which involved applying cream to his still weeping, blistered wound, was carried out by the burn nurse, a certain Nathalie who was so friendly and gentle even Oliver managed a tiny smile when he saw her. With the protective barrier of outer skin layers gone, the immediate priority was preventing infection. There was no anesthetic, just a maximum dose of Panadol and something else on arrival at the hospital. As Nathalie began unraveling the bandages, Oliver wept but didn't struggle, soothed perhaps by her words. "I know, I know, *bébé*. You're so brave. I'll be quick. Who's that watching you over there?" Inwardly I shuddered at the sight of Oliver's chest, still scarlet and raw, but I followed her lead, trying to distract him. "They're your two favorite friends, aren't they, sweetie? Ted and Totoche." Propped at the end of the hospital bed, the teddy bear and seal stared back with eyes so shiny they might have been welling with tears of sympathy.

Underpinning our anxiety was a new insecurity about Frédéric's Sydney job. There'd been a lapse in communications from the Paris head office about our move. Later it would transpire that heated disagreement had broken out over the plan to create an Australian bureau. Law firms are political beasts. Caught up in the momentum, we went ahead with making arrangements, leaving everything to the last minute in case the firm changed its mind. Finally our flights were reserved, a temporary apartment in Sydney had been rented, and our belongings were booked into a Sydney storage facility. On our packing boxes we wrote "SARAH'S OFFICE" and "OLIVER'S BEDROOM" and "KITCHEN," as though they had a home to go to.

There is an irony to a transient life. Changing country requires commitment and energy. Finding or starting work, making friends, developing new rituals, locating favorite restaurants and pastimes—the process of settling in, or "blending in," as my mother used to say, takes time and energy. Finally, if you've been diligent and your efforts prove fruitful, you end up with precisely what you left behind: routines and a regular life.

And that is usually when you leave.

Having moved a total of thirty-eight times in fifty years of marriage, my parents were well acquainted with the advantages and disadvantages of such a life. Their overseas postings within the military network were very different from the unplanned way I'd ended up in Paris or even the way Frédéric and I had come to Tahiti. Yet as our departure grew closer I found myself thinking of Mom and her emphasis on *keeping in contact* with friends around the world. The rest of the family would exchange mischievous glances at the announcement that it was high time to call so-and-so: my mother loved the telephone and these long-distance conversations were never short. They were never cheap back then, either. Letters were written, too, chatty pages of news and inquiries, to ever-expanding circles of defense force friends, Mom's physiotherapist colleagues and whoever else had been swept up in the net. In this way, what might have been a series of postings or separate lives acquired continuity—meaning, too, I think.

Imminent departure makes you look not only forward

but also back to take stock of successes and failures. We had met some lovely people on the island but I had not met the sort of girlfriend to laugh and cry with, to share the highs and lows. While it's possible that in my sorrow I had not been open to such intimacy, it's also true that such friendships are precious precisely because they are rare. My dream of having a baby had come true but that other great goal, my "novel," amounted to a meager collection of scenes and characters that stubbornly refused to connect. Perhaps I should take heart from Matisse and the long gestation of his Tahiti-inspired cutouts. Would my po-faced Bretons and apathetic artists one day march out of the bottom drawer and demand some action? What memories of this place would later dart out of the coral branches of my brain? Thanks to Tumakohua Pass, I'd had the thrill of flying through water and, who knows, maybe I did meet God. I had tried to understand many things about the islands yet there was much that had escaped me. So much for my plan to learn Tahitian. Soon after recommencing lessons I gave up, realizing my main motivation had been to fill time.

Yearnings change as we grow older. What made me leave Australia in my mid-twenties was a desire to be pulled out of my comfort zone, exposed to something exciting and new. In a foreign culture daily life retains a frisson of novelty. The constant effort to understand and be understood, to interpret the nuances, makes life frustrating and endlessly interesting. Now at forty, I longed for the intimacy of old friendships. I wanted to put down roots. Perhaps it was also having a child that made being spread far and wide feel like being spread a bit thinly. An Australian friend who lived for years in London put it this way in an e-mail: "Sooner or later we yearn for the one place we don't need to constantly explain ourselves."

The closer our departure drew, the more relieved I felt and the sadder I felt, too—sadder even than when we left Paris. France was braided into our lives. We had family there; my husband was French. Like our son, I was half French now, too: my citizenship papers had finally come through. Paris was my home as much as Frédéric's. Tahiti was different. While we would visit again, we were leaving for good. On the *Aremiti V* one day, my eyes misted over. For years now, I'd wished the ferry would change its tune but now the sappy instrumental version of "Ebony and Ivory" pulled at my heartstrings. Oliver sat on my knee, having had his bandages changed for the last time. Leaning against the window was the last bunch of twirling pink heliconias I'd ever buy from the sweet flower vendor. *"Pour toi,"* she had said, holding out her customary free stem.

At our farewell lunch we ate at a long table on the beach— "our beach" we'd always called it, though it never was ours. Thanks to the much publicized, controlled introduction of a tiny wasp, the voracious grasshoppers had been eradicated. If at first we'd been dubious about the experiment, we all agreed it was a treat to sit beneath the *mape* tree without being peed on. Butterflies of sunlight fell through the leafy canopy, flittering over the feast laid out on the long table. Clement had done the earth-oven roast suckling pig; Alain had made two types of *poisson cru*, one with vinaigrette, the other with coconut milk. The secret, we now knew, lay in seasoning the tuna generously with salt and pepper and saving the lime juice until the last minute so the fish didn't toughen and "cook." Guite made the punch, though due to complaints about the potency of her last batch, which had resulted in a particularly jolly afternoon, she'd gone easy on the rum. Joel, Alain's brother, had made coconut bread. I'd baked a chocolate cake and Nelly brought another, thickly coated in caramel icing.

Oliver, when he woke from his day sleep, was greeted with outstretched arms, joggled and admired. He in turn lurched around the table, from one friend to another, making grabs for Guite's gold earrings, sticking fingers in everyone's punch, laughing uproariously as Mo'e blew farty sounds on his belly. He was not shy, not in the least bit clingy. Later, people would remark on his outgoing nature, as though this was his parents' achievement. Certainly, he seemed to have his father's enthusiasm. Though one of the wonders of children is not how closely they resemble their parents but how quickly they become their own person.

Around Oliver's neck hung the baby-sized *tiare* garland Nelly had made for him. It almost covered the bandage that could be seen poking above his cotton T-shirt. A wide-brimmed hat shaded his face and on his chin was a daub of white sun block, thick as oil paint. Classified as a superficial burn, the redness on his face was well on its way to disappearing. By contrast, the injury on his chest was more severe: an advanced second-degree burn was the assessment at the hospital. The scar was not smooth and cleanly outlined like a lagoon but thick and fibrous, with feral crimson creeks running north and south. "Hypertrophic" is the medical term. In the future specialists would call it "nasty," and the word would spear my heart again. But for the moment we allowed ourselves to hope it might one day disappear without a trace, like one of those drought-stricken lakes in Australia. Already the soup map was beginning to shrink. In our bags were five liters of thick, green potion we hoped would eventually work wonders on the scar: tamanu oil, extracted from the inedible fruit of tamanu trees like the grand, leafy tree in our own garden. Polynesians have long used it on skin ailments but only recently have its potential benefits raised interest in Western medicine.

It wasn't customary to make speeches at social occasions, not in the Polynesian culture, nor in the French one. But there were things that needed to be said at this lunch, I felt. Everyone was here: Alain and Aima, Guite, Daniel and Catherine, Nelly and Mo'e, Aima's mother and stepfather, Alain's sister Moetu, along with a handful of other family members. Aima had even invited a local priest to bless our departure.

"I just wanted to take this opportunity to thank you all," I began a bit formally. "For all the kindness you've shown us. For including us in so many family celebrations. For the many bags of fruit and bundles of vanilla beans. For all the love you've given Oliver." My voice cracked. I squinted at the lagoon a few meters away, as clear as a child's marble. "People come and go all the time in Tahiti," I continued. "That's why we're so grateful . . ."

An incident came to mind, one that spoke for many others. The day Oliver came out of the hospital had been awful: pummeling rain and high winds made for a particularly rough ferry crossing back to Mo'orea. Oliver had thrown up all over his new body bandages. I wiped and sponged as gently and as best I could but worried that the smell would not come out. As we drove along the straight stretch to home, in the gray obscurity a bright red umbrella caught my eye. Someone was waiting in the pouring rain by our gate. Before I could jump out, Guite had rolled it open. The gate was heavy, the tracks were rusty and I needed two hands to do it. But somehow this slight, almost eighty-year-old managed, all the while balancing the umbrella in pouring rain. On our front porch, under the eaves, was a bag bulging with the home-cooked meal she'd just delivered—lamb and lentils plus baked custard for Oliver, along with our favorite tart made with guava from her garden.

"I knew you'd be on the midday ferry," she explained after. "Thought I'd wait. No point both of us getting wet."

But at our lunch, taken aback by my own overflow of feelings, I swallowed tears and simply sat down without telling the story. Around the table everyone blinked and wiped their eyes. "Ehhh!" Nelly exclaimed in surprise, as Oliver swiped the red hibiscus from her ear and made off with it, shrieking delightedly. We all joined in laughing and the mood lightened again. Aima started cutting the chocolate cake and plates were passed around; we picked up our forks. Perhaps there was no need for more words, my sentiment had said enough.

I understood then that the real issue about the comings and goings and the pain it may cause is linked to giving and taking. Tides sweep in but they also sweep stuff away. It is tempting to point to the usual suspects: the French retirees who move here for the generous pensions then save all their money for trips home to France. The teachers who come not for the experience but for the significant pay benefits. Yet we were taking much with us, too.

One of the more precious souvenirs in our bags was a stunning red and white *tifaifai*—the term for the traditional hand-sewn bedcovers that feature stylized motifs of island flora and fauna. The artisan had sucked air through her teeth when I'd chosen an especially intricate design from her show book. "*Oish!* That's my hardest one!" Cutting out each tiny dot and streak must have taken forever. With the red top sheet pinned to the bottom white layer, two local seamstresses then carried out the tedious task of hand stitching the two pieces of fabric together. Five months later, just in time for our departure, the *tifaifai* was ready for me to pick up. It was my turn to gasp then. The red quilt was covered in white constellations so delicate I wondered what kind of scissors had shaped them. The pattern was more like something you'd see in nature than anything man-made. "It's *exquisite*," I effused.

Among the items we were taking with us were some things that it might be argued were not ours to take: shells and driftwood, and also a name. Like many *popa'ā* whose children were born in the territory, we'd given Oliver a Tahitian middle name. "Isn't it a girl's name?" I'd queried but Frédéric assured me he knew of a Polynesian fellow called Orama. It means "great vision from the sky," though we had chosen the name for its sound and the natural way it flowed on from Oliver. The giving of Tahitian names to European children is a practice that has drawn interest and also criticism from some scholars, both within the territory and in France. Some see it as appropriation. Others see it as a positive sign of the strength and influence of the Tahitian culture, citing it as an example of how, in spite of colonizing efforts, it is often *popa'ā* who adopt local habits and not the other way around. To us both arguments were a bit academic. The name meant Oliver could not forget where he came from. Despite having no memory of his birthplace, he will be required to acknowledge it again and again. "Oh yeah," he will have to explain, "I was born in Tahiti."

Some art historians have gone so far as to say that Matisse appropriated the Tahitian tradition of *tifaifai*, pointing to obvious similarities between his later cutouts and the quilts in their decorative aims and techniques. Other experts counter that Matisse himself never cited the colorful bedcovers as an influence. In any event, *tifaifai* itself was a result of fluidity between cultures: it was the wives of English missionaries who taught the island women needlework, beginning with patchwork then appliqué. While the local handicraft may well have given the artist ideas, he could hardly be accused of copying the designs the women guarded so preciously. Instead Matisse created something new and exciting—which was exactly what the islanders did with old patchwork techniques.

Yet in colonies or former colonies you can never ignore the broader historical context. Virtually no one arrives here without hoping for a tiny representation of the Garden of Eden, paradise on Earth and so on. We too had arrived with our own dreams—hadn't we hoped that the natural beauty of a lush island might help us have a child? And perhaps indirectly it had, who knows? Playing on the beach one late afternoon with Oliver, I studied the footprints we'd left in the soft sand, considering the question of give and take. By morning they would be gone. What, if anything, would we leave behind?

My last swim in the lagoon was hardly an occasion for striking out in a new direction or attempting to reach the reef. It was automatic now: the diversion around the coral head belonging to the clownfish, who remained as vigilantly defensive as ever; the hard left turn at the first depth post; a long swim parallel to the shore right on up to the shelf that still made my heart thud, through the black and white fish fluttering like confetti and over the coral garden. Then home.

The return journey had always been the part I loved most. I didn't cut in too shallow but stayed out over the ribbed plains. *One two three breathe.* It was here I'd often been mesmerized by the sight of spotted eagle rays soaring into the blue. Though on this, my final swim, all I saw were the trails they'd left on the sandy floor.

It still amazed me how in this stunning clarity everything blurred. Reality felt a dream, time was an illusion and the heightened sense of being alive might have been my body dissolving like an aspirin into the water. How I'll miss you, lagoon. Keep well. May your waters stay clear and warm (but not get too warm for the coral). Perhaps Matisse was right about the healing benefits of color and light. I tilted my head back a fraction to fix my eyes not below but on the radiance straight ahead that was neither turquoise nor aquamarine but an opaline brilliance for which there is no name.

TWENTY-TWO

"How far is it to the next town?"

We'd been driving all day up a road like an interminable runway and now, with the sun on its downhill slide, the priority was to find somewhere to stop for the night. We were tired of the biscuit-dry country, the stingy highway that for nine hours hadn't given us so much as a glimpse of the Indian Ocean, which lay only a few kilometers to the west. "Incy Wincy Spider" and "Ten Green Bottles" played on in my ears though the sing-along had blessedly come to an end when I'd pulled out our big gun, the portable DVD player. In the back Oliver glowered at the small screen, his arms and legs covered in texta scribbles. Stickers of monkeys, lions, pirates and dinosaurs dangled jauntily from his nose, forehead and cheeks. A clean, unfolded diaper was propped on his head like a party hat. It was past his dinnertime.

I looked at the map open on my knees and took a guess at

the distance, glancing at its ruler scale as a guide. A few millimeters could translate into a full day's driving.

"About one hundred and fifty kilometers."

"Are there any campgrounds marked between here and there?"

I'd checked already. At this time of day I was always anxious to feed Oliver his dinner. "Nope."

Our eyes scanned the country either side of the road. From here it looked smooth as a kitchen bench, like you might drive straight onto it and set up camp anywhere, but we knew better. We'd very nearly got stuck on another deceptively flat plain, which turned out to be riddled with sly gullies and hillocks of dry grass that scraped and clawed as we rode over them. Game though she was, our caravan was not designed to go off-road. Château Pliant we called her, for the nifty way both ends folded out to create beds. I'd had to get out and find a way around the crevasses on foot, with the Prado and our tiny home hobbling behind me.

"We'll find a spot," Frédéric said lightly.

The remarkable thing about the Australian landscape is not its loveliness but its capacity for transformation. As the sun slipped lower, a flush spread across the dull earth. Now you could see it wasn't flat but rose and fell in undulations, like the ocean. Colors that had mumbled incoherently all day opened up and started to sing. Gray turned to silver, beige to gold; pale ochre flamed rose and salmon pink. The spiky spinifex clumps looked pillowy and spindly acacias threw mauve shadows three times their size. The monotonous, austere plain was now a pulsating pattern of light and shade that sounded in my ears like a drumbeat.

So engrossed were we in the spectacle that the mesa seemed to appear out of nowhere. Amid the surrounding flatness it had the majesty of an Egyptian pyramid—one sliced flat at the top. A winding dirt road led up to the plateau, where tire marks and a polite stack of wood indicated many before us had camped. We had the routine down pat now and quickly set to work, popping up the roof of the caravan, winding down its little legs, flipping out the canvas "wings" at either end, setting up chairs and table outside. At last I heard a welcome gushing sound and Frédéric emerged from Château Pliant with two cups of cask wine.

"Let's enjoy the view while there's still light."

"*Attention*, Oliver," I called. "Keep away from the edge."

On the loose at last, he was a speed demon on his push-along bike. "Look at me, look," he cried jubilantly.

Before setting out I'd been nervous about the idea of camping in isolated places. Would we be safe at night in our canvas-sided caravan? A couple of Sydney friends had talked about the outback like it was an eerie vacuum. There'd been the notorious backpacker murders during my years out of the country, and the strange and awful abduction of a young English couple. "You could fly around the country instead of driving," one urbanite had helpfully suggested, "that way you'd skip the Nothing."

But we'd learned to cherish the rare occasions we had open space to ourselves. This mesa was one of many memorable campsites. It was less than 100 meters high but it felt as safe as a hilltop fortress. Château Pliant looked cozy and comforting with the lights on inside. We sat back in the comfortable canvas chairs that were our smartest camping accessory—how glad we were now to have spent the extra and got the model with attached side trays for drinks. Oliver scuttled by on his bike with Ted the bear wide-eyed and wobbling precariously in front of him; Totoche, who was no longer a white seal but reddish, lay facedown in the dust. The Indian Ocean stretched in the distance like a prize ribbon. This was the west coast of Australia and we weren't even facing in Tahiti's direction but somehow this aperitif evoked the many we'd had on our beach.

"*Manuia*," I said and our plastic cups butted together.

I suppose it may have been a way of running from reality. The sensible thing for me to do when Frédéric's Sydney job fell through would have been to rush out and find work. After our three and a half years on Mo'orea you'd have thought we'd had enough of circling islands. But we needed time to regroup, to rethink. The bad news from Paris came at the end of our first week back in Australia: sorry guys for dragging you there, the Sydney office isn't going ahead. Though of course there was no apology and the message was worded more formally. In the days that followed, Frédéric alternated between fury and despondency. The offer of a job back in Paris did nothing to placate him. But what would a French-trained lawyer do for work in Sydney? What we both agreed was that running straight back to France was not an option. Our belongings were on a container ship somewhere in the South Pacific. In a few days Mads would be carried off the plane in a cage and checked into Eastern Creek Quarantine Station. Our hearts and minds were set on a new beginning in Australia. It wasn't just any move: it was to be Frédéric's first experience of living in my country, and my return after fourteen years living abroad.

That was where my Plan B came in. I'd formulated it before our departure from Tahiti, remembering much-repeated advice from my father, who was a big believer in contingency plans. Inside our modest orange-brick apartment I gave rousing speeches about turning a negative into a positive and not letting those bastards in Paris get us down. "You'll be able to paint all the time," I expanded. "I can write." It would be a working holiday. A chance for me to see more of my country and an opportunity for Frédéric to clear his head. I had no idea really. But I thought a bold new plan was needed to salvage this move which had gotten off to a false start. Alicia sent me Milan Kundera's novel *Ignorance*, about an émigré going home, and one particular phrase lodged in my mind like a mantra: "the return, the return, the great magic of the return." Perhaps that's what I was hoping, that the trip might restore some magic.

Six months to do the loop of Australia had sounded ample, then adequate—and at a later point, utterly unachievable unless we hopped on a plane. At first Frédéric was thrilled by the vast distances and the size of the continent fourteen times bigger than France. He wanted to go the whole circumambulation, not cut corners. Coloring in our progress on the map was a solemn after-dinner ritual.

But when after four months' traveling we still hadn't turned the bottom left corner, he grew demoralized.

"*C'est gigantesque,*" he said gloomily one night. In the low light of the gas lamp, Australia was spread out on the dirt (only in Tasmania do I recall grass). With a highlighter pen he marked up the 500 or so kilometers we'd covered that day and our fluoro trail nudged forward a couple of millimeters toward the Nullarbor. We'd covered barely a third of the total distance back to Sydney. Frédéric shook his head, "*C'est vraiment monstrueux.*" Just looking at Western Australia's long coastline gave me a feeling like vertigo but for his sake I tried to appear undaunted. "We spent a whole month in Tasmania," I reminded him. "We've really only been traveling on the mainland for *three* months." But this correction provided little comfort. It didn't help that we kept running into travelers, whiskery gray nomads mostly, who had set off from Mount Isa or Newcastle or Adelaide with the same idea and were still contentedly circling five or ten years later.

Suffice to say Frédéric didn't do quite as much painting as we'd envisaged, just as I didn't do quite as much writing. The main obstacle to this idyllic vision was, in a word, Oliver. "You do realize he was precisely *the hardest age* for this kind of thing," chuckled a family friend, a child psychologist. We were back in Sydney by then and I could laugh with her. Perhaps I should have remembered the terrible twos, along with the extra tensions created by the inescapable togetherness of travel, because my sister was the same age when our family went around Europe in a small camper van. A caravan park in Cannes was the scene for memorable tantrums, first by Anna and then by Mom, who, at her wits' end, shouted like a crazed monarch to me and my brother to *take her away*. Our Cannes moment occurred in the Kimberley, where as a birthday present to Frédéric my family had kindly booked us into the Emma Gorge Resort. Oliver marked his father's fiftieth with three days of obnoxious disobedience and tantrums. At a celebratory lunch, fistfuls of food were hurled around the restaurant, at waitresses and shocked diners; he blew apple juice through a straw at his father. So much for table manners like French children. "*Arrête*, Oliver. *Maintenant, ça suffit*," I snapped, glaring at him. "*Encore une fois et c'est la fessée*," growled his father. "Do it again and you'll get a smack." It might be a Romance language but when it comes to commands and admonishments, French has a sharp, authoritarian edge.

"Just ignore him," I urged quietly.

But it was too much for Frédéric. "Imagine what he'll be like as a teenager," he muttered through clenched teeth, furious but also despairing. Off he stormed into Emma Gorge, minus the recommended covered shoes, water bottle and hat.

"At least we weren't in France," I joked once Frédéric had returned and recovered. "Imagine if we'd been having Sunday lunch at a bistro full of perfectly behaved French children!"

Despite concerted efforts to arrive at a sensible hour, somehow it was always dark when we pulled into campsites— "wine o'clock," in the lingo of older, seasoned travelers who were gathered sociably under awnings drinking chilled beers and glasses of white. Our frenzied activity provided great entertainment. After being cooped up in the car for many hours Oliver would be revving to bolt, and one set of eyes had to be on him at all times. Campsites by rivers and lakes were always a worry, though the worst were busy caravan parks, with their constant flow of vehicles reversing into tight spaces one or two meters away. Inquiries and assurances volleyed back and forth. Have you got him? I thought you had him. Oliver? Oliver? I see him, don't worry. Only a pathetic concern for what the neighbors would think stopped me from attaching our son to a rope.

Once in a while, we put him into a child-care center, which may explain our particularly fond memories of certain places. Goldmining town Kalgoorlie might be renowned for gambling, grog and topless girls but I recall civilized mornings reading newspapers in a sunlit café, our Parisian-style round table cluttered with coffee cups and half-nibbled croissants. If these unencumbered days restored us, Oliver, too, seemed to relish the breaks. He trundled eagerly into the child-care center at Kalgoorlie. "Kids, kids, KIDS," he called, as if to say, "Boy, am I glad to see you!"

"Listen to this," said Frédéric as he read the local newspaper on one of our last mornings at the café. "It says here you can get a gold prospecting kit secondhand for under a hundred dollars." There was only a hint of jest in his tone. "What do you think about doing that for a year?" It was easy enough to picture us as a pair of jolly prospectors—it was no madder than some of our other ideas. But I told Frédéric about a conversation I'd had with the woman at the caravan park office. "Everyone comes to Kal with a two-year plan and the idea of getting rich," she'd said. She'd nodded toward the caravans made into permanent homes with picket fences and pot plants. "Ten years later they're still living here."

After the lushness of Tahiti, it took a while to readjust to the subtle palette and special charms of the Australian bush. My heart sank as we pulled into one particular camp area a few hours from Adelaide. "It's a hidden secret, really worth the detour," one couple had raved. "It's just a dirt clearing between half-dead gums," I said, unimpressed. Even their leaves were the color of dry clay. But at sunrise the next day I was up with my camera, crouching close to the river red gums, taking photos of their shredded patterns and textures. Trunks that looked pale gray from a distance were actually a patchwork of beige, ochre and dusty pink, with mottles of chocolate and maroon. "They're always so warm," Frédéric said, pressing his hand to one. "You'd think the gums had blood running through them."

I thought then of how another Frenchman had been captivated by Australia's iconic trees. Admiral Bruni d'Entrecasteaux, whose ships in 1792 had anchored lengthily off Tasmania's southernmost coast, ordinarily kept a rather dry and factual journal. But struck by the blue gum forests, dense with the trees' desiccated droppings and also new growth, he broke into luminous verse: "Nature, in all its vigor, and at the same time in decline, offers to the imagination something more imposing and picturesque than the sight of this same nature embellished by civilized man's industry."

Bear hugs, kisses and celebratory bubbles awaited us in Alice Springs. We hadn't seen Gen and Vinnie since we had fled to the Center almost three years earlier to take our minds off the "terrible two-week wait." There was a special poignancy in returning with Oliver. Day two we unhitched Château Pliant and headed off in convoy on an outback road trip they had organized, through remote country to the west—permission had been sought from six different Aboriginal communities to travel across their lands.

At Kintore we had an unscheduled all-day stop when one of the vehicles developed a mechanical problem. In the past as a journalist I often found stepping into Aboriginal communities confronting—the litter, the burned-out houses, the painful disparity between energetic kids expertly kicking a footy or back-flipping into water, and the air of defeat among adults. Kintore, or what I glimpsed of it, struck me as such a place. But invited inside the art center I got a different impression. Women of all ages sat in the dirt, barefoot and in beanies, painting ovals and minute dots, their fingers long and tapered like those of a piano player. It's in this art center that some of the world's most sought-after Aboriginal art is produced. One of the white coordinators at the center pointed out a gray-haired artist curled around a canvas in rich earthy tones and off-white. "That's Ningura Napurrula. She painted one of the big ceiling panels at the Quai Branly," he explained, referring to the grand indigenous art museum in Paris.

Watching artists at work always makes me feel like a voyeur and on this occasion the sense of intrusion was compounded by being a white person on Aboriginal territory. But it was wonderful to glimpse the women chatting and joking in Pintupi, applying color in dabs and sweeping arcs, as if obeying a rhythm. Was this the same fluidity and certitude that Matisse achieved by picking up scissors and cutting directly into paper? I couldn't help thinking back to my own angst-ridden state during unproductive writing days on Mo'orea. If only I could have been as relaxed as these women about creating! As if to underline the point, a mangy dog then strolled right across the canvas of Naparrula, the internationally acclaimed artist, stamping a trail of red dust into the wet paint. There were no shrieks or sighs of pretension, just a giggle and a flap of the hand.

Each day the roads we took grew narrower and seemed less traveled. Red earth turned to sand. By the last day our four-wheel drives were clambering up a dry riverbed. It would have been quicker to walk and we stopped regularly to confer. Is this really the way? Did we miss a turn? It was hard to say when the road wasn't marked on any map. The Aboriginal landowners had just told Vinnie about it. "Maybe your GPS could tell us if we're heading north at least," he ventured hopefully, as we squinted at the boulders ahead. I nodded doubtfully. Throughout this epic mini trip, our navigational device had provided all sorts of mad indications and the mere suggestion of relying on it now only confirmed our predicament. "We really are lost," I cheerfully announced to Frédéric in the car.

To the pair of us, losing our way was part of the adventure, along with sleeping in swags around fires while listening to the wind whistle through desert oaks and the distant, haunting howls of dingoes. We had plenty of water and enough food for a few more days. Besides, Vinnie and Gen had arranged for friends to give the alert if we weren't back by Friday. Still, in the late afternoon the neat houses of tiny Areyonga were a welcome sight. Our guides broke into relieved grins; they began to see the funny side. "The whole of Alice would have heard about it if they'd had to come looking for us," said Gen. "It's all right for you, everyone expects tourists to do dumb things."

⌒⌒

Given my romantic notions about life on the road, the grinding domesticity of the gypsy life came as a surprise. When I wasn't poring over maps figuring out where to stay or writing shopping lists or waging war with ants in our caravan, my thoughts wandered back to Tahiti. Memories can be triggered by the most tenuous connections. In the car, if I stared long enough into the distance, the heat shimmer of the road would morph into a lagoon, one illusion of bending sunbeams evoking another. It's Thursday, I'd think: Nelly will be at Guite's. Oliver hadn't forgotten the island, either, or the many hours meandering among our *tiare* bushes. All over the country he helped himself to flowers from private gardens, public parks and protected forests. I'd glance over to see him with a pilfered hibiscus bloom or rose behind his ear, and though I made a show of tutting I could hear Nelly encouraging him. "Oraamaa," she would call in her long, lilting way— our Polynesian friends always called him by his Tahitian name. "*C'est bien, Orama, tu es beau.*"

A single 15,000-kilometer journey around a continent is very different from our many trips around Mo'orea and yet in meditative moments in the car I was struck by the similarities. By definition islands are insular; each one is its own world. Clockwise or anticlockwise? you ask yourself before setting out around them. Yet it's not all smooth circling. Their coastlines wriggle and wend around peninsulas, bumps and bays, and even as you continue straight ahead there are many times when you are doubling back. Perhaps what matters in life is the momentum and not whether you go forward or backward, as the psychotherapist in Tahiti had once suggested. My thoughts drifted to Matisse again and the lesson of the artist's *découpages* that I'd once underestimated. Was that the challenge of our messy existences: to bring them back to something pure and simple? I knew what shape I would cut out. The forms that touched me most were circular: a sunflower moon, an atoll viewed from the air, a lovely embryo.

It took us nine months to get back to Sydney. With all our detours and zigzagging, we'd clocked up almost 33,000 kilometers, even though our route had lopped off much of the Northern Territory and northern Queensland. To my surprise, of the three of us it was Frédéric who felt most sorry to stop. I'd thought his innate need for his personal history—those keepsakes and treasured collections—would mean he'd be longing to unpack our paintings and set up house. But he'd grown attached to Château Pliant, which he fondly swept out each morning. Oliver and I, on the other hand, were ready to break out. Toward the end of the trip I'd started to get caravan envy. "They've got carpet and a TV and they don't have to pack up their bed, it sits there just like in a bedroom," I'd said after one house-proud owner gave me a tour of the home she shared with her husband.

I wasn't sorry to say good-bye to caravan parks with their drafty amenities blocks and traffic dangers for small children. I wouldn't miss communal laundries with their lists of Ten Commandments of Courteous Camping: Thou shalt keep your campsite tidy at all times so as not to be an eyesore to others. Thou shalt be friendly and sociable with as many fellow campers as possible without becoming a nuisance or unwelcome guest . . . In my reveries I pictured a nice, safe environment for an energetic two-year-old. A suburban house with a kitchen overlooking a fenced backyard—that started to sound like paradise.

Other priorities took precedence when we got back to Sydney. The desire to remain in Australia had become entrenched during our trip, which meant the first thing was to find somewhere to live. It was a few months before I got around to making an appointment with Dr. L and found myself back in the wood-paneled office amid the fertility statues. After Oliver, I was convinced I'd get pregnant naturally. Once my body knew what to do, once the pressure had been lifted, once the longing for one had been fulfilled—isn't that what people say? But nothing had happened and with an obvious lack of optimism, Dr. L agreed to help us have one more try. "You've had one miracle," he reminded me mildly. I felt slightly put out. Having one child doesn't prevent you wanting more, even if the longing is not underpinned by the same existential ache.

Once again everything hinged on my FSH level: we could forget about another go if the blood test result was higher than fourteen. And so when the nurse rang there was disbelief, excitement—and triumph. "I'm getting younger every year," I trilled on the telephone to Frédéric afterward. "My FSH is SIX!" My imagination took flight. With a level that low our chances were excellent. I even began calculating the age difference between Oliver and his yet-to-be-conceived younger sibling. How thrilled he would be to have a little brother or sister.

But a few days later another blood test revealed that the first result was completely unreliable. My FSH level was not encouraging—on the contrary, my hormones were all over the place. The force of the plunging disappointment took me by surprise. I knew then. "I can't do it," I told Frédéric flatly. "That's it." He nodded understandingly: we had Oliver, how lucky was that? It was exactly the message Dr. L had tried to convey to me. I realized then that this must be one of the challenges for specialists, knowing when the time has come to help patients face up to reality. Still, the unopened box of hormones that had been issued by the clinic sat in our fridge for more than a year. Even now, at forty-six, when my two inner baskets must be nearly empty of eggs, hope still flickers in an irrational corner of my mind. I rather look forward to the day Mother Nature settles the matter once and for all. Bring on menopause, I say.

EPILOGUE

"Can I get up? Is it time?" In the darkness Oliver, five, pads into our bedroom, pretending not to have heard Frédéric's reply: "*Trop tôt,*" it's too early. "What did you say, Freddie?" That is what he has affectionately called his father from the outset—and to think I waited fifty years to hear the word "Papa," Frédéric used to lament in mock despair. Though it was Oliver's French grandfather who was most alarmed by this casual familiarity: "What does he call you?" he'd asked Frédéric, his eyes widening in disbelief. Lax parenting or in some vague way Australia—perhaps he blamed both.

Allowed to slide in between us, Oliver makes a pantomime of trying to be quiet. "Oh sorry, Mama, for kicking you. Oops, who was that I poked?" There is some giggling and he forgets to be quiet. "Sssh," Frédéric reminds him. "It's the weekend, you're not supposed to come in before seven." Still jet-lagged, I feign sleep—not that this deters him. Oliver would happily chat to a sea cucumber. *Un moulin á paroles* indeed he is, just

311

like his father was as a boy: a "windmill of words." Sometimes I think Frédéric got his wish for three children—or at least the energy of three in one child. Soon Oliver is burrowing vigorously beneath the bed linen, rumpling my treasured Tahitian *tifaifai* bedcover, which despite being handsewn withstands the washing machine and all sorts of rough treatment.

"You can come into my cave," calls a friendly muffled voice. "Just say the password."

Frédéric raises his head and regards the wriggling lump. "*Ça suffit*, Oliver. It's back to your own bed if you can't keep still."

No sooner has the threat been made than from outside comes a low, irreverent chuckle. Like helpless laughter it catches on, leaping from tree to tree, until the whole, long street reverberates with it. In my mind's eye I picture the kookaburras on the high branches, large heads thrown back, fat beaks cracked open, calling out to Oliver and every other kid in the country: *ahahah-oo-oo-ah-ah, it's high time to get up!* It's the maddest, most joyful alarm I've ever heard. If only the birds would sleep in a little later.

On cue, there is a scrambling down below and then a gust as the doona is thrown back. The bedroom brightens with the day's first light. Oliver is holding up the blind, looking out the window.

"Awesome, it's *mawning*," he exclaims in his broad Australian accent. After our five weeks away he's brimming with impatience. There's no chance of ignoring his eager call, even with my head under my pillow. "C'mon Mom, c'mon Freddie!"

It's a fact of life that holidays are spent in France, though we can't quite manage annual trips. That year we went for Christmas and despite the cold, it was our most relaxing trip. Time was split between my father-in-law in the north, my parents in the southwest, and Paris, where we rented an apartment in our old neighborhood. We felt like locals but ran around like tourists, trying to cram in as many sights and museums as possible, as well as catching up with friends. At five, Oliver was at a better age to appreciate the city. He was patient with his parents' prattle: that's the café where Mommy used to write; that place makes the world's best hot chocolates; this is Mommy and Daddy's favorite park. Dear old Mads had died a few months earlier and being in Paris brought back just how much our cheerful little friend had meant to us. Our promenades around the city turned into Maddie pilgrimages. "Remember the night we ate at that bistro over there?" Seeing it, Frédéric laughed, too—he remembered all right. It was during the Paris fashion shows; the restaurant was full of models and magazine editors, and Maddie got into one of their designer handbags under the table. To a curious pup, the packet of tampons must have been enormous fun and by the time anyone noticed, the little bullet forms had been pulled and fluffed into artistic clouds. "Cotton candy," exclaimed a fashionista, quite taken with the sight until she spied the tampons' telltale tails.

Naturally we went back to Notre-Dame des Victoires, where I used to light my candles. Inside, the basilica was ablaze with votives as always. "Can we buy one of the really big candles?" Oliver whispered. I said we could. He performed the ritual solemnly, lighting the wick with exaggerated care, for he remains wary of anything that might burn. We squeezed shut our eyes. Amid the stone walls of engraved plaques, I silently said thanks.

This trip was a thrill for all of us but for Frédéric, Paris was like an elixir. *"Regarde comme c'est beau!"* he exulted, striding through Galerie Vivienne, where handsome boutiques were decorated for Christmas with twinkling curtains of gold lights, bouquets of holly and garlands of carved reindeer. I knew what he was thinking: not a gaudy Aussie bauble or shred of tinsel anywhere. One morning strolling through a quiet square, we passed a café where a man in a heavy coat sat outside in a sunbeam, reading. Maybe it was his dark, handsome looks, or the fact he was smoking so early in the day, or that the book was by Nietzsche. To our eyes, accustomed now to Australia, this everyday Paris scene was exotic. *"Cela me réjouit,"* Frederic confided—the sight filled him with joy. He seemed overcome by a sense of recognition. In our previous life, the one we led before Tahiti, he *was* that man.

France is where he doesn't have to explain himself, to use my friend's expression. Australia is that place for me. It may not be my *fenua*—that emotive Tahitian word for home—but it's the closest thing I have to it. My years away have changed me and I am no longer wholly an insider. Yet Australia is where I grew up, mostly; here my nationality is of no interest to anyone. Of all places in the world it is where I stand out least.

Learning a language as an adult is very different from imbibing a language from birth, and it is our hope that Oliver is bilingual in a way that we are not. It's not that Frédéric and I aren't comfortable switching between French and English—we do so often, sometimes mid-sentence. *J'ai trouvé le* screwdriver, I might say lazily. Oliver, *mets tes crayons dans ta* pencil case. Words elude us and even ones that look familiar can turn out to be *faux amis* and mean something different. Thinking to have found the English translation for *se forger*, Frédéric recently began an e-mail to an Australian client with the statement: "I forged the legal opinion"— a claim that may have given cause for alarm coming from a lawyer.

Not having grown up speaking French, I take liberties with it. I like to think I use swear words judiciously in English but in my second language they roll easily off my tongue, their sound no cruder to my ears than any other word. A memory springs to mind of a Paris dinner party some years ago that I went to on my own—a stroke of luck for Frédéric, as it turns out. With the other guests, I was nibbling marinated olives and sipping summer rosé when cries from the street below drew us off the plush sofas to a window. "Leave me alone! Don't touch me!" A woman was struggling with a guy who was yanking her into his car. She's being attacked, I thought in horror—though admittedly it was hard to tell in the dark, five floors up. "Hey you, STOP!" I might have yelled in English. "PISS OFF ASSHOLE," I screeched in French, my voice projecting to the far corners of the genteel 6th arrondissement. "Just fuck off!" Even the couple in the street appeared stunned. They looked up, muttering to each other.

Who was that raving *poissonière* screaming from the pretty window? Their domestic dispute apparently forgotten, the pair hopped in the car and drove off. In the awkward silence that opened up inside the apartment, there was no laughing off my outburst. The wary distaste on the faces of the other guests said it all.

That's why we badger Oliver, so that he might be a true bilingual. *"C'est le weekend,"* Frédéric insists, *"le weekend on parle français."* To our consternation he nearly always replies in English. Before leaving for France, Frédéric fretted how his own father would react to this affront. Doting grandfather though he is, Alain is also a staunch defender of French culture. As the Australian parent, privately I feared blame would be laid on me. But in the end Oliver made the switch seamlessly, if not effortlessly, proving the point that children will pick up whatever language is being spoken in the wider community and by their peers. He particularly relished the many colorful expressions with which his grandfather regularly cursed the bleak weather so characteristic of northern France in any season. On a day of unrelenting rain, Oliver was heard to aptly observe, *"il pleut comme une vache qui pisse"*—literally, it's raining like a peeing cow. Alain's eyes brimmed with emotion. *"Mon petit poulet,"* he said, patting his grandson's head proudly.

Naturally we tell Oliver he is French *and* Australian, half-half. But biculturalism is not a neat equation. What we want will have little bearing on how he feels in his heart, and what he feels in his heart may change with time. For the moment his effervescent energy seems wholly Australian. So it appeared to me in Paris, watching him walk through gilt-fenced *jardins* in his usual way—that is to say, in bursts of running, hopping and skipping with skidding stops to poke a pile of dog poo or bat a fallen chestnut with a stick.

～～

It may be only a 24-hour flight but the other side of the world feels far away. When we landed back in Sydney I knew Frédéric was thinking of his father, in his eighties now and living alone. On the drive home from the airport he was pensive. I felt unsettled, too. Our decision to remain in Sydney might feel right to us but were we being a little selfish when our parents were in France? Wouldn't it be nice if they were a more constant presence in our son's life? North of the city, we finally arrived at the familiar streets near home. It was barely after ten at night but everything was dark, the houses were shut, lights were off, people were in bed. I couldn't help thinking of Paris and how alive and lit up its streets were at this hour.

A rush of air made me turn around to the back, where Oliver was furiously winding down a window. His face was as bright as a bulb; you'd never guess he'd come straight off a long-haul flight. "Helloooo, helloo," he called to the blank houses. "It's me, Oliver. Hello school, hello toy shop, hello friends, I'M BACK!" The elated salutations continued through the front door until we were all laughing, swept up by his evangelistic fervor: "I love my room, I love my house!"

He's right, this old beach house does feel like home. Its

floors slope every which way and when the westerly blows it feels to me that the whole flimsy place might blow away, but it has loads of character and a lovely view across the Pittwater estuary. It hasn't been easy for Frédéric work-wise, but when things get tough he can still look through the majestic spotted gums to the scalloped bays in the distance and find a reason for being in Sydney. To a Frenchman, the peeling trunks, olive hills and sailboats are every bit as exotic as the sloping jumble of Paris rooftops had been to me.

Gum trees aside, the first time I stepped into the garden I'd thought of Tahiti. Despite the different climate and soil, the same plants seem to thrive. At times of big change, any thread of continuity can appear quite significant and the *taina* gardenias with their floppy, fragrant blooms, seemed a good sign, along with hibiscus flowers the same crimson color that Tahitians often wore. We've even got another gangly papaya tree that doesn't bear fruit and a palm that I was convinced would produce bananas until it grew fantastic beaks and spiky white flowers. Our giant bird of paradise is a favorite with the sulfur-crested cockatoos, which nibble on the seeds. When the sunlight falls through the fanning foliage onto their plumage, the pure brilliance reminds me of a freshly cracked wave on a reef.

That first Sunday back from France we head to the beach straight after breakfast. Already it's one vivid, shifting pattern of red, white and green surf caps: several hundred nippers are separated into age groups and spread along the sand.

The big tide means the waves are breaking high on the shore and the ocean pool churns like a washing machine. The parents of the Under Sixes trudge on the soft sand after the children, lugging bags and boogie boards, as the group searches for a calm spot. It's too rough to venture in so instead they run races on the beach under the direction of Dave, their ebullient group leader, who wears a broad-brimmed hat, zinc on his nose and a grin as wide as the beach. "Under Sixes RULE!" he bellows, along with endless encouragements: "good work," "well done," "awesome job."

"Get ready," he cries next. "Heeeereshhheecoomes . . ."

This is the part I love. It's the simplest exercise—fifty-odd Under Sixes kneel in a line along the shore, hanging on to a rope held by moms and dads. At this age the emphasis is on building up confidence and the idea is to get them used to the waves. With the stretchy nylon caps pulled smooth and tight over their scalps, the kids' faces look like balloons with smiles drawn on them.

Foam rushes up around my shins, zapping my skin. I'm still a warm-water girl and for a moment I pause. Who'd guess it's the same ocean that flushed us through those tremendous atoll channels; the same one I swam in each morning on Mo'orea? That sun-laced lagoon that had valiantly borne my weight. Here there's no liminal fringe, no blurring of realms. Compared to the air the water is freezing. For a moment my eyes are drawn to the horizon and the blueness that continues beyond the curvature, sprinkled with unseen islands.

The kids' shrieking makes me turn. Standing in the surf holding the rope, Frédéric grins back. From where I stand I can't see Oliver's face, but my ears pick up his excited yell amid the crescendo, "WaaaOOOO." *Life begets life. Energy creates energy.* It's only a little wave but when it rushes over their laps it's like a chemical reaction. All of a sudden there's nothing but froth and fizz and above the rumbling ocean I hear the vital ring of young laughter.

ACKNOWLEDGMENTS

Among the many books that were helpful to me in writing *All Good Things*, certain titles deserve special mention. I first read *Matisse the Master*, the second volume of Hilary Spurling's marvelous biography of Henri Matisse, while we were living on Mo'orea. It was there, too, that I came across Paule Laudon's evocative account of the artist's trip to French Polynesia, *Matisse, Le Voyage en Polynésie* (also published in English under the title *Matisse in Tahiti*). These richly researched books painted vivid images of Matisse that stayed with me throughout my time on the island, and they greatly nourished this memoir.

In addition to Paul Gauguin's published journals, *Noa Noa* and *Avant et Après*, several other sources illuminated the artist's years on Tahiti and Hiva Oa for me, including *Gauguin in the South Seas* by Bengt Danielsson, and David Sweetman's biography, *Paul Gauguin: A Complete Life*.

Aphrodite's Island by Anne Salmond is a fascinating, in-depth account of the European discovery of Tahiti. In his essay "The Atoll," published in *Return to Paradise*, James A. Michener writes inspiringly about the allure of these strange coral causeways. Though hard to come by, Tom Neale's account of living on a desert atoll, *An Island to Oneself*, is a must read for "islomaniacs." Maco Tevane's valuable insights on the meaning behind the Tahitian word *fiu* are published in *101 Mots Pour Comprendre La Polynésie Française*.

Inconceivable Conceptions, edited by Jane Haynes and Juliet Miller, helped me make sense of my own experiences and greatly furthered my understanding of the psychological impact of unwanted childlessness, as well as the effect it may have on the creative impulse.

Nothing If Not Critical and *The Shock of the New*, both by Robert Hughes, provided perspective on art and color, as well as specifically on Gauguin and Matisse.

~~

For bringing this book into the wider world, I am indebted to the dedicated team of people at HarperCollins Australia: Publishing Director Shona Martyn embraced this book with unfailing enthusiasm; Amanda O'Connell helped pull everything together. Above all, heartfelt thanks go to my publisher Fiona Henderson, who remained steady and supportive from beginning to end—even when I broke the news that the book I was supposed to be writing about traveling around Australia had wandered off into a completely different part of the Pacific. Her calm response—"I have faith"—gave me essential encouragement when I most needed it. In the United States,

I am deeply grateful to my agent, Liv Blumer, as well as the wonderful team at Gotham Books, led by my publisher William Shinker and editor Lauren Marino.

A memoir not only exposes the writer's life but also intrudes into the lives of others. I wish to thank all the people who have allowed me to include them in this book. Some names have been changed and out of respect for privacy I have mostly used first names only. Deep thanks go to our friends on Mo'orea—the best neighbors one could wish for—who welcomed us into the fold and showed us the huge value of small gestures: Alain, Aima, Guite, Moetu, and their extended families, along with the irreplaceable Nelly. I'm grateful as well to our dive buddies, Daniel and Catherine, now back in France, who never needed an excuse to open one of their best bottles of Bordeaux.

My thanks to Katy Young for letting me use the Aisle of White office when I needed to get out of the house to write. To all the loyal friends who continued to ask how the book was coming along, even when they were probably scared to—thank you. I'm especially grateful to Bitsy Harper, for her loving care of Oliver, and to the school moms who have kindly helped out when I needed more hours to work. My thanks to Sue Quill, too, for always being there no matter where I live.

My family has encouraged me in all my endeavors and my parents, Jan and Murray Turnbull, graciously allowed me to draw on their experiences for this book. Thanks to my sister, Anna Turnbull, for her generosity and support in so many ways. Precious encouragement also came from my father-in-law, Alain Venière, who has made two trips to see us in Sydney, where he threw himself into just about everything except the surf.

I am deeply grateful to my readers, including Phoebe Damrosch at Gotham Writers' Workshop, whose early feedback helped steer the book in the right direction, and to my dear friends Stephanie Williamson and Helen Anderson. From Paris, Alicia Drake sustained me with her wise counsel, honest feedback and uplifting e-mails; Moya Sayer-Jones pushed me through the end and her insights and thoughtful suggestions helped make this a better book.

A huge hug to my son, Oliver, for his sweet humor and endless encouragement, as well as practical writing tips: "just write *The End*, Mom, it's easy!" To my husband, Frédéric, who believed in this book before it remotely resembled one, and read countless drafts, jogged my memory and checked my French, no words can adequately express my gratitude. This is your story, too, Freddie, and if I have managed to write from the heart and tell it truthfully, it is thanks to the love and courage you gave me.